Tables and Chairs

Tables and Chairs

The Best Of Fine WoodWorking

The Taunton Press

Cover photo by Wesley Bender

BOOKS & VIDEOS

for fellow enthusiasts

First printing: 1995
Printed in the United States of America

A FINE WOODWORKING Book

FINE WOODWORKING® is a trademark of The Taunton Press, Inc.,
registered in the U.S. Patent and Trademark Office.

The Taunton Press, Inc.
63 South Main Street
P.O. Box 5506
Newtown, Connecticut 06470-5506

Library of Congress Cataloging-in-Publication Data

Tables and chairs.
     p. cm. – (The best of fine woodworking)
    "A Fine Woodworking book" – T.p. verso.
    Includes index.
    ISBN 1-56158-100-3
    1. Tables.   2. Chairs.   3. Furniture making.
 I. Fine woodworking.   II. Series.
TT197.5.T3T327   1995
684.1'3–dc20   95-1912
                                             CIP

Contents

Introduction

Tables and chairs are the workhorses of furniture. They are at the center of our lives as we sit down to enjoy a meal and some conversation, or maybe just take a break from the hectic pace of modern living. A table may be called upon to serve a banquet and then be cleared to handle a family craft project or a teenager's homework. Chairs are called to duty as everything from instant step-stools to quick places for a nap. It's no wonder then that so many woodworkers want to build tables and chairs.

These 28 articles from the pages of *Fine Woodworking* magazine offer a wide variety of styles and types of tables and chairs for woodworkers to build. Tables include everything from a dining table that expands to accommodate 14 people to a simple end table. Chairs range from the refined beauty of a bowback Windsor to the sturdy comfort of a Morris chair. But it's not all just projects: Mixed into these pages are countless practical techniques that can be applied to other furniture-making endeavors. There are tips on carving chair seats, working green wood and designing chairs that fit. A whole menu of joinery techniques is also served up.

So, lay the book out on a table, pull up a chair and read. I suspect it won't be too many pages before you start fidgeting in your seat, wanting to move to your shop to build some new tables and chairs.

—The Editors

The "Best of *Fine Woodworking*" series spans ten years of *Fine Woodworking* magazine. There is no duplication between these books and the popular *"Fine Woodworking on..."* series. A footnote with each article gives the date of first publication; product availability, suppliers' addresses and prices may have changed since then.

Making a Walnut Occasional Table

A *simple project from a single plank*

by Richard Kapuaala

Cutting up a large, rough plank of wood is always exciting for me, but I can't help feeling a little anxiety. I worry whether the furniture I intend to build will enhance or detract from the wood's natural beauty. This was my dilemma when I set out to build an occasional table from a roughsawn, 4x13x96 walnut plank. It was hard to tell what the piece of wood was like beneath its exterior; but upon resawing, I saw the lovely color and grain pattern inside, and I adapted my design ideas to fit the character of the wood. The resulting table, shown here, has a single drawer with all-wood guides, a custom-made wooden pull, and a top large enough for a lamp, magazines or other accessories. Construction is based on joinery that you're probably familiar with: dovetails for the drawer, mortises and tenons for the legs and aprons, sliding dovetails for the aprons and bridle joints for the partitions. Even with the small details I've added to make the table more visually interesting, building it should take you about 30 hours. The drawing on the facing page and the bill of materials on p. 11 include the dimensions for all the parts. To help you get started, I'll tell you how I built my table.

Sawing the parts—After a little handplaning, I knew my walnut planks were richly colored with deep crimsons and purple streaks. What I couldn't see until after I had resawn the planks was the wood's beautiful flame-figured grain pattern, with dark, wing-shape intrusions at the edges. When I set the pieces side by side and in mirror symmetry, I knew the figure would look best if the tabletop was book-matched. Since the table's legs required the thickest material, I cut them out before resawing the plank to ¾-in.-thick stock for the other parts. Because the plank was more than twice the thickness needed for the 1⅛-in.-square legs, I cut them out in pairs, so they would match and the grain would be symmetrical. It's a good idea to match the legs of any piece to minimize problems in case there is any moisture-related twisting or bowing: The opposing pairs of legs will warp symmetrically. If you can't saw matching legs from the same piece of stock, choose stock with straight grain for less chance of warping.

After crosscutting the plank into more manageable, shorter lengths with my radial-arm saw, I jointed the bark-side edge to remove sapwood from the walnut, and then I ripped the sections to rough widths. Using a standard bandsaw fence and a ¾-in.-wide blade, I resawed the sections of the plank to about ⅞ in. thick (except for the legs). This left enough stock to thickness-plane the sections to ¾ in. or thinner, as required for the parts. Before final thicknessing, sticker the resawn stock and let it stabilize at shop temperature and humidity for a few days. This way, you can take out slight warping with the jointer or planer and set aside any stock that warps more severely. Finally, I use the tablesaw and radial-arm saw to cut all the parts to width and length, following the bill of materials. If some of the parts on the bill appear to be oversize, the extra stock is either for joinery or it will be trimmed away later.

Cutting the joints—First cut the 5-in.-wide by 1-in.-long tenons on the ends of the front and back aprons that will join the legs. There are many good machine or hand techniques for cutting tenons, but I prefer to use my tablesaw and a shopmade tenoning jig, which holds the stock upright during the cut. My procedure is similar to the one described in *FWW* #66, p. 70. Next, I cut the sliding dovetails on the ends of the side aprons, again using my tablesaw and the tenoning jig. As with tenons, the jig holds the workpiece vertically, but the blade is tilted 12° to cut the male dovetail (see the left photo on p. 10). I prefer this method to using a router and a dovetail bit because it allows me to change the angle of the dovetail if I desire.

Next I cut the female dovetail slots into the front and back aprons. A regular miter gauge fitted with a special wooden fence is

The author's occasional table was designed to fit the character of the wood: a single plank of ¹⁶/₄ walnut that he resawed for the book-matched top, matched pairs of legs and most of the other parts. The top has room for magazines, a lamp or other accessories. The table has a single drawer with all-wood guides and a custom-made wooden pull.

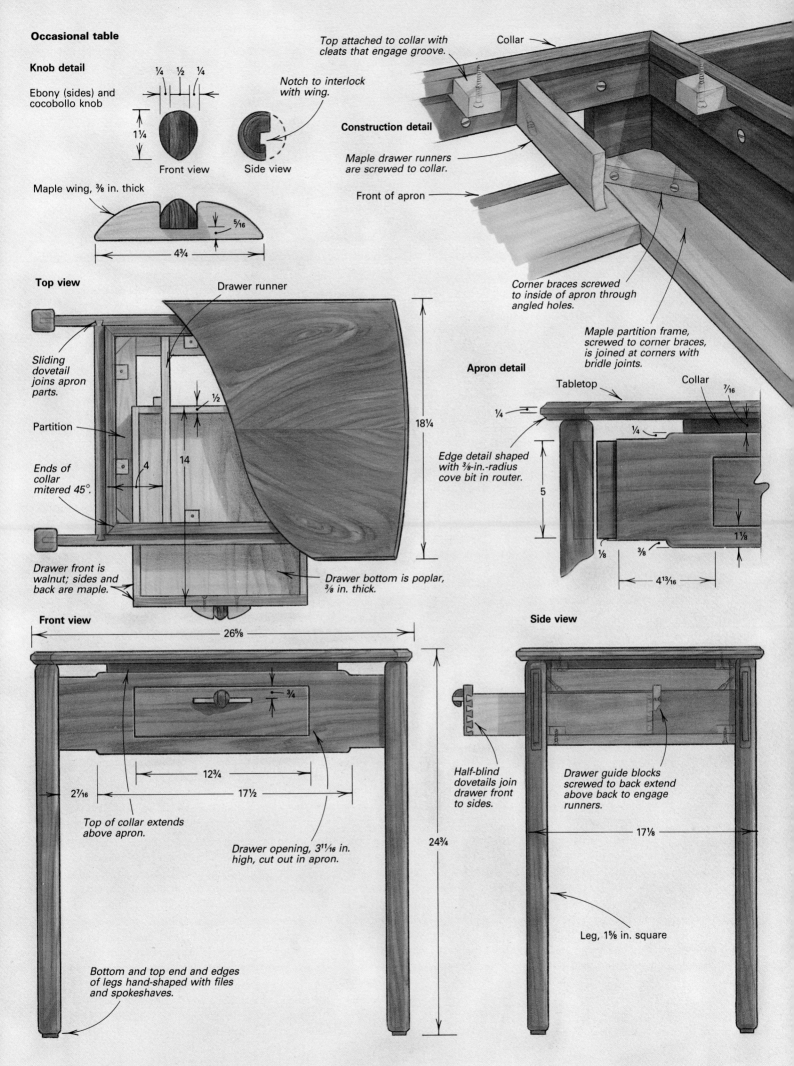

Occasional table

Knob detail

Ebony (sides) and cocobollo knob

1/4   1/2   1/4

1 1/4

Front view

Side view

Notch to interlock with wing.

Maple wing, 3/8 in. thick

5/16

4 3/4

Top view

Drawer runner

Sliding dovetail joins apron parts.

Partition

Ends of collar mitered 45°.

1/2

4

14

18 1/4

Drawer front is walnut; sides and back are maple.

Drawer bottom is poplar, 3/8 in. thick.

Top attached to collar with cleats that engage groove.

Collar

Construction detail

Maple drawer runners are screwed to collar.

Front of apron

Corner braces screwed to inside of apron through angled holes.

Maple partition frame, screwed to corner braces, is joined at corners with bridle joints.

Apron detail

Tabletop

Collar

7/16

1/4

1/4

Edge detail shaped with 3/8-in.-radius cove bit in router.

5

1/8   3/8

1 1/8

4 13/16

Front view

26 5/8

3/4

2 7/16

12 3/4

17 1/2

Top of collar extends above apron.

Drawer opening, 3 11/16 in. high, cut out in apron.

Bottom and top end and edges of legs hand-shaped with files and spokeshaves.

Side view

Half-blind dovetails join drawer front to sides.

Drawer guide blocks screwed to back extend above back to engage runners.

24 3/4

17 1/8

Leg, 1 5/8 in. square

Drawing: Bob La Pointe

Tables and Chairs   9

Left: To cut the male dovetails on the ends of the side aprons, Kapuaala uses his tablesaw and homemade tenon jig, which supports the workpiece vertically as it is guided past the tilted blade. Center: After crosscutting the female sliding dovetails in the front and rear aprons with a miter gauge on the tablesaw, Kapuaala pares the bottom of each flat with a chisel. Right: To cut out the drawer opening in the front apron, the author uses a plunge router fitted with a guide bushing that follows a rectangular hole cut into a particleboard template. With the template clamped on top of the apron, he plunges the bit and follows around the template clockwise, cleaning up the corners of the opening with a chisel after routing.

used to push the stock through, again with the blade tilted 12°. The fence I made is as long as my saw table and has a wooden runner that fits in the slot on the right side of the blade. I cut one side of the dovetail, rotate the piece around and then cut the other side, repositioning the stop between cuts. After cutting both sides of each female dovetail, I remove the waste in the center by crosscutting with the blade squared and lowered; then I pare the bottom flat with a chisel (see the center photo). Now trial-fit the apron pieces, and if necessary, trim the male dovetail until the joints slide smoothly, yet fit snugly together.

With the joints done, it's time to trim the aprons to their final width. I joint both edges *after* cutting the dovetails so that all traces of tearout disappear. You may decide that you don't need to do this, but if your joints aren't perfect, it helps keep the apron looking good.

Shaping the aprons—To lend a decorative element to this occasional table, the corners of the front and back aprons are cut back and rounded. I bandsaw four 2$\frac{7}{16}$-in.-long pieces from each apron, as shown in the drawing. I first make the rip cut using the fence on the bandsaw as a guide. Don't go too far or you'll cut into the sliding dovetails. Then, crosscut with the bandsaw's miter gauge to remove each corner strip, and use a rasp or file to round over the corners on the new stepped areas. Next, I chuck a $\frac{1}{4}$-in.-radius roundover bit into the router table to shape the entire edge on the outside faces of the front, back and side aprons, stopping short of the tenons.

Now comes a potentially tricky step: cutting out the drawer opening in the front apron. I use a $\frac{1}{2}$-in.-dia. straight bit in a plunge router with a guide bushing fitted in its base. The bushing follows a rectangular hole cut into a Masonite or particleboard template. I waste the cut-out piece because it's too tedious a job to saw it out with a thin-kerf sawblade and save. I substitute a piece with similar grain for the drawer front. With the template clamped on top of the apron, I plunge the bit down about $\frac{1}{4}$ in. and then follow around the template clockwise (see the photo at right). I repeat this till the bit cuts all the way through. I clean up the rounded corners of the opening with a chisel, but before routing, you could cut these corners square with a hollow-chisel mortiser if you have one. Routing sometimes tears up the wood, so it's wise to make an extra apron front, just in case. Finally, glue up the aprons without the legs.

To complete the apron assembly, I make and attach the collar: a thin frame that fits around the apron assembly's top inside edge and sticks up $\frac{7}{16}$ in. above the apron assembly. A $\frac{1}{4}$-in.-wide by $\frac{3}{8}$-in.-deep groove around the inside of the collar, cut with a dado blade on the tablesaw, provides a means for attaching the top with small cabinetmaker's buttons, as described further on. The ends of the collar are mitered, and the four pieces are screwed to the apron through countersunk holes. Take care not to drill a hole where the drawer runners will be attached later (see the drawing). I use a marking gauge to scribe orientation lines on the inside of the apron to help align the collar as it is screwed into place.

Making the drawer—Having routed the opening earlier, handplane the piece for the drawer front until it fits snugly. Now you're ready to make the drawer. I won't go into detail on drawer construction since it's covered in other texts (see *FWW* #73, p. 48). I prefer to make all my drawers with hardwood rather than softwood because I think it lasts longer and looks better. For my occasional table, I made the drawer sides and back from maple, which contrasts nicely with the walnut. The drawer bottom is $\frac{3}{8}$-in.-thick poplar, but a $\frac{1}{4}$-in.-thick plywood bottom works also. The dovetails on my drawer aren't sized in any fixed way: I lay them out so they look pleasing. With a sliding T-bevel, I mark the angle of the half-blind dovetails at the front of the drawer and the through dovetails at the back. To keep the drawer from rubbing on the sides of the opening, make the front of the drawer slightly wider than the back. Cut the pins on the drawer back slightly deeper, between $\frac{1}{64}$ in. and $\frac{1}{32}$ in., and then handplane them flush with the sides after assembly.

The drawer-guide system I use is a bit unusual, but it is relatively easy to install, is adjustable and keeps the drawer running smoothly. This system consists of two hardwood runners screwed to the apron's collar that keep the drawer aligned via two small guide blocks screwed to the back end of the drawer. For strength and wear resistance, I make the runners out of $\frac{1}{2}$-in.-thick maple. The runners are attached with screws in countersunk holes drilled at an angle through both ends. Be sure to countersink the holes deep enough to keep the screw head from sticking out and interfering with drawer operation. Before screwing the runners in place, check that they are flush with and at perfect right angles to the bottom edge of the collar and are parallel to each other and the apron sides.

Next, turn the apron assembly upside down so that it rests on the collar and insert the drawer so that it rests on the drawer runners. Drill oversize pilot holes in the guide blocks (made from maple scraps) so you can shift them around to adjust the drawer tracking in the future. With the drawer front flush with its opening in the apron, position each guide block to lightly contact the outside edge of each runner, and screw both to the back of the drawer with round-head screws and washers.

Before flipping the apron assembly over, I make the table's partition and the four corner braces it will be screwed to. In addition to keeping the apron from racking, the partition supports the drawer, like a dust-panel frame in a dresser, and provides a surface for the drawer to slide on. The ¾-in.-thick partition frame is joined at the corners with bridle joints. These joints are cut on the tablesaw in much the same way that the apron tenons were earlier.

The corner braces, made from maple scraps with 45° cuts on each end, are screwed to the inside corners of the apron through angled holes (see the drawing on p. 9). Before securing the braces, I scribe a line around the inside of the apron to mark where the top edge of the partition will be when installed. This way, when the table is upright, the top of the partition is flush with the bottom edge of the drawer opening. Since the partition screws to the braces, this line also determines where the bottom edge of each brace will be. When everything jibes, I screw on the braces, but I leave the partition off until the top has been attached.

Gluing up the tabletop—If you haven't already glued up your tabletop, do so now. I used blind splines to join the two 9⅛-in.-wide book-matched walnut boards, but you may prefer biscuit joints or just glue. In any case, after the glue is dry and the excess is scraped off, I lay out the top's curved outline with the spline-and-weight method described in *FWW* #71, p. 45. However, I didn't have real architect's weights; so I used regular C-clamps to hold the spline I made from a ⅛-in. maple strip, and then I bandsawed the top. The table's edge detail consists of two small cove cuts, one on the top of the edge and one on the bottom. I would have preferred to use a ⅜-in. ball-bearing-piloted cove bit in the router to shape the detail, but since I didn't have one, I used the cove portion of my Roman ogee bit.

Small cabinetmaker's buttons are screwed to the underside of the top and attach it to the table; a small tongue cut on one end of each cabinetmaker's button engages the groove around the inside of the collar. The buttons allow the top to float: an important feature since wood can get very cranky if it's denied freedom to expand and contract. I space the six cleats around the collar; you might want to use more than six, but don't use fewer or the top will move whenever you touch it. When you set the cabinetmaker's buttons, make sure the tongues don't bottom out in the grooves, as that would restrict the top from moving and defeat the purpose of the cleats. Once the top is attached, screw the partition to the braces. Now, flip the apron/top assembly over and make sure the drawer slides smoothly. Adjust the guide blocks if they rub too hard against the runners and wax them if necessary.

Shaping and mortising the legs—With the top on and the drawer in place, it's time to attach the legs to the occasional table. Taking the blanks that were cut out earlier, hold the top end of each leg against the bottom of the tabletop with one edge butted to the apron tenon it will join. Now, with a marking knife, scribe lines at the top and bottom of the tenon to show where the mortise will begin and end. Repeat with all the legs, and then lay out the width of the mortises, centering them ¹¹⁄₁₆ in. from the outer face of each leg. To chop the mortises, I used the mortising table attachment on my combination jointer/planer. However, a router with a straight bit and a good mortising jig, like the one described in *FWW* #80, p. 46, will also work. If you chop the mortises by hand, you may wish to leave a "horn" at

the top of each leg to prevent the short endgrain at the top of the mortise from splitting out (it gets cut off after mortising).

I wanted the tops and bottoms of the legs to be slightly rounded, and so instead of shaping those profiles on the router table or shaper, I used a combination of files, planes and spokeshaves. First, I ease the edges with a small block plane, and then use the files and spokeshaves to create the soft contours on the edges and ends. Finally, I finish-sand the legs before gluing them to the apron, since it's a real pain to try to sand after glue-up.

Making the drawer pull—Since I built my occasional table from an original design, I wasn't about to settle for a store-bought pull for the drawer. For this design, I came up with the pull shown in the drawing because it seemed to fit the mood of the piece. The design has a central knob glued up from small pieces of ebony and cocobolo, with a horizontal maple "wing" intersecting the knob.

To make the knob for the drawer pull, I cut out three round blanks using a 1⅜-in.-dia. hole saw in the drill press. This yields three 1¼-in.-dia. discs that I laminate together: two ¼-in.-thick ebony with one ½-in.-thick cocobolo in between. After the glue dries, I clamp the knob in the vise on my workbench and cut out the notch for the wing, proportioned as shown in the drawing. I used my Japanese dovetail saw for the cuts, but any thin-blade, sharp handsaw will do. I then shape the knob to its soft contour on a stationary belt sander, holding the knob in a pair of channel locks with padded jaws so I don't sand my fingertips.

The pull's maple wings are marked out with a compass and then cut out on the scroll saw. I set my pencil compass to a 3⅞-in. radius, and then sketch an arc on the ⅜-in.-thick maple stock. After sawing the arc, I cut out the notch to fit the knob with a standard dovetail saw. Next, dry fit the pieces and trim the notches to fit. Gradually use finer and finer grades of sandpaper to polish the pull. Finally, glue the knob and wing together, drill two ¹⁄₁₆-in.-dia. holes on the back of the wings, and screw the pull to the drawer front.

By now your occasional table should be ready for a good finish. I used several coats of tung oil, with a final coat of beeswax after the tung oil had dried. All the work I put into my table seemed worthwhile the first time I saw the midday sun hit it, sending shimmering ripples of light across the walnut top.　□

Richard Kapuaala is a professional woodworker in Salinas, Cal.

Bill of Materials

No.	Description	Dimensions (T × W × L)
4	Legs	1⅝ × 1⅝ × 24
1	Top	¾ × 18¼ × 26⅝†
2	Aprons (front and back)	¾ × 5¾ × 24⅜*
2	Aprons (sides)	¾ × 5¾ × 15½**
2	Collars (front and back)	¾ × 1¹³⁄₁₆ × 16††
2	Collars (sides)	¾ × 1¹³⁄₁₆ × 14¾††
1	Drawer front	⅝ × 3¾ × 12¾†
2	Drawer sides	½ × 3⁵⁄₁₆ × 14†
1	Drawer back	½ × 3⁵⁄₁₆ × 12¾†
1	Drawer bottom	⅜ × 16 × 12¾†
2	Drawer runners	½ × 1⁷⁄₁₆ × 13⅜†
2	Drawer guide blocks	½ × ¾ × 2
2	Partition frames (front and back)	¾ × 2 × 16##
2	Partition frames (sides)	¾ × 2⅛ × 14¾
4	Corner braces	¾ × 2¼ × 2††
6	Cabinetmaker's buttons	¾ × 1½ × 2

*	Includes 1-in.-long tenons on both ends.	††	45° miter on both ends.
**	Includes ⅜-in.-long sliding dovetails on both ends.	#	Includes ¼-in.-thick tongue on one long edge.
†	Trim to final size.	##	Includes bridle joints on both ends.

Knockdown Red-Cedar Trestle Table Works Well Indoors or Out

Hand-chopped mortises complement simple design

by Tony Konovaloff

This red-cedar table's mass is lightened visually by its gently rounded and bevel-edged top, tapered foot and thin, slightly tapered wedges. Just the same, the table is built solidly to withstand years of use and abuse, both indoors and out.

When I was a student at James Krenov's woodworking program at the College of the Redwoods, money was tight. Having virtually no furniture, though, I needed to make some basic utilitarian pieces including a kitchen table. I went to the local lumberyard and purchased just enough 2x stock to make a trestle table like the one in the photo above. I liked that first table's lines and wanted to try it in a nicer wood, so I chose clear, vertical-grained red cedar because it's highly rot-resistant: The table can be used outside as well as in the kitchen or dining room.

Building this table can be done just as easily with power tools as with hand tools and may even be slightly quicker. But the scale of the joinery and the simplicity of the design also make this an ideal project on which to practice cutting joints by hand.

I use hand tools exclusively, partially because acquiring and practicing hand-tool skills is what initially attracted me to woodworking. But mostly I use hand tools because I really enjoy planing and cutting joinery by hand, and I really don't enjoy the scream of electric saws, routers and sanders.

The trestles

I built the two trestles first, then the related pieces (stretcher, wedges and battens) and, finally, the top. By having the trestles and related pieces ready when I finish the top, I can attach the battens to the underside of the top right away, connecting top and base before there's any chance of major wood movement. If I built the top first, it could have warped while I was building the base, making it difficult to connect the two.

I used dimensional red cedar for this project, which I cut to length, planed smooth and laid out for mortises and tenons. I clamped each of the trestle members in my bench vise and bored holes for the mortises using a brace and expansion bit (see the top left photo on p. 14). I set the expansion bit to the width of one of

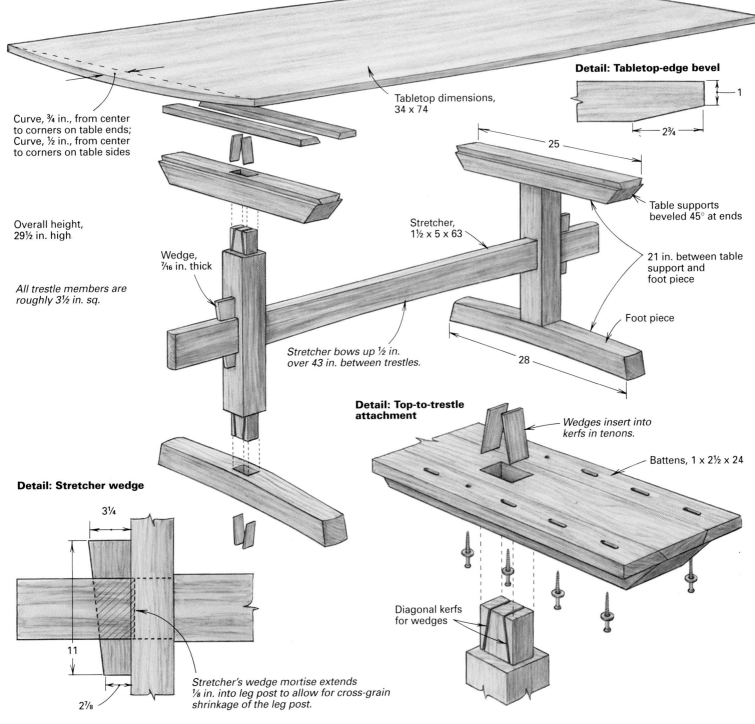

Indoor/outdoor trestle dining table

Curve, ¾ in., from center to corners on table ends;
Curve, ½ in., from center to corners on table sides

Tabletop dimensions, 34 x 74

Detail: Tabletop-edge bevel

1

2¾

Overall height, 29½ in. high.

All trestle members are roughly 3½ in. sq.

Wedge, 7/16 in. thick

25

Table supports beveled 45° at ends

Stretcher, 1½ x 5 x 63

21 in. between table support and foot piece

Stretcher bows up ½ in. over 43 in. between trestles.

Foot piece

28

Detail: Top-to-trestle attachment

Wedges insert into kerfs in tenons.

Battens, 1 x 2½ x 24

Detail: Stretcher wedge

3¼

11

2⅞

Stretcher's wedge mortise extends ⅛ in. into leg post to allow for cross-grain shrinkage of the leg post.

Diagonal kerfs for wedges

my mortise chisels and positioned a depth stop to just less than half the depth of the mortise. To ensure the holes are perpendicular to the surface of the workpieces, I clamped the work so that my drilling motion keeps the bit naturally level. I sight along the bit and the sides of the workpiece to keep the bit from wandering to the left or right. After boring to the depth stop, I repeat from the other side, leaving just a wisp of wood in the middle.

I cleaned out the mortises with a mallet and a registered mortise chisel, which has square sides but is not as thick as a standard mortise chisel (see the photo at right on p. 14). I kept the blade perpendicular to the length of the mortise, and I chopped from one end of the mortise to the other, staying just shy of the marked top and the bottom shoulder lines. After hogging out most of the mortise with the bit and brace and the registered mortise chisel, I came back with a paring chisel. I pared the mortise clean, squaring the ends and making sure the sidewalls are relatively smooth

and square (see the bottom left photo on p. 14).

Once I've finished all six trestle mortises (four for trestle assembly, two for the stretcher), I cut the shoulders and then the cheeks on the tenons of the vertical trestle members, smooth all tenon surfaces with a shoulder plane and kerf the tenons diagonally (see the drawing above). Kerfing the tenons diagonally, toward the outside of the tenon (see the drawing), causes the outer sections of the tenon to splay, almost like a hinge. Diagonal kerfs reduce the likelihood of a crack extending beyond the tenon when I drive the wedges home later. Cracks are also less likely with diagonal kerfs because the plane of the sawkerf does not follow the grain.

Next I shaped the two horizontal trestle members: a 45° bevel at the ends of the top pieces (which support the tabletop), a ⅜-in. taper on either side and a ⅝-in. taper on the top of the foot piece (see the drawing). I also planed dovetail rabbets into both sides of both top trestle members where they'll slide into the battens on

BORING, CHOPPING AND PARING WIDE MORTISES

Boring holes perpendicular to the face of a workpiece (left) *with a brace and bit isn't difficult if you position the workpiece vertically and at a height that automatically levels the bit. To keep the brace from wandering left or right, just align the bit visually with the sides of the workpiece.*

To clean large, pre-drilled mortises, use the registered mortise chisel (below). *Its square sides and thick blade keep it snug against the sides of the mortise and parallel to the ends. With a sharp edge on one of these chisels, its mass will make quick work of any mortise.*

A sharp paring chisel will smooth and square the walls of the mortise (above), *ensuring a good, snug fit of an accurately sized tenon in the trestle.*

the underside of the tabletop. I rounded the ends of the foot pieces slightly to reinforce that motif in the tabletop. Then I relieved the bottom of the foot so that it would rest on its two ends, and I slightly chamfered all sharp edges. With all trestle pieces finished, I applied glue to all mating surfaces, started the wedges into the tenons, inserted the tenons into the mortises and then clamped the trestles closed. I tapped the wedges home. The next morning, I sawed them flush and then planed smooth those surfaces on which the tenons were exposed.

Stretcher and wedges

I planed the stretcher stock smooth, crosscut it to length and marked out the tenons. Then I crosscut the shoulders, ripped the cheeks and cleaned up the tenon surfaces with a shoulder plane. I installed the stretcher tenons into the two trestle mortises, marked the stretcher for the wedge mortises (see the drawing for taper) and then disassembled and chopped the mortises (see the photos on the facing page).

Because this mortise is so narrow ($7/16$ in. wide), I skipped drilling it and just pounded out the mortises with a mallet and a sash mortise chisel. Some furnituremakers like to work from the middle out when chopping mortises. I prefer working from one end (just shy, actually) to the other, being careful at the ends not to round over or crush the crisp shoulder of the mortise. Also, because this mortise is tapered, I was particularly careful not to gouge the inclined plane against which the wedge will bear. The more perfect the wedge and this inclined plane mate, the less prone the wedge will be to slip and the more solid will be the table's structural elements.

As a final touch on the stretchers, I rounded the ends side to side, using a rasp and a file, to go along with the foot and the tabletop.

From *Fine Woodworking* (May 1994) 106:60-63

CHOPPING NARROW MORTISES

Chopping from just shy of one end nearly to the other loosens the top layer of the mortise (left). Keeping back from the marked lines at either end keeps the shoulders from being crushed.

Continuing to remove one level of chips at a time (below), as deep as a mallet blow takes you, yields a mortise quickly. The thickness of the mortise chisel blade keeps the mortise true between the marked lines.

I cut the wedges from scrap. The taper is slight: ¾ in. over a foot. It's important that the taper not be too steep because that would cause the wedges to become unseated with the slightest bump to the table. I chamfered the top of both wedges, so they wouldn't split out when tapped into their mortises. I did the same to their bottoms for the sake of symmetry. I left the sides with crisp edges to maximize the bearing surface in the mortises.

Tabletop

For the top, I edge-jointed, glued and clamped three red cedar 2x12s. I sprang a batten on each of the two sides to mark subtle fair curves that sweep from the centers of the sides in ½ in. to the ends. I also marked fair curves along the ends in ¾ in. from the centers to the sides (see the drawing on p. 13). These curves make the table. I scrub-planed top and bottom roughly flat, left the bottom that way (I like the texture) and smooth-planed the top.

I scribed the underside of the table 2¾ in. in from the edge, and then I marked the edge down 1 in. from the finished top surface for a bevel to lighten the appearance of the tabletop. I used a drawknife to eliminate most of the waste, followed up with a scrub plane and finally took the bevel to the two scribe lines (and to a finished surface) with a smooth plane. I chamfered both top and bottom arrises of the table's edge with a block plane.

I ripped, crosscut and planed the four battens that connect the tabletop to the trestles (see the drawing) and drilled and elongated screw holes in the battens. I screwed them to the underside of the table using the stretcher-connected trestles as spacers. ☐

Tony Konovaloff is a professional furnituremaker in Bellingham, Wash.

To square the end of the mortise, position the chisel bevel side in, and chop down along the marked line (above), being careful to keep the chisel perpendicular to the face of the piece. For the tapered (outboard) end of the mortise, pare gradually from both sides until you have a straight uninterrupted plane, top to bottom.

Gate-Leg Table Is Light but Sturdy

*Precisely routed and tablesawn joinery
gives the table its strength*

by Gary Rogowski

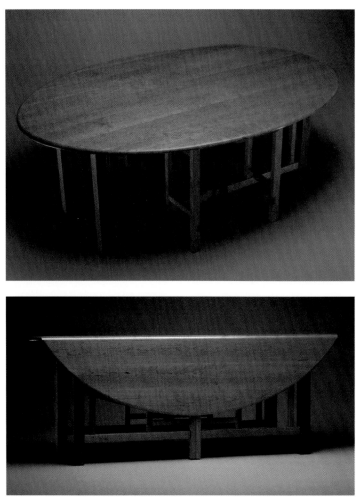

***Contemporary lines and thin gate legs
give this table a light feel** (top). The
table's size, 60 in. by 84 in., seats eight, but
when the leaves are down, the table is
more compact and can be moved against
the wall for more floor space (bottom).*

I was shown a picture once of a gate-leg dining table. It had eight cabriole legs, and it looked like an insect with a tabletop on it. I delicately convinced my prospective clients to let me design a table with a little more grace that still had the drop leaves and gates they wanted. The tabletop was to be an oval large enough to seat eight comfortably. My concern was to lighten the base visually and still provide adequate support for the leaves. The table that resulted satisfied my clients' needs for utility and complemented its surroundings well (see the photos above).

Gate-leg tables were designed to save space. A leg-and-apron assembly, or gate, hinged to the table or pivoting on pins set into the table's framework, swings out to support a leaf that's hinged to the tabletop. In this way, a small table can be transformed easily into a larger one. A single gate can support a leaf on a smaller table, or double gates can be used for larger leaves, such as on this dining table. The gates can also be on one or both sides of the table, depending on the function of the table and how much extra space is desired. When not in use, two leaves take up hardly more space than one. For the finest appearance, rule joints are used between the leaves and top. This joint looks clean and provides support for the leaves. (For how to rout rule joints, see *FWW* #80, p. 48 or the reprint of that article in *The Best of FWW: Router Projects and Techniques,* p. 106.)

Double gates can pivot either toward or away from each other. I decided to have the gates pivot away from each other so that with the leaves down, the gate legs would sit side by side. Measured together, the pair of gate legs are 2½ in. wide, or the same width as one of the outer table legs. This lightens the table visually by making it look like there's only one leg in the center of the table rather than two.

Joinery and pivots

The table is made of cherry. I used 12/4 stock for the legs to avoid laminating thin-

Photos this page: Jim Piper

Drill bit marks pivot point. *After trimming pivot posts to size and checking the fit of the gates, the author marks where he'll drill for the bushing and hinge pin. He drops a drill bit through the bronze bushing in the rail to make a mark.*

ner stock to get the 2½ in. I wanted. Crosscutting something this thick can be a problem. A 2½-in. leg is too thick for a 10-in. tablesaw blade when the leg is riding in a crosscut carriage with a ¾-in. base. I got around this by using two miter gauges with a fence screwed on between them. With this two-miter-gauge setup, I can cut all the way through the legs in one pass. The two gauges also minimize any side-to-side slop that might occur with just one gauge, and the long wooden fence between the two gauges lets me clamp a stop to it to index the length of my cuts for accurate multiple cuts.

I used mortise-and-tenon construction for all the joinery on this table, routing the mortises and cutting the tenons on my ta-

blesaw. The jigs I used for these two operations are as simple as could be, but they do their jobs well and take practically no time to make (see the box on p. 20).

The leaves needed to fold down without binding on the top of the gate. For this to work out, the gates had to pivot out of the way into the table base itself (see figure 1 on the following page).

After cutting, routing and dry-fitting all the joinery, I cut notches in the top and bottom rails where the gate legs will nest, dadoing them just ¾ in. deep. Keeping the

dadoes this shallow ensured I didn't weaken the rails. It also meant I'd have to notch the legs later, so they'd tuck into the rails inside the plane of the table's outer legs. I made the notches in the rail a little wider than the combined width of the two gate legs to allow for the swing of the legs as they open and close.

I debated between using wooden dowels or steel pins for hinging the gates and ended up opting for the steel pins, which I set in bronze bushings. This choice allowed me to deal with glue-ups with something approaching leisure, letting me add on the two gate assemblies later. Another advantage of using steel pins and bronze bushings is that they will probably last through more than a few dinner parties.

Fig. 1: Gate-leg table

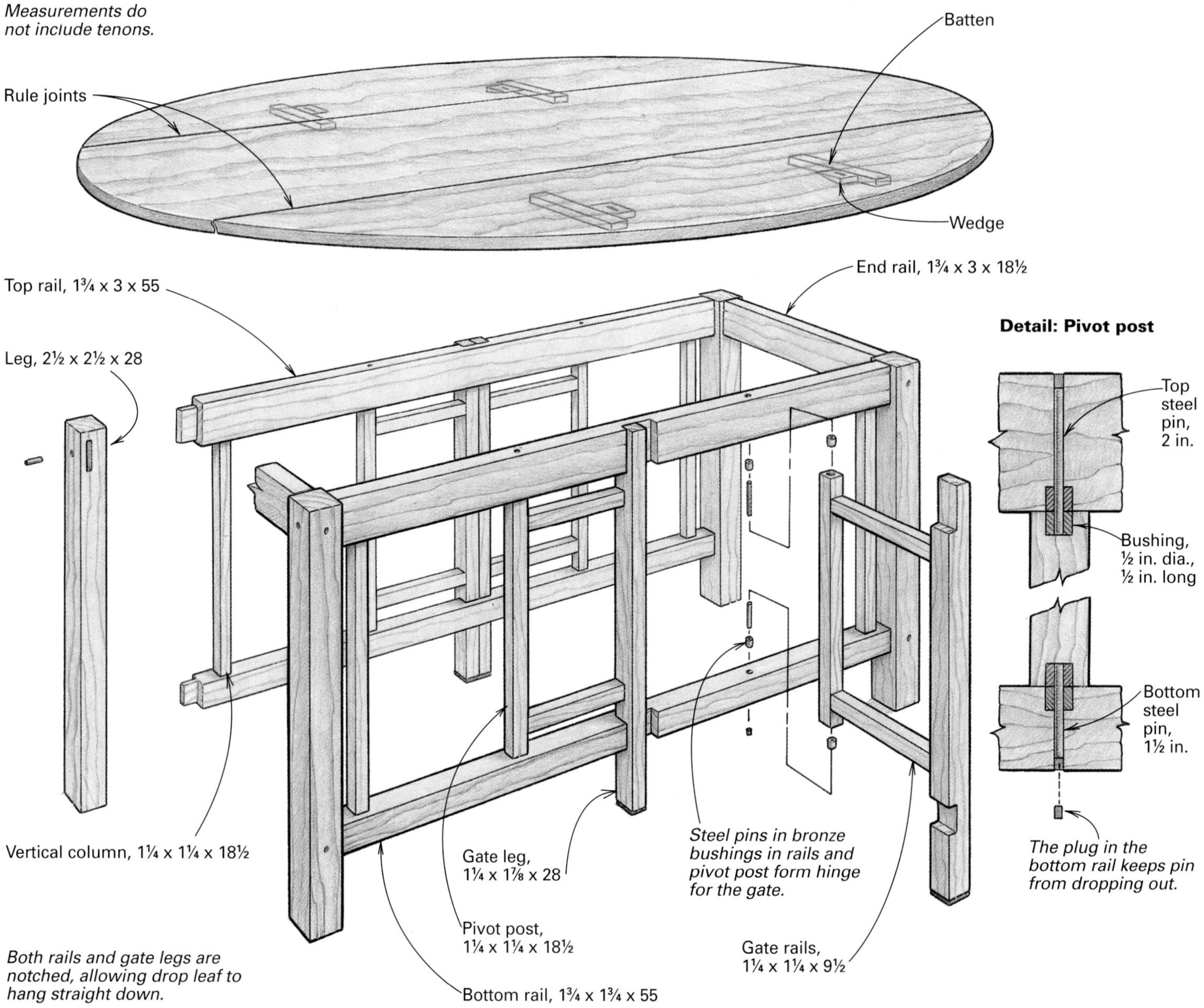

Measurements do not include tenons.

Batten

Rule joints

Wedge

Top rail, 1¾ x 3 x 55

End rail, 1¾ x 3 x 18½

Detail: Pivot post

Leg, 2½ x 2½ x 28

Top steel pin, 2 in.

Bushing, ½ in. dia., ½ in. long

Bottom steel pin, 1½ in.

Steel pins in bronze bushings in rails and pivot post form hinge for the gate.

Vertical column, 1¼ x 1¼ x 18½

The plug in the bottom rail keeps pin from dropping out.

Gate leg, 1¼ x 1⅞ x 28

Both rails and gate legs are notched, allowing drop leaf to hang straight down.

Pivot post, 1¼ x 1¼ x 18½

Gate rails, 1¼ x 1¼ x 9½

Bottom rail, 1¾ x 1¾ x 55

Fig. 2: Mortising fixture

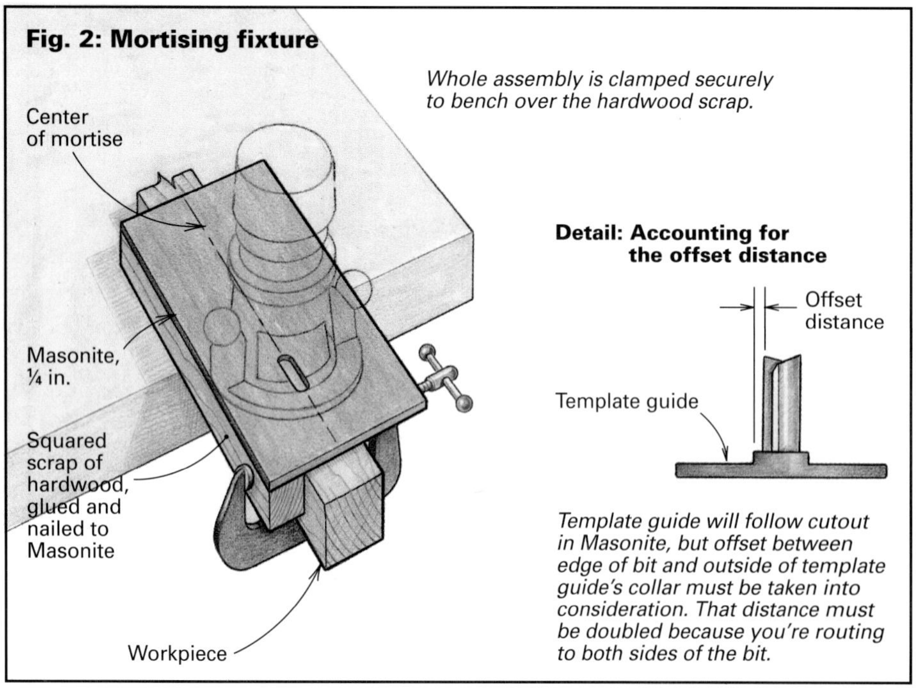

Whole assembly is clamped securely to bench over the hardwood scrap.

Center of mortise

Masonite, ¼ in.

Squared scrap of hardwood, glued and nailed to Masonite

Workpiece

Detail: Accounting for the offset distance

Offset distance

Template guide

Template guide will follow cutout in Masonite, but offset between edge of bit and outside of template guide's collar must be taken into consideration. That distance must be doubled because you're routing to both sides of the bit.

Fig. 3: Tablesaw tenoning jig

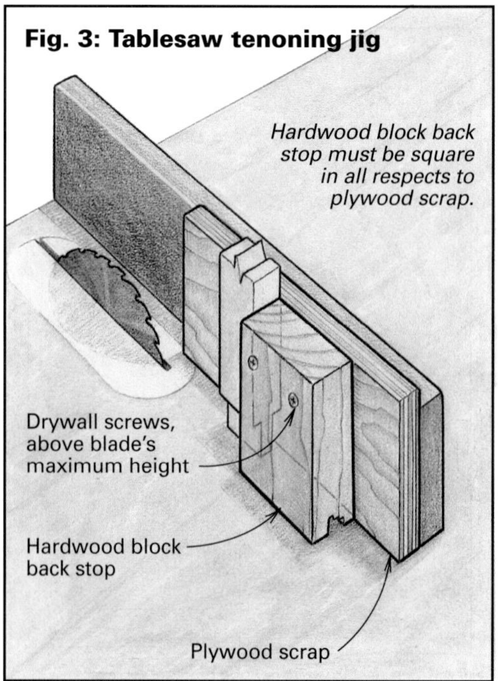

Hardwood block back stop must be square in all respects to plywood scrap.

Drywall screws, above blade's maximum height

Hardwood block back stop

Plywood scrap

I drilled the rails for the gate-pivot pins and bushings on my drill press. For the ½-in.-OD, ⅜-in.-ID bushings I found at my hardware store, I used a ½-in. brad-point bit and drilled exactly ½ in. into the rails. Next I centered a ¹³⁄₃₂-in. bit (⅜ in. was just a little too snug for the steel pins) on the dimple at the bottoms of the bushing holes in the rails and drilled all the way through the rails into scrap to prevent tearout. Then I took a smear of epoxy and glued the bushings into their holes in the rails.

The bushings were twice as long as I needed, so I came up with a simple, quick way of turning one into two. I marked the bushings with a pencil midway along their length, stuck a ⅜-in. dowel most of the way through the bushing and then chucked the dowel into the drill press.

I set my hacksaw on a wooden block and adjusted the drill-press table so that the hacksaw blade was even with the pencil mark and the blade's teeth face into the rotating bushing. I cut the bushing with the drill press set at its lowest speed (see the photo at right). I could tell when I was through the bushing because the blade started spitting sawdust. I deburred the inner edges of the bushings before epoxying them into the legs and pivot posts.

As a last step before gluing, I dry-clamped each half of the base together to ensure that everything fit well. And then I marked and mitered the ends of the upper rail tenons on both the ends and sides.

Glue-up sequence
I glued the vertical columns to the long rails first, taking care to make sure that the frame went together perfectly square by temporarily dry-clamping the legs to the rails. Next I glued the long side rails to the legs. After that joint set up, I joined the two long assemblies with the short end rails. It helps not to be too liberal with the glue for the long side rails because you'll have the glue puddling up inside the mortise for the end rails. Then you'll have to wipe or chip the mess out.

I checked both gates as I was gluing them up to ensure they stayed flat, and I was careful not to overclamp. A twisted gate will cause major problems when you

try to fit it to the table. I sighted across the posts and rails of the gate to see that they were in line. If they had been out of alignment, I would have used some judicious clamp-tweaking to pull them flat. After the gate assemblies had dried, I notched the gate-leg posts on the tablesaw so that

A hacksaw blade makes quick work of an overlong bushing. With his drill press set at its lowest speed, the author makes two ½-in. bushings from one 1-in. bushing. It's easy to tell when you're through the bushing because sawdust from the dowel starts coming off the blade.

they would mate with the notches on the rails and be out of the way of the leaves.

Fitting the gates
I set the two gate assemblies in place so that the center of the pivot posts lined up with the centers of the bushed holes in the rails. I trimmed the pivot posts as necessary to fit between the top and bottom rails without binding and without too much play. I also checked to ensure that the reveal between the gate legs was even top to bottom. Once I was satisfied with how the gates looked in relation to the rest of the

table, I marked centers on the pivot posts by dropping a ⅜-in. bit down through the bushing in the top rail and pushing it up through the bushing in the bottom rail (see the photo on p. 17). Then I just repeated the procedure I went through for the rails on the pivot posts, drilling for the bushing first and then for the steel pin. I plugged the hole in the bottom of the bottom rail later to keep the pin from dropping out with the gate attached to the base.

I also slightly beveled the insides of the outer gate legs where they come together, so they wouldn't bind when both were opened together. Then I marked and trimmed the bottoms of the legs so that with plastic glides on them, they're just touching the floor. If the legs are too short, they won't support the leaves. If they're too long, they'll lift the table and stress the hinges connecting the leaves to the table.

Each gate leg also needs to be tall enough to support its leaf without any sag. Leaves that are perfectly flush with the center portion of the tabletop are what you're looking for. The problem is that if your leg is at just the right height, there's virtually no clearance to swing the gate by the leaf without scraping the bottom of the leaf. To prevent this scarring, I cut the leg between ¹⁄₁₆ in. and ⅛ in. less than I really wanted it to be, and later I screwed a wedge in place on the underside of the table to make up for that shortfall (see figure 1). This provides the necessary clearance and gives a nice flat appearance across the whole top.

Making the oval tabletop
The tabletop is an oval measuring 60 in. by 82 in. I laid out a quarter of an oval on some thick paper folded in quarters. I cut out the quarter-oval, unfolded the paper and retraced the whole oval onto a sheet of cardboard to get some idea of how the tabletop would look. I used this rough pattern to lay up boards for the tabletop. If a board had a knot or defect at one end, I used it where that end would be cut off during the final shaping. I glued up my top and leaves, sanded them, cut and shaped the rule joints and hinged the leaves to the center of the top, all before I cut my oval.

I roughed out the oval with a sabersaw, a good blade and a steady hand. For the finish-cut, though, I created a router jig based on the instructions for drawing an ellipse in Ernest Joyce's *Encyclopedia of Furniture Making* (Sterling Publishing Co. Inc., 1987). A similar jig is shown in *FWW* #82, p. 88. I used my plunge router to make the cuts just ⅛ in. deep each pass. I took my time to minimize tearout, espe-cially at the two sections where I was cut-ting against the grain. The final pass, which uses the entire cutting edge of the router bit, needs to be done very slowly and carefully. Once it's cut, though, you have a perfect oval that needs just a bit of sanding along its edge.

One other feature I added to the top is a pair of battens beneath each leaf to keep the leaves flat. I positioned them right be-hind the wedges, so they also prevent the gates from rotating too far. The center part of the tabletop extends far enough out to the sides that the top rail doesn't get in the way of the battens or prevent them from hanging straight down. ☐

Gary Rogowski designs and builds custom furniture and teaches woodworking at the Oregon School of Arts and Crafts.

Jigs and fixtures: They don't have to be fancy to work well

I like low-tech solutions, and I'm not giv-en to buying expensive jigs or fixtures when I can make my own. For the mor-tises on this table, I made a template-routing fixture for my plunge router. It consists of a little piece of Masonite nailed to a squared scrap of hardwood, and it takes less than a half-hour to lay out and build (see figure 2 on p. 18).

I use a piece of Masonite wider than my workpiece and the scrap hardwood side by side to give my plunge router a stable platform. The hardwood scrap should be a little less deep than the workpiece, so the workpiece can be clamped to the bench. I figure out the distance from the inside edge of the hardwood scrap, which sets against the face of my workpiece, to the center of the workpiece and mark this distance on the underside of the Masonite.

I make the cutout in the Masonite as wide as my template guide. To get the correct mortise length, I add twice the offset distance (from the edge of my router bit to the outside of the template-guide collar) to the mortise length and mark that overall length on the under-side of the Masonite (see the detail in fig-ure 2 on p. 18).

To make the cutout in the Masonite, I set up the fence on my router table so that the bit is centered on what will be the center of the mortise cutout in the Masonite, and I rout away. I use the pen-ciled marks on the underside of the Ma-sonite as my stop marks. Because the hardwood block is squared, I can use it as a reference surface against my router table's fence.

To rout the mortise, I simply clamp the fixture to my workpiece, clamp the workpiece to my bench and have at it (see the photo at left). The template guide takes care of the rest.

My tablesaw tenoning jig is simpler yet. I take a length of plywood a bit shorter than my rip fence and glue and screw a 4- or 5-in.-high block of hard-wood scrap to it so that the forward face of the block is at 90° to the table (see fig-ure 3). If you screw the block to the ply-wood as I did, make sure you do so above the maximum height of your ta-blesaw blade. My right hand presses the workpiece and plywood tight against the rip fence. My left hand keeps the work-piece snug against the plywood and the hardwood block as I guide the work-piece through the blade (see the photo at left). You could also attach a toggle clamp to the hardwood block to hold the workpiece in place for more safety.

I cut the shoulders of the tenons first using a regular crosscut box, and then I rough-cut the cheeks on the bandsaw. I take the cheeks down to final thickness (dictated by my mortises) on the table-saw with this simple jig. —*G.R.*

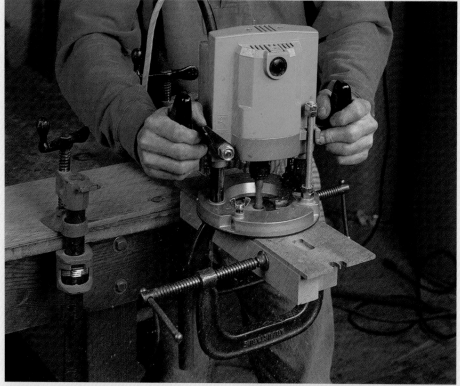

Simple and accurate mortising. The author's template-guide fixture makes for accurate mortises as long as they're laid out properly and the router is held square to the workpiece. He plunges and routs a little at a time to save wear on the router's bearings.

From the scrap bin, a serviceable, de-pendable tenoning jig. It may not look like much, but the author's tenoning jig has seen more than a few projects go out of the shop over the years. An accurate 90° back stop is all it takes; careful guid-ing of the workpiece does the rest.

A Table for Breakfast or Banquets

Drop down legs support expansion mechanism

by Steven M. Lash

Extra legs add support and rigidity to tables that expand beyond the usual additional 2 ft. or 3 ft. Drop-down legs hidden in the expansion mechanism enable this Queen Anne dining table to expand to more than 14 ft. long.

With the center legs retracted into channels in the beams of the expansion mechanism, the ends can be pushed together to shrink the table from 14 ft. long to just 60 in. long.

A s a reproduction cabinetmaker, I am constantly looking for examples of 18th-century American furniture that can inspire new projects. My unsuccessful search for an expandable Queen Anne dining table led me to design and build a table with an unusual extension slide mechanism: It incorporates hidden legs that can be dropped down to provide extra support as the table is expanded. The legs remain concealed inside the beams of the slide mechanism when they're not needed.

The convenience of drop-down legs was a crucial factor in my overall table design. I wanted my table to have a pair of fluted, pillar-and-claw pedestals (rather than four legs) as its principal supports. I also wanted significant expansion capacity—from 5 ft. long in the closed position to over 14 ft. long with all the leaves in place (see the photos above). In this article, I'll describe a smaller version of the extension slide mechanism that I used in my table.

How the extension slide works

Like many table extension mechanisms, mine extends and retracts in telescope fashion. Fixed to one end of the table is a central beam—the narrowest part of the telescope. The remaining beams in the mechanism function in pairs, sliding against the edges of adjacent beams as the table is extended. The outermost pair of beams is fixed to the opposite end of the table (see figure 1 on the following page).

Although I knew that drop-down legs would help to stabilize my table in stretched-out form, I still wanted to minimize sag when the mechanism was fully extended. A good way to do this is to maximize beam overlap when the mechanism is fully extended. I divided the 48-in.-long beam into thirds, allowing for an overlap of two-thirds and an extension of one-third, or 16 in. (The beam length is determined by the size of the tabletop, allowing space for overhang and apron thickness.) Once you know the maximum beam extension, you can calculate how many beam pairs will be required to achieve the full extension of your table.

The only major limitations in designing a table around my extension mechanism are the width and thickness of the mechanism. It can't exceed the space you have available beneath the table and between the table aprons (see figure 1). The extension-assembly

Photos: Dirk Bakker; drawing: Bob La Pointe

beams are paired around a larger central beam (see figure 2 on the facing page). The wide central beam is mortised to receive a tenon that extends from the top of one pedestal.

As in any expanding table design, it's very important for the extension mechanism to be solidly anchored to the table ends. In a pedestal-type table like mine, table-end construction must include solid connection details for the pedestals as well as for the extension mechanism. With this in mind, I designed a drawer-like compartment, or sleeve, formed by the tabletop, two side aprons and a bottom support board in each table end. A pair of steel angles and a ¼-in.-thick steel plate reinforce each sleeve.

The extension mechanism and the pedestals are secured to the bottom support, not to the tabletop. The tabletop, fastened to the aprons with machine screws and threaded inserts, is easily removed for access to the entire extension mechanism.

One pedestal has a tenon that extends through the bottom support board, through the steel plate and through a mortise cut in the central beam. Wedges and screws add rigidity at this critical connection. The other pedestal is screwed to a 3-in.-dia. pipe flange that is, in turn, screwed to the steel plate.

Wood dovetails and brass guides

In a well-functioning extension mechanism, the beams are coupled together and glide smoothly against one another. In my initial design, I planned to couple the beams with sliding dovetails—beam-long dovetail pins that would slide in dovetail slots milled along beam edges. To test the design, I built a mock-up mechanism out of 2x4s.

The mock-up was a good idea. I learned that the overall weight of my test mechanism caused the dovetails to bind. This prevented the beams from sliding smoothly against each other. If weight was a problem with fir 2x4s, it would only get worse with the maple I planned to use for the finished version.

To solve the binding problem, I added some guides made from brass angle stock. The guides have a leg that rides in a slot milled along the edge of the adjoining beam (see figure 2). There are more guides on top of the beams than on the bottom because the hollow section in the bottom of each leg-carrying beam doesn't leave enough wood for guide slots or mortises.

To make the sliding surfaces more slippery, I let in a pair of plastic strips on either side of each beam's dovetail slot. The central beam has dovetail slots and strips on both sides. I cut the plastic from a sheet of high-density polyethylene (HDPE), available from Laird Plastics, Inc., 1400 Centrepark Blvd., Suite 510, West Palm Beach, Fla. 33401; (407) 689-2200. Similar to teflon, but less expensive, HDPE is easy to cut on the tablesaw.

I made some staple-like stops from brass rod (which is available at most hobby shops) and drove them into the upper guide grooves to prevent each beam from sliding beyond its maximum extension of 16 in. Also, I screwed a small stop into the dovetail slots to prevent each beam from sliding beyond the closed position. To close against this stop, the adjacent beam's dovetail pin needs to be trimmed. By removing the end stops, and a few central brass guides, it is possible to completely disassemble the mechanism.

Making the beams was fairly straightforward. I milled the dovetail slots on my shaper, using a ½-in.-dia. dovetail bit. The rest of the work was done on the tablesaw: cutting out the dovetail pins, rabbeting beam edges to receive plastic strips and cutting guide slots. Making multiple passes with the dado cutter, I cut the channel for each drop-down leg. This channel needn't extend the full length of the beam. Instead, it can be stopped a couple of inches from where the base of the leg will fit.

The drop-down legs

I carved the drop-down legs in Queen Anne style, tapering from the square top section to just above the carved pad foot. The top edges of each leg are radiused so that the leg can swing freely without binding against its channel.

Removable, brass pins hinge the drop-down legs to their respective beams. I made the pins from brass rod, threading one end of each pin and cutting a straight screwdriver slot in the other. Then I held the leg in its correct position in the beam and drilled a pilot hole through the beam and leg. Next, I enlarged the pilot hole in the leg to accept a length of brass tubing. The tubing prevents the

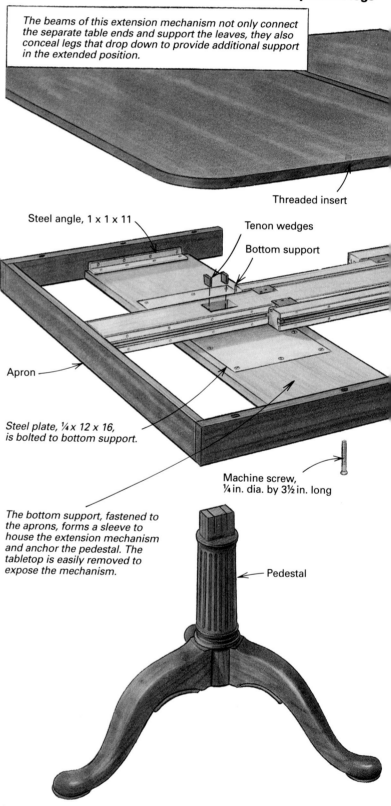

Fig. 1: Table expansion mechanism houses drop-down legs

The beams of this extension mechanism not only connect the separate table ends and support the leaves, they also conceal legs that drop down to provide additional support in the extended position.

Threaded insert

Steel angle, 1 x 1 x 11

Tenon wedges

Bottom support

Apron

Steel plate, ¼ x 12 x 16, is bolted to bottom support.

Machine screw, ¼ in. dia. by 3½ in. long

The bottom support, fastened to the aprons, forms a sleeve to house the extension mechanism and anchor the pedestal. The tabletop is easily removed to expose the mechanism.

Pedestal

pin from enlarging the hole with use. After installing a threaded insert in the beam to receive the threaded end of the pin, I installed the leg by inserting the pin through one installation hole and through the leg and screwing the pin into the threaded insert.

A brass ball catch holds each leg in place in the beam channel until the leg is pulled free. I used a Brusso ball catch (available from The Woodworkers' Store, 21801 Industrial Blvd., Rogers, Minn. 55374; 612-428-3200). For more holding leverage, install the catch as far down the square section of the leg as possible.

Adjustable floor glides are an important feature on my drop-down legs. The threaded insert that fits in the bottom of the foot

enables me to fine-tune the leg length to accommodate floor irregularities.

I glued some felt in the channels where the drop-down legs fit. The felt is most useful near the base of the leg to protect the carved foot from scraping against the beam as a leg is returned to its concealed position. In addition to its protective function, the felt is a fine finishing touch for a mechanism that you're bound to be showing off.   □

Steven Lash builds furniture as an avocation in Bloomfield Hills, Mich.

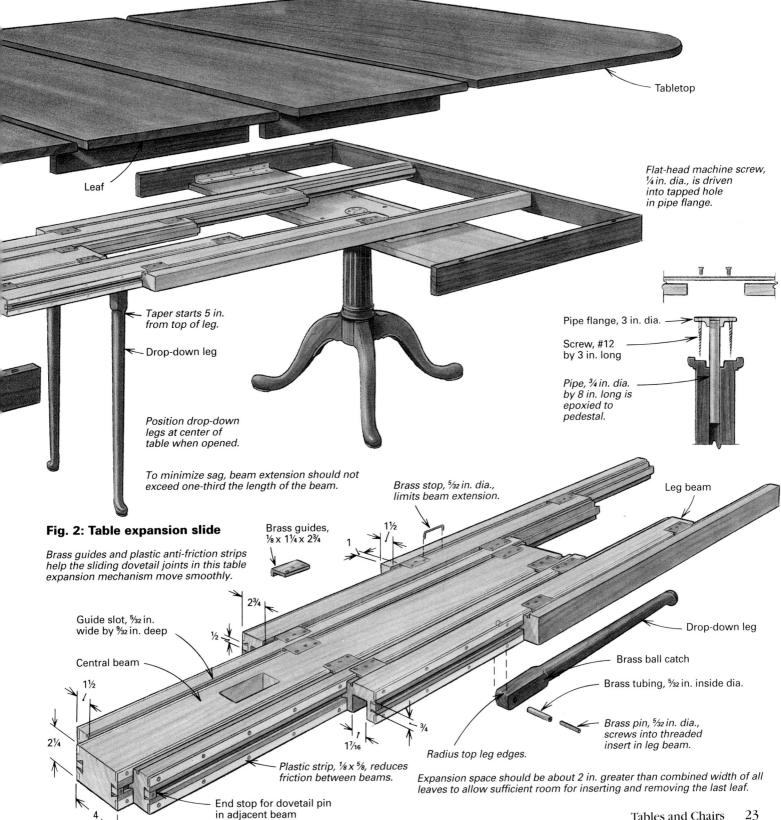

Tabletop

Flat-head machine screw, ¼ in. dia., is driven into tapped hole in pipe flange.

Leaf

Taper starts 5 in. from top of leg.

Drop-down leg

Pipe flange, 3 in. dia.

Screw, #12 by 3 in. long

Pipe, ¾ in. dia. by 8 in. long is epoxied to pedestal.

Position drop-down legs at center of table when opened.

To minimize sag, beam extension should not exceed one-third the length of the beam.

Brass stop, ⁵⁄₃₂ in. dia., limits beam extension.

Leg beam

Fig. 2: Table expansion slide

Brass guides and plastic anti-friction strips help the sliding dovetail joints in this table expansion mechanism move smoothly.

Brass guides, ⅛ x 1¼ x 2¾

1½
1

2¾

½

Guide slot, ⁵⁄₃₂ in. wide by ⁹⁄₃₂ in. deep

Central beam

1½

2¼

1⁷⁄₁₆

¾

Drop-down leg

Brass ball catch

Brass tubing, ⁵⁄₃₂ in. inside dia.

Brass pin, ⁵⁄₃₂ in. dia., screws into threaded insert in leg beam.

Radius top leg edges.

Plastic strip, ⅛ x ⅝, reduces friction between beams.

End stop for dovetail pin in adjacent beam

4

Expansion space should be about 2 in. greater than combined width of all leaves to allow sufficient room for inserting and removing the last leaf.

Shaping refines a table's design. The author first uses models, measurements and full-scale drawings to work out a dining-table design. Plywood templates (foreground) help execute that design. But even so, subtle shaping in the shop makes the table more inviting to the touch and to the eye.

Making Dining Tables That Work

Careful measuring and common sense ensure stability, comfort and good looks

by Peter Tischler

"Make furniture that people can be comfortable living with." So said Sam Maloof, the noted chairmaker, and this same guiding principle is at the heart of the furniture I build. Optimum comfort certainly applies to chairs, and the same holds true for dining tables. When building a dining table, I start by finding out how the owner likes to dine and where the table is going. I use this information to come up with rough sketches and scale models, which convey material and proportions better than drawings. Then I measure everything—people, dining room, rugs, existing furniture and china—so I can translate dimensions to drawings and occasional mock-ups. This multi-step process almost always leads to a table that best suits the customer.

Design is always a compromise

How a dining table relates to its users is just as important as how it relates to its surroundings. The best tables are the ones that make tiny compromises. For example, when building a table for a family with children, the durability of the finish on the tabletop outweighs the need of the finish to be authentic to the table's style period. Fortunately, there are some simple guidelines that will help with design decisions.

Seating—The first step is to determine the number of people to be seated, so you can figure the table size that will fit them comfortably. If the owner entertains regularly, you'll want to make a table with an expanding top that doesn't require a complicated leaf system or a forest of legs. I consult a number of references (see the further reading box on p. 26) to get ideas for seating needs. They are only a starting point, though. General rules (for example, the commonly given 24 in. of elbow room per person) may have to be increased or decreased to take into account the type of table, the space needed for the chairs or how else the table might be used. Figure 1 on p. 25 shows a typical table plan for seating six people.

Basic dining dimensions— I've found that the most comfortable height of a dining table is between 28 in. and 28½ in., which is a bit lower than what the textbooks say. But for a family, that height is more informal and makes the sitters feel relaxed. The height, of course, depends on the chairs and whether the table has an apron that will limit leg clearance (see figure 2 on p. 26).

The width and shape of a dining table's top also affect seating arrangement. Most chairs are 20 in. wide or so, but you will need better than 24 in. of place-setting width for most people and even more if you're dealing with squirming teenagers. For the minimum overall width of the table, I use 36 in. A table much over 40 in. wide will lose any feeling of intimacy between eaters on opposite sides. An oval top offers more side seating than a rectangular top of similar square footage. (It's easier to squeeze two more people

It takes more than a measuring tape for good table design. The author uses small models, full-size chair and sideboard mock-ups, full-scale drawings and templates.

Quarter-scale models show table options—From the left, the model bases are single pedestal, double pedestal, trestle and leg and rail. Models also present wood choices.

may have to do some hybrid designing to come up with a table that matches a sideboard or china hutch. Similarly, if you're making a contemporary table, it's useful to know the tastes of your client because you're likely to borrow the lines or elements of his or her favorite furniture pieces. Here's where models can help.

When I build quarter-scale table models, I make several variations to help the customer visualize differences in proportions and materials. I use various woods to show what color, figure and grain patterns will look like in the room. Alternative shapes for the top, such as free-form edges and book-matched halves, are another example of what models can depict. Models can also present a variety of base forms, which show how much room there will be under the top and how stable the footprint will be (for more on this, see *FWW* #92, p. 28). The following are the four most common base types I use.

in at the ends of an oval when company comes over.) But because square and round tables take up less space, they often fit better in small dining areas.

Measure everything before you cut anything

After you've figured out the seating and overall table size, take out a tape measure, sit at a comfortable dining table and think about the relationships of sitter to chair to table.

Then start taking real-life dimensions. With the biggest sitter in a relaxed, seated position, measure the distance between his or her elbows and knees. Measure knee heights, and add a little extra to establish the bottom of the apron height. Measure how far forward the person likes to put his or her feet. Measure dinner plates, serving platters and the room where the table is going. Exact dimensions aren't as important as how they all relate. Once you get to the final shop drawings (see the top photo), you'll already have a good idea of how the table will look, and consequently, how it will match the room and furnishings that surround it.

Models show table proportions and styles

Most styles of furniture offer variations for dining tables, such as top shapes, woods to use and options for bases. It's worth looking at lots of examples of the period you're working in because you

Fig. 1: Dining dimension guidelines

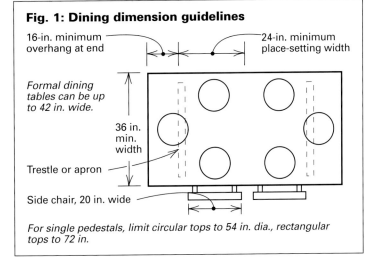

16-in. minimum overhang at end

24-in. minimum place-setting width

Formal dining tables can be up to 42 in. wide.

36 in. min. width

Trestle or apron

Side chair, 20 in. wide

For single pedestals, limit circular tops to 54 in. dia., rectangular tops to 72 in.

Single pedestal—In terms of stability and looks, the mahogany model (the first one in the bottom photo) shows the relative proportions a single-pedestal table should have. An oval top resting on a single-pedestal base is probably my favorite dining table, partly because it allows for extra sitters. Because this type of table has a central column, it makes sense to have an even number of people on each side (an odd number can cramp the person sitting in the middle).

Single pedestals also lend themselves well to a round top, but there is a size limit that the pedestal will support. I limit round tops to 54 in. dia., unless the undercarriage is quite heavy. A rectangular top on a pedestal shouldn't be much over 72 in. long.

Double pedestal—A double-pedestal table (the second model in the bottom photo) will fit an odd number of sitters per side staggered around the columns. The model shows how a free-form top, here in wormy red maple, looks over a walnut base. The top's slightly asymmetrical shape, which widens in places, actually offers extra knee space where the curved vertical members are. The two pedestals spread out the center of gravity, so the table can be quite long. Double-pedestal tables are good for expansion (using draw leaves) because the place settings will be in the right spots.

*Trestle—*Trestle tables (see the third model in the bottom photo on the previous page) are great for accommodating many people because there are lots of expandable-top options. Even without leaves, a trestle table can be long because the length mainly depends on the strength of the stretcher and how far the top boards can span. In the case of the trestle model, the bookmatched cherry top has butterfly keys joining two large boards, similar to classic George Nakashima tables. The model also shows that the base uprights are shaped inward at knee level to accommodate sitters at the ends of each side.

There are two major drawbacks of a trestle table: First, it requires lots of overhang (compared to a leg-and-rail table) at each end to give enough room for end sitters. To allow for this, pull a chair up to the edge of a dining table, and measure how far in the ends are. I generally allow 16 in. as a minimum amount of overhang all around the tabletop. Second, the trestle's feet interfere with people seated at the ends of each side.

*Leg and rail—*Leg-and-rail tables, such as the fourth model in the bottom photo on the previous page, can be strong, as well as quick and economical to build. But because a table's legs can take up much of the sitter's leg room, I give each sitter at least 28 in. of width for comfort because about 3 in. is lost around each post. Or a

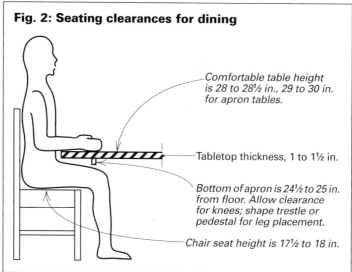

Fig. 2: Seating clearances for dining

Comfortable table height is 28 to 28½ in., 29 to 30 in. for apron tables.

Tabletop thickness, 1 to 1½ in.

Bottom of apron is 24½ to 25 in. from floor. Allow clearance for knees; shape trestle or pedestal for leg placement.

Chair seat height is 17½ to 18 in.

Further reading

Designing Furniture by Seth Stem, The Taunton Press, PO Box 5506, Newtown, CT 06470

Encyclopedia of Furniture Making by Ernest Joyce, Sterling Publishing Co. Inc., 387 Park Avenue South, New York, NY 10016

Fine Woodworking on Tables and Desks, The Taunton Press, PO Box 5506, Newtown, CT 06470

Designing for family needs—The author had the family in mind when he designed this table to seat six comfortably, with room for a high chair. He used end leaves to allow plenty of elbow and leg room without dividing or disrupting the figure in the tabletop's center.

But to work out final construction details and to produce templates, I usually make full-scale drawings. I then use the templates to shape the parts (see the photo on p. 24).

There are benefits to using solid wood for the whole table, including the top. For me, the durability, variation in grain and smooth transition of top to edge make solid-wood tops worth the effort (see the photo). Though veneered tops may be stable and show consistent pattern and color, there are ways of achieving similar results in solid wood.

For stability, I use only well-seasoned stock. To keep the boards flat, I rough-mill in several sessions over two weeks to acclimate the wood to my shop. The best way I've found to keep consistent grain and figure patterns is by using the widest boards available. Wide boards are usually much easier to match than narrow ones.

For color continuity, I like the logs that are to be cut into tabletop stock to be sawn clear through. If this isn't practical,

leg-and-apron table can be fitted with a bow-sided top, like the model, and the legs spread out to the corners to provide more seating room. I build leg-and-rail tables slightly higher—about 29 in.—to allow enough leg clearance because the apron will take up some height. To do this, determine the bottom of the apron height by measuring the largest sitter in a chair. Chairs are typically 17½ to 18 in. high at the seat. Allowing 6 to 7 in. for the thighs to go under the top, the bottom of the apron should usually be 24½ to 25 in. above the floor (see figure 2).

The importance of scale drawings and materials

Proportions are such an important part of overall design. I've found that one-quarter scale drawings and models bring up the design issues and questions that I need to present to the customer.

select boards from the same lot, and buy all your wood at the same time. Then when gluing up the top, go for the best grain match rather than trying to orient all the end grain a certain way.

Changes in top thickness as small as ¹⁄₁₆ in. can have a dramatic effect on how we perceive the table as a whole. My tops vary from 1 to 1½ in. thick. I allow extra thickness for planing the wood a few times before matching up the boards for glue-up. Longer boards will likely be cupped or twisted, so give yourself enough wood rather than under-sizing the top's thickness just to get it flat. When connecting the top to its base, allow for seasonal movement by using screws in slotted holes or cabinetmaker's buttons. ☐

Peter Tischler is a North Bennet Street School graduate who runs a chairmaking and cabinetmaking shop in Caldwell, N.J.

From *Fine Woodworking* (January 1995) 110:61-63

Sofa Table Complements Antiques

This eclectic design blends styles and joinery

by Gene McCall

By skillfully combining mahogany and glass, Gene McCall met his clients' need for a sofa table that fit aesthetically within a room of mixed styles. To do this, McCall designed the piece with a variety of decoration, like the corner fret detail (below).

W hen a husband and wife asked me to design a sofa table for them, I knew that the piece would have to go with the other furniture in their living room and fit easily into the context of their home. The room in question was decorated with an eclectic mix of formal 18th-century American and English antiques. The imposing look of the room was softened by colorful floral fabrics and oriental rugs, as well as by a contemporary coffee table. Even the house itself was eclectic architecturally. Because of these things, I decided that the sofa table should incorporate different design motifs (see the photos on this page) and joinery that would harmonize with the restrained elegance of the home and its furnishings.

Design and materials

Aside from lovely wood and a rich finish, I felt the real snap of my clients' sofa table should come from details, like delicate moldings and lively frets. The design I arrived at (Chinese Chippendale in spirit) blends well with most any room featuring English or American period furniture.

In the corner of my shop was a particularly lovely piece of highly figured mahogany with wild dark grain streaks. It was ideal for the table's lower shelf. To make the shelf more visible and also to help maintain a feeling of lightness about the table, I chose to inset the tabletop with three pieces of glass. This meant I needed to finish the aprons and corner frets inside and out. For the aprons, moldings, legs and top-frame parts, I selected pieces of straight-grain mahogany.

I cut all the pieces to rough width and length, leaving extra length for end tenons. After I squared all edges to their faces, I thicknessed the pieces. I cut the leg mortises and apron tenons and drilled and countersunk holes in the aprons (see the drawing on p. 29) for screwing on the top and shelf.

Shaping the legs

To create the profile on the outside corner of the leg faces, I first shaped the corner bead. I adapted a cutter by grinding down

a standard ¼-in. beading cutter until each shoulder came to a point. Beading the legs required only one depth and one fence setting, but I had to make four passes for each leg: two passes (each in a different direction) for the center bead and one pass each for the two other corner beads. Although I used my shaper to do this, a router table would also work.

I used similar multi-step cutting to form each face's swell. Using two passes, I

From *Fine Woodworking* (May 1993) 100:63-65

To cut chamfers with a jointer, McCall clamps a stop on the outfeed table, tilts the fence to 45°, sets the infeed side for a full cut and passes the leg corner over the cutterhead up to the stop. Once the chamfer's ending arc is cut, he backs and lifts the leg off.

Rabbets cut on the shaper connect the tabletop's crosspieces to rails. Using rabbet-and-dowel joinery in the top frame allows McCall to inset the glass panels easily and precisely. He drills the dowel holes before rabbeting the rail edges and crosspiece ends.

shaper-cut two curved flutes to form a gentle crest in the middle of each face. Again, single depth and fence settings did the trick. A couple of passes with a block plane, followed by hand-sanding, rounded off the center crest of the swell. Finally, I cut off the leg blanks' tops and bottoms.

To lighten the legs visually, I chamfered the inside corner of each from the floor up to a point slightly below the frets. To cut the chamfer and its graceful lamb's-tongue-like arc, I pressed my jointer into unusual service. I carefully marked and taped (to prevent tearout) each leg where the chamfer ends in the upper leg. Then I clamped a stop block to my jointer's outfeed table the same distance from the cutterhead. Finally, I set the jointer's fence to 45° and the infeed table to the chamfer depth. Because depth of cut is critical, it's a good idea to make a few trial passes on a scrap of 1⅞-in.-sq. stock before you risk your good wood. For safety, make sure the test piece is at least 16 in. long. Once your jointer is adjusted properly, slowly feed each leg until the end butts the stop (see the top photo). Back the piece off an inch or two from the stop, and lift the leg from the jointer.

Preparing the shelf and apron
After cutting out the shelf to dimension, I routed the half-round on the shelf edges. Next I made a ⅛-in.-thick plywood template to lay out where the legs would meet the shelf corners. I sawed along the shelf's marked off corners and edges, while checking to see that each cutout fit against the chamfer of the corresponding leg.

I fit the under-shelf aprons and corner blocks next. Each end of the apron meets at a 45° angle to fit the leg chamfer and is mitered to fit the adjoining apron. I secured the aprons and corner blocks to the underside of the shelf and drilled holes in the corner blocks to accept screws that fasten each leg.

Framing the tabletop for glass
The table's three pieces of ¼-in.-thick plate glass are inset within a top framework rabbeted and doweled together. The frame's rail-to-crosspiece joinery is the same for the ends and the intermediate crosspieces. I marked and bored dowel holes in the ends of all four crosspieces and in the inner edges of the rails where the crosspieces join. By doing this now instead of waiting until the glass rabbets have been cut, you avoid the nightmare of trying to drill into a profiled edge. After I dry-assembled the parts with the dowels to check their fit, I shaper-cut the ¼-in.-deep, full-length rabbets for the glass. I also cut the mating rabbets in the ends of the crosspieces (see the bottom photo). Again, I dry-assembled the entire frame, so I could check the joints before gluing up.

After I removed the clamps, I shaped the frame's outside bead (the same size as the one in the legs) and the curved edge leading to the bead. The coved molding, which goes under the bead, should not look applied, but instead, should appear integral to the tabletop. To achieve this effect, I extended the molding underneath the top, which also let me easily glue and screw the molding to the underside of the frame.

When sizing the glass for the inset in the frame, don't go by the opening sizes. The length and width of the glass will actually be ½ in. larger to allow the glass to rest on the rabbeted edges. Because the glass is not retained by applied moldings, the inset fit is critical for appearance. To get a precise fit (no more than 1/16 in. between the glass edges and the wood), I cut out paper templates for the three glass pieces. Instead of ordering the plate sizes from a glass shop, I sent the templates to a glass factory, which furnished me glass with 90° polished edges. Before I inset the sections of glass, I darkened all the edges with a walnut-colored design marker. Darkening the edges makes the inset look neater.

Marking and carving the frets
The ⅝-in.-thick frets, which visually brace the leg-to-tabletop corners, are made of solid mahogany. Before I cut out the frets, I made a template from ⅛-in. birch plywood. The template extends past the actual fret pattern (see the drawing detail); once the shape is cut from mahogany, the extra wood at the edges reinforces the unsupported fret spokes. These edge stiffeners strengthened each fret while I was sawing and carving its shape.

I traced the template onto eight pieces of mahogany that had the grain running at a 45° angle to the edges. I then cut the frets' corners square. (If the leg-to-apron angle is not exactly 90°, fitting the frets will be difficult.) I bandsawed the frets' outer curve, and with scroll and coping saws, I cut away the interiors, leaving the edge reinforcement intact. Because the frets must be carved in pairs with their grain opposing (four left and four right), I marked the front face of each. Next I drew ridge and depth carving guidelines on all the front faces. Much like the roof of a house, the ridge line describes where the two sloping faces of a fret spoke meet; the depth lines indicate the bottom of each slope.

While carving the frets, be mindful of short-grain and the inherent delicacy of the fret spokes. I've found that gently paring away thin slices of wood with a razor-sharp chisel is best. Once I carved all the frets, I sanded them smooth. Then, to remove the edge stiffeners squarely, I used my tablesaw as follows: First, I set my Accu-Miter gauge to 90° and positioned its fence close to the blade (because the fence supports the work right up near the cut, I didn't have to use a hold-down, which might fracture the delicate spokes). Then, holding the piece tight to the fence with my hands well clear of the blade, I cut an edge stiffener off each fret. It's best to make the cut in a few passes, as you grad-

Sofa table assembly

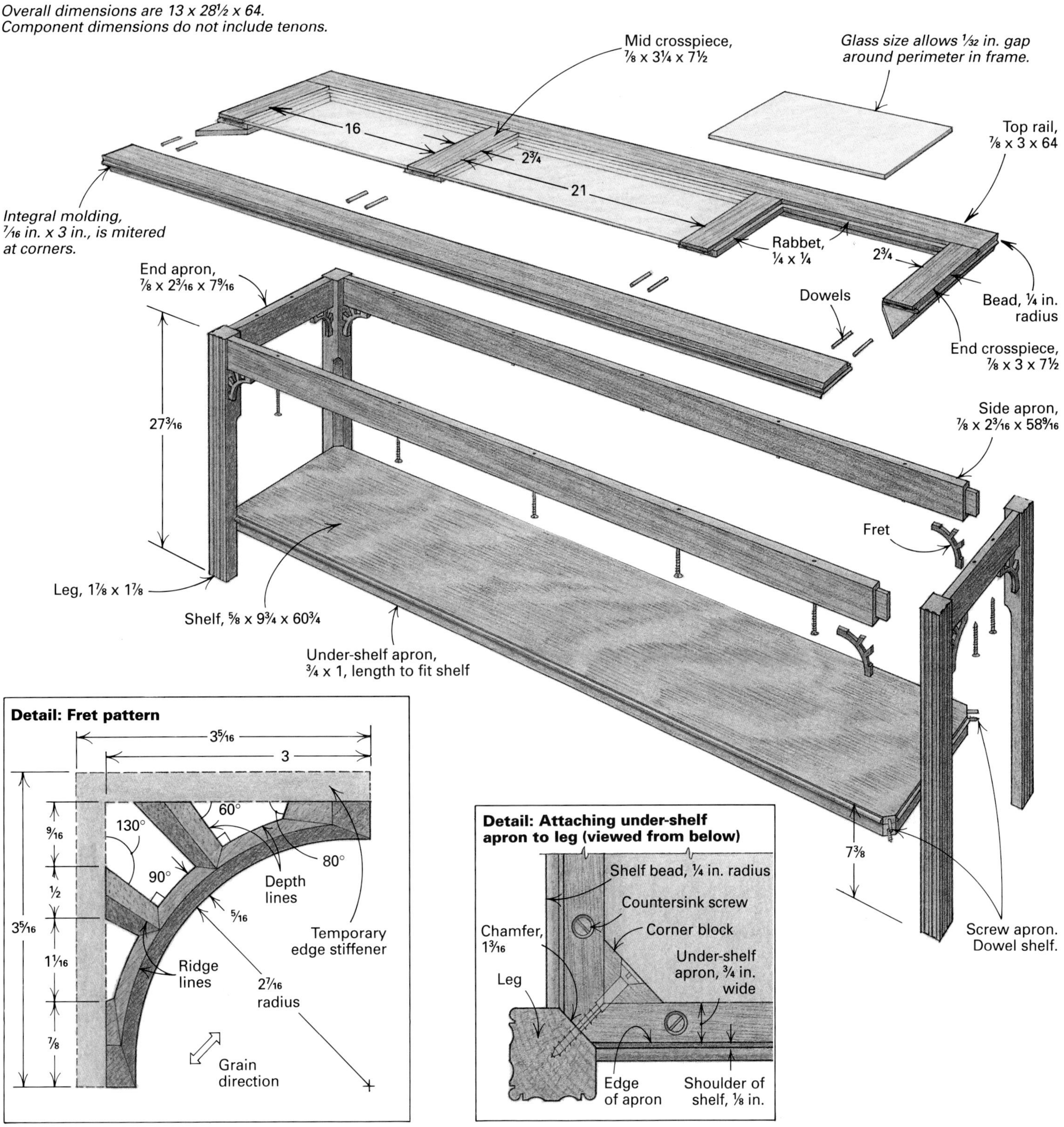

Overall dimensions are 13 x 28½ x 64.
Component dimensions do not include tenons.
Mid crosspiece, 7/8 x 3¼ x 7½
Glass size allows 1/32 in. gap around perimeter in frame.
16
2¾
21
Top rail, 7/8 x 3 x 64
Integral molding, 7/16 in. x 3 in., is mitered at corners.
Rabbet, ¼ x ¼
2¾
End apron, 7/8 x 2 3/16 x 7 9/16
Dowels
Bead, ¼ in. radius
End crosspiece, 7/8 x 3 x 7½
27 3/16
Side apron, 7/8 x 2 3/16 x 58 9/16
Fret
Leg, 1 7/8 x 1 7/8
Shelf, 5/8 x 9¾ x 60¾
Under-shelf apron, ¾ x 1, length to fit shelf
7 3/8
Screw apron. Dowel shelf.
Detail: Fret pattern
3 5/16
3
60°
130°
9/16
90°
80°
1/2
Depth lines
5/16
3 5/16
Temporary edge stiffener
1 1/16
Ridge lines
2 7/16 radius
7/8
Grain direction
Detail: Attaching under-shelf apron to leg (viewed from below)
Shelf bead, ¼ in. radius
Countersink screw
Chamfer, 1 3/16
Corner block
Leg
Under-shelf apron, ¾ in. wide
Edge of apron
Shoulder of shelf, 1/8 in.

ually approach the pattern lines. Finally, I rotated the fret 90° and repeated the process to remove the other stiffener.

Assembling and finishing

I drilled ¼-in. holes to receive dowels that attach the shelf corners to the inner chamfers of the legs. Before assembling the table, I sanded any parts that weren't already sanded and stained the table a mahogany color. When the stain was dry, I assembled the major components, and then I finished the table with lacquer and a topcoat of padding lacquer, which I rubbed out by hand.

To attach the frets, I drilled one edge of each fret where it would be doweled to the leg and drilled a corresponding hole in each leg. I positioned each fret by aligning its dowel to the leg and carefully drilled up through the fret into the underside of the apron. With the fret and its leg dowel glued in place, I inserted another dowel into the apron hole. I trimmed the end of this dowel flush to the fret. Although the dowels won't be visible once the table is in place, I stained and lacquered all the dowel ends, so they'd match the frets before I waxed the entire table. □

Gene McCall is a furnituremaker in Englewood, Fla. He also teaches sculpture at the Ringling School of Art in Sarasota.

Photos: Charley Robinson; drawing: Vince Babak

A Butterfly Expansion Table

Self-storing leaf hides under the top

by Paul Schürch

I n a butterfly-leaf table, a hinged leaf stored under the top pivots up and unfolds to extend the table. This leaf-storage system
eliminates the need to handle the heavy, bulky leaves normally
used in an extension table and also avoids the possibility that for-
gotten leaves will be left behind in the excitement of loading up
the moving van. Just this past year, I've had two jobs making and
matching table leaves to replace ones that had been lost. So when
commissioned to design and build an extension table, I decided
on the butterfly-leaf table for its practicality, aesthetics and absolute ease of operation.

The butterfly mechanism is not as complicated as it may appear,
and once the basic geometry is understood, the mechanism can be
built easily. The hinged-leaf sections counterbalance each other, as
shown in the photo below, and move almost effortlessly. The key

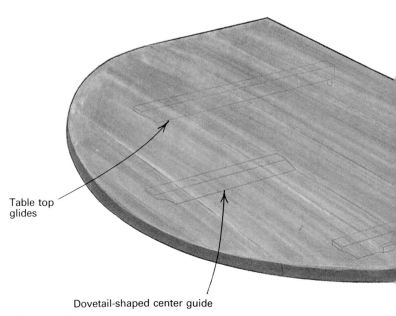

Table top glides

Dovetail-shaped center guide

*The butterfly-leaf table derives its name from
the motion of its folding leaf as it is moved from the
stored position between the rails to the open position in the extended table.*

Photo this page: Paul Schürch; drawings: Bob La Pointe

Fig. 1: Butterfly-leaf table construction

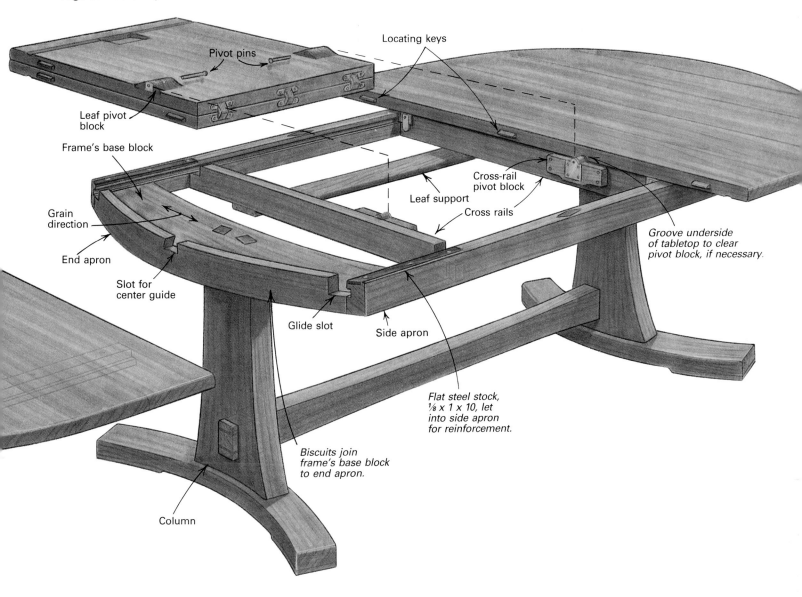

Locating keys

Pivot pins

Leaf pivot block

Frame's base block

Grain direction

End apron

Slot for center guide

Glide slot

Side apron

Cross-rail pivot block

Leaf support

Cross rails

Groove underside of tabletop to clear pivot block, if necessary.

Flat steel stock, 1/8 x 1 x 10, let into side apron for reinforcement.

Biscuits join frame's base block to end apron.

Column

to laying out the mechanics of the leaf is to build a full-scale mock-up based on the cross-sectional view of the butterfly leaf and aprons shown in figure 2 on p. 32. You must take into consideration that the leaves need space to swing freely under the table and that the aprons are an important structural part of the table. With the exception of these restrictions, there is considerable flexibility in designing a butterfly-leaf table. The top can be just about any shape or size and can be supported by a trestle base like the one shown in the photo at left or with a more traditional four-legged base. The table's base-and-apron assembly are stationary, and the ends of the tabletop are screwed to glides that ride in grooves cut into the side aprons. For greater extension capabilities, the table could include multiple butterfly leaves.

In addition to the mechanics of the folding leaf, there are some other key areas that this article will touch on. The material from which the table is made will not only affect the appearance but also can have an impact on the function of the mechanism. For example, woods with excessive seasonal movement may interfere with the operation of the leaf. The hardware for the folding leaf is surprisingly simple, and much of it is easily shopmade, as are the guides and glides that the table ends slide on. And, finally, I'll discuss the pivot blocks, which ensure smooth operation and the locating keys, which position the leaf in relation to the tabletop. In

the sidebar on p. 34, I'll describe the simple templates I use to rout the mortises and tenons that connect the top to the base.

Making a mock-up of the butterfly mechanism

A full-scale drawing of the leaf in both the open and closed position and a working mock-up of the table-leaf mechanism are essential for planning and laying out a butterfly leaf that opens easily, aligns properly with the tabletop and stores without interference below the top. To make the mock-up, draw a cross-sectional view, as shown in figure 2 on p. 32, on a smooth piece of plywood. Two thin strips of plywood, fastened together with a fabric hinge at one end, represent the hinged table leaf. Drive a nail through the mock leaf at the approximate pivot point, as shown in figure 2. Put another nail into the plywood drawing to represent the edge of the leaf support. Now you can move the mock leaf through its entire range of motion and experiment with the location of the pivot point and the leaf support. As the top half of the leaf is lifted, the bottom half should ride on the leaf support and just barely clear the apron. To gain more clearance, you could move the aprons farther apart, but having the aprons as close to the folded leaf as possible provides the best balance and support for the open leaf.

To make the mock leaf, rip two strips of 1/2-in.-thick plywood as wide as the tabletop is thick (1 1/4 in. for the tabletop shown in this article). A piece of fabric glued onto the ends of the plywood strips simulates the action of the Soss hinges used in the actual leaf. The location of the folded leaf between the side aprons of the table is not critical, although I positioned my folded leaf so that it is centrally located between the aprons and parallel to the top. The space between the folded leaf and the underside of the tabletop must accommodate the pivot block without interfering with the top as it slides open and closed. As this space becomes larger, however, the side aprons must become wider to conceal the leaf below the table. About ⅝ in. clearance is ideal, but because I wanted narrow aprons, I left only ⅜ in., and, consequently, had to groove the underside of the top to pass over the protruding cross-rail pivot blocks, as shown in the bottom photo on the facing page.

Pivot-point placement is very critical and needs to be carefully laid out. After positioning the folded mock leaf on the drawing in the closed position, outline the leaf's exact location on the plywood and remove the leaf mock-up. Then draw a line from the closed leaf-joint center (point A in figure 2 below) to the open leaf-joint center (point B, which must fall at the table's center). The pivot point lies at the middle of this line.

Now, reposition the mock leaf on the drawing and glue a semicircular block with a small hole drilled through it onto the leaf, so the hole aligns with the pivot point. A finishing nail, driven through the hole serves as the pivot point while a second nail driven into the plywood drawing simulates the contact point between the leaf and the edge of the leaf support. Clamp the plywood drawing in a vertical position so that the leaf hangs on the pivot nail and gravity holds the bottom half of the leaf against the leaf-support nail. Pull the top half of the leaf up, over and into the open position, while checking that the lower half of the leaf slides properly on the leaf support and clears the side apron by at least ¼ in. Also, be sure the trestle or other substructure does not interfere with leaf movement. Although the leaf is balanced and moves with very little effort, it should not open on its own. If the leaf does not stay in the closed position, the pivot point needs to be moved toward the hinged edge of the leaf, which in turn necessitates repositioning the leaf and possibly the leaf support. It takes some experimenting, but once this mock-up functions properly, you are assured that the actual tabletop will operate flawlessly.

Choosing the right wood for the top and leaf

Most of the references I found on making butterfly-leaf tables recommended against using solid wood because seasonal movement or warping can cause the mechanism to bind or cause a mismatch between the leaf and the tabletop ends. My solid-wood table, now six years old, was built with wood movement in mind. Even though the table is subjected to humidity swings of 25 percent to 55 percent, it still works very well.

Wood selection is very important. I used teak for this table, but mahogany, oak or even pine will do, if it is high-quality, stabilized wood. The wood must be properly air- or kiln-dried (with no internal tension) and stabilized to the shop's environment. Boards with a wild and undulating grain pattern or those that bind or warp when ripped are sure to have internal tension and should be avoided. The grain of the tabletop should run across its width, and to equalize or minimize warping, I recommend using the opposed-heart method when gluing up the top, as shown on the table's edge in figure 1 on p. 31. To allow for seasonal movement of the leaf, I left ¼ in. between the leaf and each pivot block. And because the aprons are the main structural support and form the glide system for the tabletop, quarter-sawn defect-free wood, with its grain oriented as shown in figure 2 below, is preferred.

Selecting and making the hardware

I joined the leaf halves with three heavy-duty Soss hinges (see the Sources of supply box on p. 34) that permit the halves to fold back on themselves yet are completely invisible when the leaf is open. The pivot pins that hold the leaf in the table are two ¼-in.-dia. by 3½-in.-long solid-brass hinge pins. I had to scavenge them from a set of brass butts after I found out that I couldn't just buy the pins. I might have been able to use the butt hinge leaves to make the

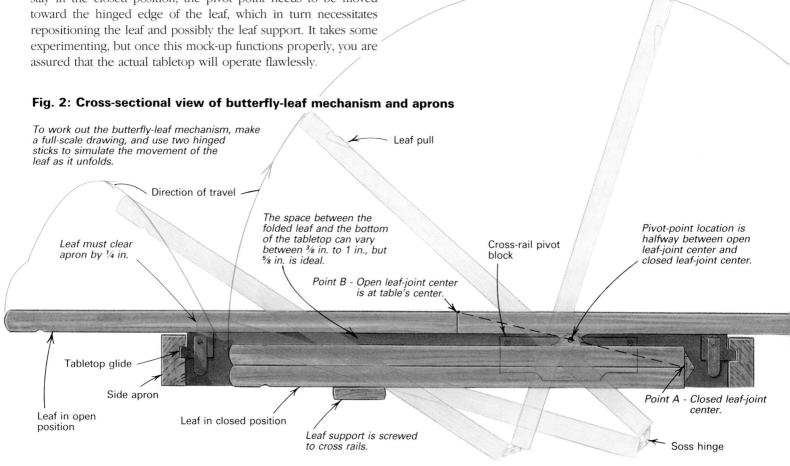

Fig. 2: Cross-sectional view of butterfly-leaf mechanism and aprons

To work out the butterfly-leaf mechanism, make a full-scale drawing, and use two hinged sticks to simulate the movement of the leaf as it unfolds.

Leaf pull

Direction of travel

Leaf must clear apron by ¼ in.

The space between the folded leaf and the bottom of the tabletop can vary between ⅜ in. to 1 in., but ⅝ in. is ideal.

Point B - Open leaf-joint center is at table's center.

Cross-rail pivot block

Pivot-point location is halfway between open leaf-joint center and closed leaf-joint center.

Tabletop glide

Side apron

Leaf in open position

Leaf in closed position

Leaf support is screwed to cross rails.

Point A - Closed leaf-joint center.

Soss hinge

pivot plates or table stops if I hadn't already cut them from some ⅛-in.-thick by 1½-in.-wide flat, brass bar stock. I also made a table lock from the brass stock. I cut the brass with a coarse metal-cutting blade mounted in a sabersaw and used drops of water as a cooling lubricant. I recommend wearing safety glasses to protect your eyes from flying brass chips. After roughing out, the brass is easily filed to shape, buffed to a bright shine with a felt buffing wheel and soft-metal rouge compound, and, finally, sprayed with Agateen 2-B cellulose-nitrate lacquer. Because these brass pieces are rarely handled, the lacquer provides a durable shine and prevents tarnishing.

To facilitate the removal and reinstallation of the tabletop, I screwed a threaded insert into the end of the tabletop glide, so the brass end stop could be fastened with an easily removed machine screw, as shown in figure 3 below. A hook-and-screw table lock, which holds the table ends together when the leaf is not in use, is mounted about 3 in. from the perimeter and across the joint on the underside of the table ends. When the table is fully extended, the weight of the leaf on the locating keys prevents the table ends from being accidentally pulled apart. But if you prefer, locks also could be installed on the leaf.

To strengthen the aprons against the leverage exerted by the extended tabletop, I reinforced the top ends of the side aprons with 1-in.-wide strips of ⅛-in.-thick by 10-in.-long flat, steel bar stock, as shown in figure 1 on p. 31. I screwed the steel to the side aprons with three #12 by 2½-in.-long flat-head screws, positioned to avoid the slide groove on the aprons' inside edges. The steel, located under the table ends, is not visible even when the table is fully extended on its glides.

Guides and glides

For each table end, there are two tabletop glides and one center guide, as shown in figure 1 on p. 31. The guides and glides should be made from a dense wood with the grain angling across the stock at 45° when viewed from the end (as shown in figure 2 on the facing page), which offers more lateral and shear strength. The end aprons and the cross rails are notched to allow passage of the tabletop glides, as shown in the top photo at right, and the end aprons are also notched for the center guides. The dovetail-shaped

The table glide extends through the end apron, which is dovetailed to the side apron. Also shown are the dovetail joints that connect the frame's base block and the cross rail to the side apron.

The butterfly-leaf mechanism includes the cross-rail pivot block, the leaf pivot block and pin, and the Soss hinges that join the two halves of the leaf. The author grooved the underside of the tabletop to accommodate the pivot blocks' knuckles, but this could be avoided by lowering the pivot point slightly.

Photo: Paul Schürch

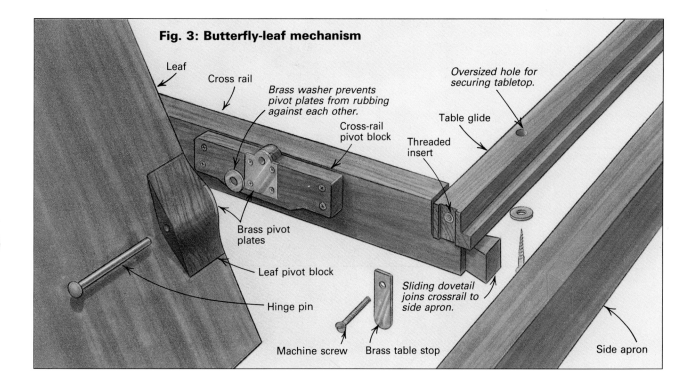

Fig. 3: Butterfly-leaf mechanism

Leaf
Cross rail
Brass washer prevents pivot plates from rubbing against each other.
Cross-rail pivot block
Oversized hole for securing tabletop.
Table glide
Threaded insert
Brass pivot plates
Leaf pivot block
Hinge pin
Machine screw
Brass table stop
Sliding dovetail joins crossrail to side apron.
Side apron

center guides provide additional support and prevent undue stress on the glides if the table is picked up by the top. The guides also prevent racking when the top sections are slid in and out and even can serve as stops if positioned to hit the cross rails when the top is fully closed.

The guides and glides are screwed to the underside of the table-top with round-head screws and flat washers through oversized holes. The oversized holes permit adjusting the glides and guides to their respective slots and allow for normal wood movement with seasonal changes in humidity.

Locating keys

Although locating keys and their corresponding mortises along the mating edges of the leaf and table ends, shown in figure 1 on p. 31, may be optional on other types of extension tables, they are necessary on a butterfly-leaf to secure the folding leaf in the open position. The locating keys also align the leaf with the table ends and when the leaf is folded, align the table ends to each other. I have found that three keys across the width of the table are sufficient. The key located near the leaf joint is positioned on the lower half of the leaf (when the leaf is closed), so it will clear the pivot block on the cross rails when opening or closing the leaf. The 1-in.-thick cross-rail pivot block automatically provides ample clearance between the locating keys (which should protrude about ⅝ in.) and the table's ends. I've found that it's best to wait until the leaf is ready to be installed in the table before cutting the mortises and setting the locating keys into the edges of the table ends and leaf. Then I can make last minute adjustments to be sure everything is perfectly aligned.

Mounting the pivot blocks

Because the leaf pivot blocks bear considerable weight and are subjected to some abuse as the leaf swings in and out of the table, I dovetail them into the leaf. Each of these joints is further reinforced with a brass pivot plate mortised into the side of the leaf, as shown in figure 3 on the previous page, and screwed to both the leaf and the block.

Before installing the cross-rail pivot block, make sure that the table ends slide freely together and apart in a smooth, predictable fashion, and then mortise for and install the locating keys. To locate the cross-rail pivot blocks, clamp the tabletop ends and leaf together in the full extension position, and from under the table, screw the pivot blocks to the cross rails with a single screw. Gently swinging the leaf open and closed will reveal if any final adjustments are needed before securing the pivot blocks with three more screws. □

Paul Schürch is a custom furnituremaker in Santa Barbara, Cal.

Sources of supply

Soss hinges and threaded brass inserts are available from Woodcraft Supply, 210 Wood County Industrial Park, PO Box 1686, Parkersburg, WV 26102; (800) 225-1153.

Brass bar stock for making pivot plates, stops and table locks is available from Industrial Metal Supply Co., 3303 N. San Fernando Blvd., Burbank, CA 91504; (213) 849-3184.

Agateen 2-B lacquer for coating brass is available from Agate Lacquer Manufacturing Co., Inc., 11-13 43rd. Road, Long Island City, NY 11101; (718) 784-0660.

Templates for through-mortises and tenons

I connect the trestle base of my butterfly-leaf table to the upper assembly with a through wedged mortise-and-tenon joint, as shown in the photo below. It's a challenge to lay out and cut this joint exactly where I want it, with tenons that fit tightly into their mortises. However, the simple templates shown in the drawings at right make lay out easy and ensure perfect-fitting joints every time. —*P.S.*

Trestle mortise-and-tenon templates

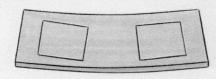

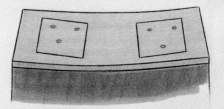

Step 1: Cut a piece of ¼-in.-thick Masonite to match the top of the trestle column. Cut the mortise openings; then scribe, cut and fit the tenon templates to the opening.

Step 2: Position the mortise template on the column end, drop the tenon templates into place and, after predrilling the Masonite, nail the tenon templates onto the column with brads. Remove the mortise template.

Step 3: Rout away the waste, taking about ⅛ in. per pass with a flush-trimming bit with the bearing mounted above the cutter. Be careful not to contact the template until you've cut deep enough for the bearing to ride along the template.

Step 4: Position the mortise template on the frame's base block and rout away waste in the center of the mortises. Again, keep the router bit away from the template until the bearing will ride on it. Square up the mortise corners with a chisel.

Becksvoort made this glass-top coffee table from ³/₄-in.-thick stock rescued from the scrap bin. The legs are mitered together at the corners and also mitered to the aprons, so there is no endgrain showing on the finished table. The inset photo shows the gently curving shapes created by the bent-laminated glass supports.

Glass-Top Coffee Table
Bent-laminated glass-supports within a mitered base

by Christian Becksvoort

W hen a client asked me to design a glass-top dining table, I decided to build a coffee table as a prototype to work out the joinery and design details. The resulting table (shown above) turned out well and required less than 7 bd. ft. of 1-in.-thick scrap lumber.

The table's construction is relatively simple. The four leg-and-apron units are assembled with miter joints strengthened with floating tenons. These units come together with glued miter joints that run the length of each leg. The glass top sits in rabbets in the top inside edges of the aprons and is further supported by glue-laminated diagonal rails joined with half-laps and screwed into the inside corners of the aprons (see the drawing on p. 37). Using

miter joints throughout the table's design resulted in an unexpected benefit: I didn't have to contend with finishing any endgrain.

Mitering and joining the leg-and-apron units

I cut and assembled the four leg-and-apron units before tapering the legs and shaping the underside of the aprons to ensure a smooth transition. To make the leg-and-apron units, I first cut the eight legs and four aprons to the dimensions in the drawing. I then mitered each leg on one end and each apron on both ends. Whether you cut miters on the tablesaw by setting the miter gauge to 45°, as I do, or on a radial-arm saw or a chopsaw, always test the setup by mitering two scraps and checking the joint with a square.

Large photo: Kip Brundage

Because end miters, like those on the legs and aprons, are structurally weak joints, I strengthened them with ¼-in.-thick floating tenons, which also increases the gluing surface. I laid out the mortises for the tenons so that they would be ½ in. from both the top of the aprons and the outside edge of the legs, as shown in the drawing on the facing page, to keep the tenon from interfering with the rabbet for the glass. I used a slot mortiser to cut the mortises, but you could also bore them on a drill press or with a doweling fixture and portable electric drill. The mortises could also be cut with a table-mounted router and fence or a hand-held router and template. Whichever method you use, be sure the mortises are centered so that the surfaces of the legs and aprons will be flush when assembled. Making passes with each side of the leg or apron against the fence or table will automatically center the mortise but may also leave it a bit wider than ¼ in. However, this is not a problem because the tenons will be cut to fit into the mortises, and tenons should be 1/32 in. shorter than the combined depths of the mortises. A few test cuts will yield a perfect fit.

Dry-assembling each leg-and-apron unit ensures that the miters are tight, that the tenons don't bottom out in the mortises and that the legs are square to the aprons. I did most of my gluing on my saw's outfeed table since its plastic-laminate surface is easy to clean. After applying glue to the miter faces and inside the mortises, I reassembled the first leg-and-apron unit, holding it together with three bar clamps. I laid the first clamp flat and parallel to the apron, to squeeze the top of the legs to the apron miters, and tightened it slightly until the joints began to slip. Then I positioned the two remaining clamps upright from the bottoms of the legs to the top of the apron, as shown in the top photo on this page, and began tightening them. The trick was to tighten all three clamps alternately so the miters pulled together perfectly without slipping.

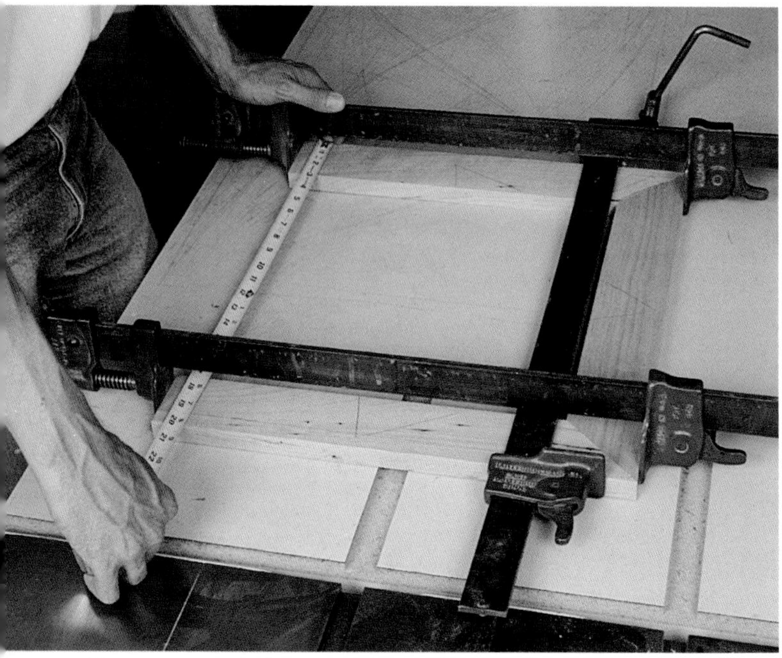

Three clamps pull the miters together and prevent the pieces from slipping when the leg-and-apron units are glued up.

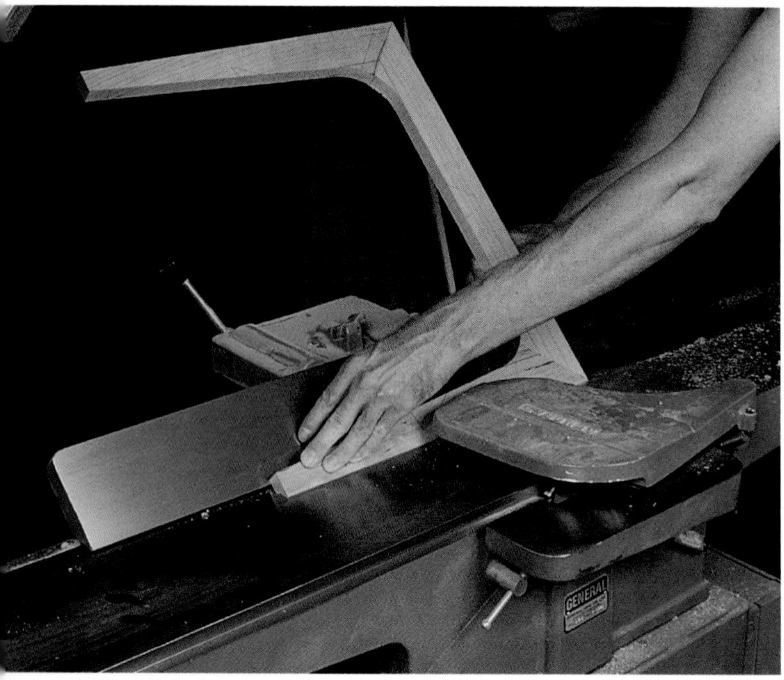

Mitering the edges of the legs on the jointer is easier and provides better results than doing them on the tablesaw.

Tapering and shaping the legs and aprons

Next, I laid out the curves and profiles of the tapered legs and underside of the apron, as shown in the detail of the drawing. I drew the curve between the legs and apron using a coffee can. I bandsawed to the waste side of the line and then finished to the line with a belt sander, a pneumatic sander and by hand-sanding.

After all four leg-and-apron units were bandsawn and sanded, I mitered the outer edge of each of the eight legs. My first inclination for cutting these long miters was to use the tablesaw with the blade tilted to 45°. However, this didn't work well because the rip fence was too far away from the cut, resulting in chatter and vibration at the unsupported bottom end of the legs. I found that I could get nearly perfect miters by tilting my jointer's fence to 45° and making a series of passes until the last pass just met the face of the leg, as shown in the bottom photo at left. After both legs of all four units were mitered this way, I used the tablesaw to rip the rabbet for the glass top in each apron. Because this rabbet will be visible through the glass, it had to be sanded carefully. Before gluing up the leg-and-apron units, I also sanded all inside surfaces, starting with 120-grit paper and working up to 320-grit.

Joining the four leg-and-apron units

Gluing the leg-and-apron units together is an ideal job for an eight-armed Hindu goddess. It's not difficult, but it must be done quickly and efficiently, so laying out the clamps and planning ahead are essential. Almost any clamping arrangement will work. I used a band clamp around the apron and spring clamps and rubber bands along the legs. Before gluing, I dry-assembled the four units, using tape and rubber bands, checked the miters along the legs and touched them up as needed with a handplane. After gluing up the table, I allowed it to dry and then sanded the outside faces to 320-grit.

Making and installing the glass support rails

The curved support rails were made by laminating three strips of cherry over a curved plywood form. To simplify the procedure, I first laminated two wide strips and then ripped them to form the four required rails.

The form for the laminations is simply a stack of five pieces of ¾-in.-thick plywood glued and screwed together into a block. I laid out and bandsawed a 36-in.-radius convex curve along one edge of the block and then disc-sanded the curve fair and smooth.

I made the strips for the laminations by first resawing two ⅞-in.-thick pieces of cherry, 3¼ in. wide by 44 in. long, into six 3/16-in.-thick pieces on the tablesaw. Then I planed each strip to its ⅛-in. final thickness. Because my planer has a minimum capacity of only ¼ in. thick, I used a piece of ¾-in.-thick plywood as a tem-

From *Fine Woodworking* (January 1992) 92:67-69

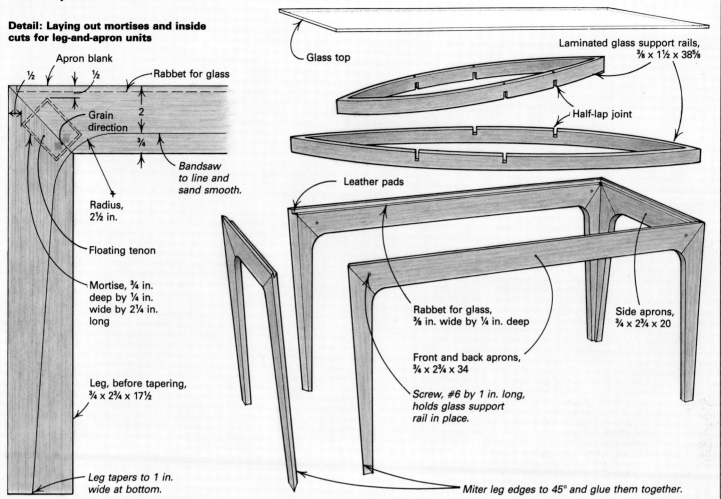

Glass-top coffee table

Detail: Laying out mortises and inside cuts for leg-and-apron units

Apron blank

½

½

Rabbet for glass

Grain direction

2

¾

Bandsaw to line and sand smooth.

Radius, 2½ in.

Floating tenon

Mortise, ¾ in. deep by ¼ in. wide by 2¼ in. long

Leg, before tapering, ¾ x 2¾ x 17½

Leg tapers to 1 in. wide at bottom.

Glass top

Laminated glass support rails, ⅜ x 1½ x 38⅝

Half-lap joint

Leather pads

Rabbet for glass, ⅜ in. wide by ¼ in. deep

Front and back aprons, ¾ x 2¾ x 34

Screw, #6 by 1 in. long, holds glass support rail in place.

Side aprons, ¾ x 2¾ x 20

Miter leg edges to 45° and glue them together.

---

porary planer bed and screwed a lip to the underside of the plywood to keep the bed from being drawn through the planer.

To laminate the curved rails, I applied glue to three of the strips with a narrow paint roller, wrapped them in plastic to minimize the mess and held them tightly to the form with a 3-in. heavy-duty band clamp. After the first lamination had dried for 24 hours, I repeated the process for the second set of rails. When the second lamination had dried, I scraped off all the excess glue and jointed one edge. Then I ran the jointed edge against my tablesaw fence and ripped the laminations into the four 1½-in.-wide rails.

The placement of the miter joints between the two pairs of rails is taken from the table, but the table must first be square. Measuring the diagonals will reveal problems, and a clamp can draw the table back to square if necessary. I placed one rail at a time diagonally across the top of the table, so the outside edge of the rail intersected the inside corners. With a square, I transferred these intersecting points along the side of the rail and marked the top edges at each end. Then I aligned a straightedge with both marks across the top of the rail to define the table's diagonal and to bisect the angle between the rails. I scribed lines across the top of the rails with a knife, bandsawed close to the lines and disc-sanded to them. With the first rail marked and cut, I clamped it in place inside the table to help align marks for the second rail. I repeated these steps to mark and cut the other rails. After sanding the rails to 320-grit, I glued pairs of them together, taping across the miters, to form football-shaped glass supports (see the inset photo on p. 35).

When the glue was dry, I dry-assembled the glass supports into the table to mark for the half-lap joints where the supports intersect. First I slid one support into place diagonally between the corners of the table frame until it was about ½ in. below the rabbet. Then I positioned the second support unit diagonally between the opposite corners, directly on top of the first. Spring clamps on the table legs prevented the supports from slipping farther down. With a knife, I scribed the bottom of the top support and the top of the bottom support where the curves intersected. Then I removed the supports and extended these lines halfway up the sides. After cutting along the lines with a dovetail saw, I chiseled the bottoms flat. Finally, I slid the two units together and trimmed them with a sharp chisel to get a perfect fit.

Once the glass supports fit properly, I glued them together and inserted them into the table. With spring clamps holding the supports in position, I drilled a hole for a wooden plug and then a pilot hole for a screw in each of the long aprons' corners and into the curved supports' mitered corners, as shown above. After inserting the screws and plugging the holes, I gave the entire table a final sanding with 320-grit paper. Four hand-rubbed coats of Watco oil provided a satisfying satin sheen.

Experience has taught me that it's better to take the finished table to a reputable glass shop and have a glass top cut to fit than it is to phone in the dimensions of the glass. For a finished look, I had the edges of the ¼-in.-thick plate glass ground, and to protect both the glass and the table, I glued round leather pads in each corner of the table and at the intersections of the supports. □

Christian H. Becksvoort builds custom furniture in New Gloucester, Maine, and is a contributing editor to FWW.

This table's open framework has an open feel, making it stronger than it looks. The one-piece top seats eight comfortably, and the components are easily shaped using templates.

Building an Open-Pedestal Table
Doubled members simplify joinery; templates make shaping parts quick and easy

by John Burchett

The open framework that supports the elliptical table shown in the photos on this page has a light and airy look that belies its strength. Doubled members that form the feet and tabletop rails, as shown in figure 1 on the facing page, reduce overall mass, add interesting detail and simplify joining the legs to the feet and rails.

In addition to the elementary joinery, I used some template-shaping tricks to greatly simplify construction. The elliptical top, with its gently curved edges, was shaped and edge-molded with a template-guided router. And the many duplicate

Doubling the frame members reduces the mass in the feet, legs and tabletop supports. It also simplifies the joinery and adds visual interest.

parts of the base were all quickly and easily cut on a spindle shaper using a template that rides against a special fence.

Working with templates

Templates are particularly useful for speedier and more accurate small production runs. I added extra length to the templates for tenons and for fixing the templates to the stock during machining. Templates that are slightly long are safer to use because they begin rubbing against the guide bearing or fence before the stock hits the cutter. Any errors in the templates will be reproduced in every cut

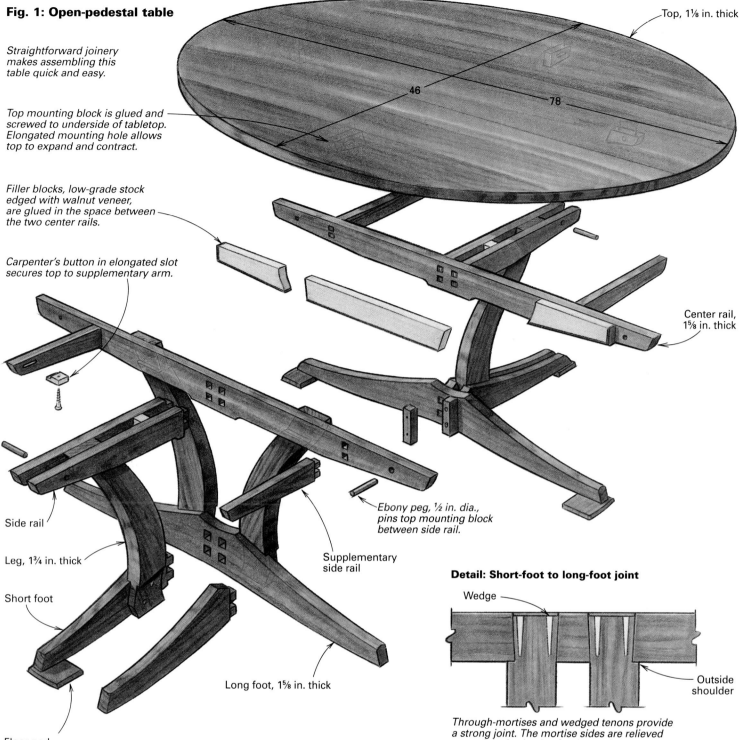

Fig. 1: Open-pedestal table

Straightforward joinery makes assembling this table quick and easy.

Top mounting block is glued and screwed to underside of tabletop. Elongated mounting hole allows top to expand and contract.

Filler blocks, low-grade stock edged with walnut veneer, are glued in the space between the two center rails.

Carpenter's button in elongated slot secures top to supplementary arm.

Top, 1⅛ in. thick

46

78

Center rail, 1⅝ in. thick

Side rail

Leg, 1¾ in. thick

Short foot

Floor pad

Long foot, 1⅝ in. thick

Ebony peg, ½ in. dia., pins top mounting block between side rail.

Supplementary side rail

Detail: Short-foot to long-foot joint

Wedge

Outside shoulder

Through-mortises and wedged tenons provide a strong joint. The mortise sides are relieved toward the back edge for the wedges.

part, so it's worth some extra time to be sure that the templates are perfect.

From the full-sized front and side elevations of the table's base (see figure 2 on p. 40), I made templates for each part from ¼-in.-thick medium-density fiberboard (MDF). I also made a quarter-arc template of an ellipse for cutting and shaping the top. I allowed the template to extend slightly beyond the quarter of an ellipse limits and outside the true circumference. That eliminates the possibility of the router cutting a depression where one quarter meets another when moving the template to shape the four quarters of the top.

I've also found templates helpful for selecting stock and laying out the cuts. I juggled the templates around to find the most satisfying grain configuration and economical use of timber before cutting out the blanks of American walnut. Then I surfaced and thicknessed the blanks for shaping. I also machined the boards for the top, so they could settle before re-machining.

When shaping large pieces, I prefer to use a hefty, hand-held router guided by a collar or bearing. But for pieces small enough to handle comfortably, I prefer a spindle shaper. The larger table, arbor and cutters of a shaper produce a smooth,

clean cut. A shaper fitted with an ordinary pair of straight-edged steel cutters and a shopmade ring fence works great for template shaping. A different fence is needed for each diameter cutter used, as shown in the photo on p. 40.

I make my ring fences from birch plywood with an arc to match the cutter's diameter and infeed and outfeed areas. The infeed and outfeed areas make shaping safer because the template can be registered against the fence, and the stock is supported before it reaches the cutter. I set the height of the ring fence with plywood spacers of varying thickness.

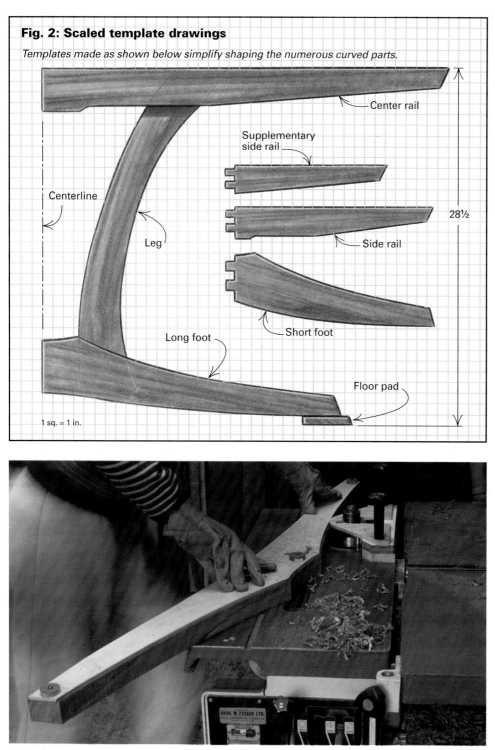

Fig. 2: Scaled template drawings

Templates made as shown below simplify shaping the numerous curved parts.

Center rail

Supplementary
side rail

Centerline

Leg

Side rail

28½

Long foot

Short foot

Floor pad

1 sq. = 1 in.

***Ring fence makes shaping easier**—It's easier to spindle-shape curved pieces with a shop-made ring fence that follows a template attached to the stock.*

The templates are screwed to the blanks in areas that are cut off later. With the machine set perfectly and the waste to be removed at a minimum, the operation is safe and pleasant. After the joints were cut, I molded gentle curves on all the show edges with the shaper. I left the edges square at the leg intersections.

Cutting the joints

Ordinarily, I cut my joints before shaping a piece, so I can lay out from flat and square faces. But for this table, the base framework was bandsawn from large slabs and tem-plate-shaped to conserve timber. The only pieces that had straight reference edges were the top rails. For laying out joinery on the feet, I established a reference surface by extending a straightedge from the flat floor-contact area of the foot to the joint area. A block between the straightedge and the foot's curved section (see the top photo on the facing page) kept the straightedge positioned while I marked the joint lines with a try square.

The first joints I cut were the tenons of the short feet and their mortises in the long feet, using the full-sized drawings to deter-mine joint positions, as shown in the drawing detail in figure 1 on p. 39. The tenons on the short feet and side rails are wedged. I left them about 1⁄16 in. shy of the full thickness of the long foot and center rail to allow for any possible shrinkage in the thickness of the mortised members. The mortises were cut with a square, hollow-chisel mortiser, and I relieved the sides of the mortises at the back with a chisel to al-low for the expansion of the wedges.

To mark the tenons at the bottom of the four legs, I clamped each leg between its corresponding feet and scribed the curved shoulder line on each side of each leg. I hogged off the tenon waste on the radial-arm saw and cleaned up the tenon surface with a shoulder plane. The convex curves of the shoulders were pared with a chisel.

I dry-assembled and clamped the legs and feet to mark the tenons at the upper ends of the legs. The shoulders were scribed and the tenons cut as before. At this stage, I marked and cut one joint at a time and assembled and clamped it together while I marked the next joint. Assembling a project one step at a time seems the only way to proceed in custom work involving curved shapes. In fact, this is the way I ap-proach most of my cabinet work. Still, I've found it necessary to make small adjust-ments to the top joints at final assembly af-ter the bottom joints were glued.

The assembly procedure

To simplify assembly, I glued up the base into two units, each consisting of a long foot, a pair of short feet and a leg.

Clamping shaped work calls for some in-genuity, but I find it is this sort of challenge that makes woodworking interesting. I overcame the problem of clamping the short feet to the long foot by adding blocks to the outside faces of the short feet, as shown in the bottom photo on the facing page. These blocks provide a bearing sur-face for clamps to pull the joint together. A softwood block between the pair of short feet holds the feet at the correct spacing. I glued abrasive to the blocks on the outside of the feet to prevent slipping when the joint is clamped. I checked this assembly dry and pulled the joint apart with the short feet still clamped together with their spac-ing block. Then I glued the mortises and re-inserted the tenons. The two main clamps were tightened, everything checked for alignment and the wedges driven home. I cut the wedges flush with the ends of the tenons. The same clamping arrangement was used to glue the side rails and the sup-plementary side rails into the long rails.

I checked the accuracy of the shoulder

lines of the legs to the feet and made fine adjustments to the tops of the feet using a scraper rather than trying to alter the shoulders themselves. To clamp the leg in place during glue-up, I screwed through a block spanning the bottom of the feet and into the end of the leg to pull the shoulder tight to the top of the foot.

The upper part of the frame was fairly straightforward; it glues into two half-assemblies consisting of one center rail, a pair of side rails and two supplementary rails. One of the half-assemblies was glued and clamped in place to three of the legs. Filler pieces, their lower edges already veneered with walnut, were then glued and screwed in place, as shown in figure 1, to form tight-fitting mortises at the tops of the legs. The second half-assembly was then glued in place.

Apart from making the four floor pads, the only remaining work on the frame was shaping and drilling the four walnut blocks that attach the top. These blocks, which fit between the ends of the paired rails, are screwed, counterbored and plugged on the underside of the tabletop. The blocks are held to the rails with ½-in.-dia. ebony pegs. The holes in the blocks between the short rails are elongated to allow the top to expand and contract.

Gluing up the top

I handplaned the edges for the simple butt joints I used to glue up the top. Two details are worth mentioning when handplaning or shooting a joint: controlling the plane and checking for square.

To control the cut, the left hand does not hold the plane's foreknob but grips the plane's side near the front with thumb on top and index finger rubbing against the side of the wood being jointed. The rubbing finger provides the control needed to move the plane either left or right to adjust the squareness of the cut.

When checking for squareness, the square should be held with its body on the planed edge and the blade extended down the face of the timber. The angle between the long blade and the face exaggerates error, making inaccuracies obvious.

I glued up the top with the heartwood facing up to avoid any exposed sapwood on the tabletop. That way, any cupping would be convex on the upper surface and easier to restrain than a concave top.

After edge-gluing the timbers, I cut the completed slab to a rough elliptical shape and handplaned it flat, planing first across the grain and then along the grain. I cut the slab to a true ellipse with a straight, two-flute router bit using the ellipse template

Laying out joinery on curved pieces is difficult because there are no straight reference surfaces. The author adds blocks and straightedges as needed to overcome this problem.

Clamping long and odd-shaped pieces—Blocks are clamped to the sides of the short feet with a properly sized spacer between each pair of feet. The blocks provide surfaces parallel to the long foot to apply clamping pressure during glue-up.

and a collar-guided router. I couldn't find a stock router bit to cut the gentle curve I wanted on the top's edge, and I didn't want to wrestle the heavy top across the spindle shaper. So I reground a straight router bit and worked the lower part of the curve first with the top upside down. Then I reground the cutter to a slightly more pronounced curve before turning the top over to work the upper part of the curve. I finished off this asymmetrical scotia shape by fairing the two cuts together with a curved scraper, constantly referring to a template to keep the edge uniform.

Finishing up

I gave the underframe a couple of coats of linseed oil and polished it off with three coats of dark wax. Because the top receives more abuse, I applied several coats of a mix of linseed oil, polyurethane and mineral spirits as a base for 14 coats of hand-rubbed, hot, raw linseed oil applied over a month. The client continued the finishing process by applying a coat each month for the next 12 months. □

John Burchett is a custom furnituremaker in Copnor, Portsmouth, England.

Drop-Leaf Breakfast Table

Cabriole legs and knuckle joints make it compact and versatile

by Robert Treanor

As an apartment dweller, I am constantly fighting a losing battle for space. In one small, narrow hallway in my apartment, the phone and its paraphernalia has to share space with one of the precious closets. Little room is left for a table on which to write messages or to place small items. It seemed to me that a drop-leaf table, narrow when closed, would fit the space and provide terms for a truce in my little battle. And as a peace dividend, I could always open up the table and use it elsewhere for special occasions.

The small table I made, as shown in the photo at right, is a good example of a late Queen Anne breakfast table. The 18th-century form combines grace and versatility, and making it demands the same attributes in the craftsman. The half-blind dovetailed aprons, rule-jointed leaves and the knuckle joints on the swing legs all require precise work. And shaping the compound curves of the cabriole legs needs a steady hand and eye. The skills are not difficult to master, and the effort will be rewarded with a useful and elegant table. The original on which my table is based was made of walnut, but I built mine of cherry. Maple or mahogany would also be appropriate. I used pine for the small amount of secondary wood.

***Modesty and majesty**—This small Queen Anne breakfast table contains a broad range of joinery. Pinned tenons, knuckle joints and half-blind dovetails connect the aprons and legs, and rule joints run between the leaves and fixed top.*

Taking stock

Begin the table by milling the required material. Leave the leg billets slightly oversized, and set them aside for a few days so any movement can later be planed out. The pieces that will form the side aprons should be left a few inches over finished length at this point. The extra length will allow you to recut the knuckle joint for the hinge of the swing leg if necessary. Cut the fixed top and the leaves from the same board, so color and figure will be consistent.

Knuckle joint is linchpin

The knuckle joints are at the heart of the table, and I start with them. The joint and the aprons it connects must be accurately aligned to ensure the fly leg stands vertically both in its home position, where it must meet the end apron squarely, and in its open position, where it must support the leaf at just the height of the fixed top.

A knuckle joint is basically a finger joint with its fingers rounded over and the bottoms of its sockets coved. To provide a positive stop for the swing leg at 90°, the joint has mating 45° chamfers on both aprons, as shown in the drawing detail. The knuckles can be cut on the tablesaw with a finger-joint jig and then finished with hand tools. With only two joints to cut, though, I opted to make the entire joint with hand tools.

Cutting and fitting the joint is not difficult, but accurate layout is essential to success. Begin the layout by marking in from the end of each piece by the thickness of the material. Then carry a line around the apron at that point. Draw diagonal lines in the square you've created on the top and bottom edges of the stock, and draw a circle, as shown in the top photo on p. 44.

The short section of the diagonals between the circle and the original layout line is the chamfer line. To make chamfering easier and more accurate, you'll need a relief cut. Draw a line parallel to the first layout line, and score along it with the corner of a sharp chisel guided by a square. Then chisel a shallow V-groove on the side of the line nearest the end of the board. The groove provides a channel for your saw to ride in as you start the relief cut. Make the relief cut with a tenon saw or dovetail saw, stopping just as the kerf touches the circle laid out on the edge of the board. Now make a guide block beveled at 45°, and ride a rabbet plane on the

Photos: Jonathan Binzen

Drop-leaf table

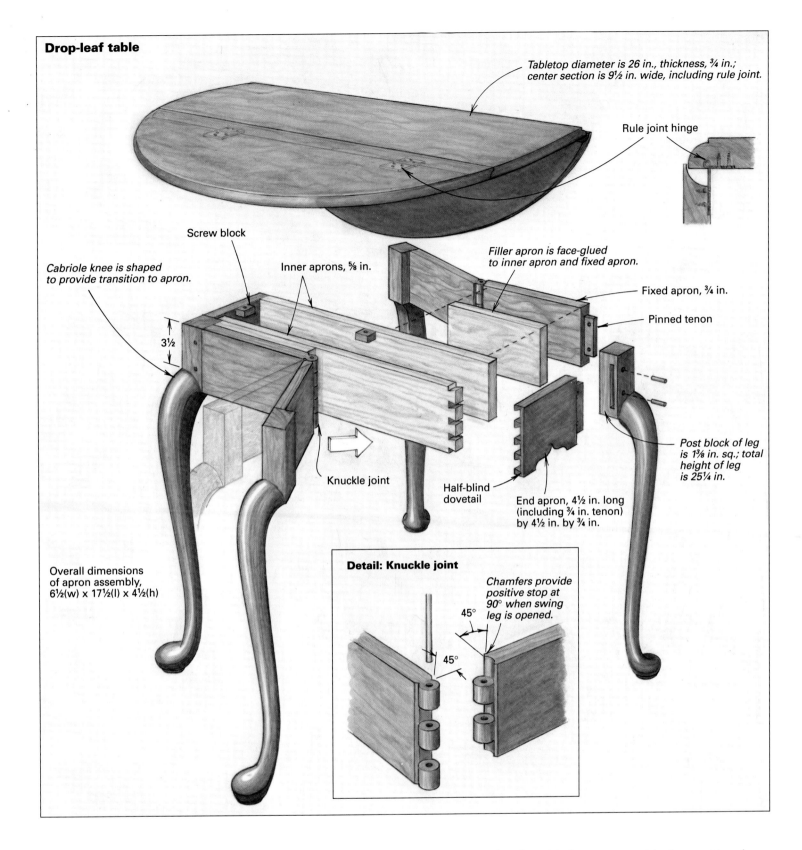

Tabletop diameter is 26 in., thickness, ¾ in.; center section is 9½ in. wide, including rule joint.

Rule joint hinge

Screw block

Cabriole knee is shaped to provide transition to apron.

Inner aprons, ⅝ in.

Filler apron is face-glued to inner apron and fixed apron.

Fixed apron, ¾ in.

Pinned tenon

3½

Knuckle joint

Half-blind dovetail

End apron, 4½ in. long (including ¾ in. tenon) by 4½ in. by ¾ in.

Post block of leg is 1⅜ in. sq.; total height of leg is 25¼ in.

Overall dimensions of apron assembly, 6½(w) x 17½(l) x 4½(h)

Detail: Knuckle joint

Chamfers provide positive stop at 90° when swing leg is opened.

45°

45°

bevel to cut the chamfers, as shown in the center photo on p. 44.

Shape the barrels of the hinge with chisels and a block plane. Refer to the circles on each edge of the board as you proceed. Begin the rounding by planing a series of facets from end to end. Continue cutting narrower facets until the barrel is round. You could also use a router for some of the rounding over. A piece of scrapwood can be coved to the same radius as the barrel and used as a sanding block for final smoothing.

Lay out and cut the sockets between the knuckles next. Divide the board into five equal units across its width, and extend the division lines around the barrels. Using a backsaw, cut down the waste side of the lines to the chamfer, and then chop out the waste material with a chisel, as you would when cutting dovetails, working from both sides to avoid chipout.

The bottoms of the sockets must be coved, so they mate with the radius of the knuckles. Use gouges that match the sweep of the cope for the end sockets and a straight chisel to shape between the knuckles, as shown in the bottom left photo on p. 44.

I used a piece of ³⁄₁₆-in. drill rod for the hinge pin. A length of brazing rod or dowel rod would also work. To drill the hole, assemble the joint on a flat surface, and clamp it together end to end with a pipe clamp. Then clamp the whole assembly to a fence on the drill-press table, and drill the hole. To avoid bit wander, drill a little more than half way through the joint, and then flip the

Lay out the knuckle joints accurately, and you're halfway to a good hinge. The diagonals determine the hinge center point.

Run a rabbet plane along a guide block to cut the chamfer that limits the swing of the knuckle joint hinge.

assembly and complete the hole from the opposite edge.

Drive the hinge pin into the joint, and check the action of the hinge. It should move smoothly without binding or much squeaking. When the joint is open to 90°, the two chamfers should form a gapless line. Set the aprons on a flat surface to ensure that they sit perfectly flat both when in line and at 90°.

Joining legs and aprons

It is best to cut the leg-to-apron mortise-and-tenon joints before shaping the legs. With the legs square, the whole process is easier and more accurate. The fly legs each have one mortise and the fixed legs have two. I cut the mortises with a plunge router, holding the legs in a simple box on which I guide the router. You could also chop them by hand or with a hollow-chisel mortiser. I find it quick and efficient to cut the tenons with a dado head on the tablesaw. For these tenons, which are ¾ in. long, I stacked the dado set ¾ in. wide and made the whole cut in one pass.

The end aprons have a tenon cut on one end and a half-blind dovetail on the other. Start the dovetailing by laying out and cutting the tails on the pine inner apron. Then use the tails to lay out the pins on the end apron. Before putting the end aprons aside, cut the ogee detail on their bottom edge.

Cabriole curves emerge

Named after the French dancing term for a leap, cabriole legs do give furniture a certain vitality or spring. And they're not all that difficult to make. A small portion of the work is done on the lathe—the foot and the pad beneath it. The rest of the shaping is done with the bandsaw and hand tools.

The leg blanks have been milled square and mortised by now. Leave the horn at the top (the extra inch that reduces the risk of a split during mortising) to provide waste for chucking on the lathe. Make a full-sized template of the leg out of thin plywood or poster board, and use it to lay out the cabriole curves on the two adjacent inside surfaces of the leg. Then cut out the legs on the bandsaw. Cut the curves only; don't cut out the post block (the section above the knee) until you've turned the feet. If you were to cut away the post-block waste now, it would be difficult to center the leg blank on the lathe. When you've cut one curve, tape the cutoff back into place, and cut the second face (see the bottom right photo).

Untape the cutoff, and mount the leg between centers on the

Scoop out the center sockets with a straight chisel. Cove the outside sockets with a gouge of appropriate radius.

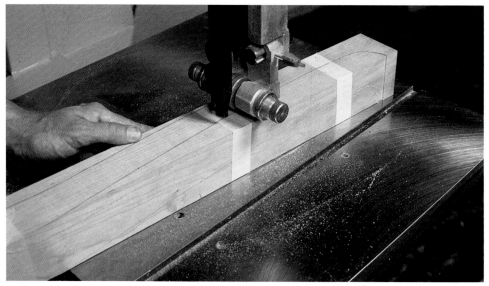

Billet rebuilt—With the blade guide lowered to just above the stock, bandsaw along the layout lines. Tape the cabriole cutoffs back in place, and turn the billet 90° to make the second pair of cuts. After turning the foot, clean up the bandsawn curves with a spokeshave.

From *Fine Woodworking* (January 1994) 104:90-93

lathe. Then turn the major diameter of the foot. Measure up from the bottom ¼ in., and use a parting tool to establish the pad of the foot. With the major and minor diameters defined, use a small gouge or a scraper to shape the foot's profile, as shown in the bottom left photo below. Finally, before removing the leg from the lathe, sand the foot. Then you can take the legs to the bandsaw and cut away the waste above the knee.

The remainder of the leg shaping is done at the bench with an assortment of hand tools. You can hold the leg with a bar clamp clamped in your bench vise. The first step is to fair the bandsawn curves with a spokeshave. Be particularly careful working at the top of the foot because this is end grain and will chip easily. The front arris of the leg, though it moves in and out, should be a straight line when seen from the front.

Once the spokeshave work is complete, use a cabinetmaker's rasp to cut chamfers on the corners of the leg. Leave the corners sharp in the area above the knee. Next use the rasp to round over the chamfers and blend the curves of the leg, as shown in the bottom right photo below. The cross-section of the leg should be circular at the ankle and square with rounded corners just below the knee. When you've finished the coarse shaping with the rasp, refine the curves with a file. Further smoothing can be done with a hand scraper and sandpaper.

Next shape the knee to provide a transition between the leg and apron, as shown in the drawing on p. 43. Lay out a curved line from the top of the knee to the point where the apron joins the leg. Then cut away the waste above the line with a sharp bench chisel. With the same chisel, shape the knee in a smooth curve. Once the shaping of the legs and knees is complete, saw the horns from the legs. Give all the parts a final sanding, and you are ready to glue up the table base.

Assembly and subassembly

With 10 separate pieces comprising its apron, this table presents an unusual challenge in the gluing up. The way I do it, there are three stages. First glue up the half-blind dovetail joints that link the end aprons to the inner aprons. Make sure the aprons meet at exactly 90° before setting them aside to dry. Next glue one fixed and one swing leg to each of the hinged aprons. A bar clamp with pads on the jaws will work well. To keep the hinge from pivoting, use handscrew clamps with light pressure to clamp the hinge to the

bar clamp. Set all four subassemblies aside to dry overnight.

To complete the base assembly, you'll need two filler aprons made from secondary wood. They are face-glued between the fixed section of the hinged apron and the inner apron (see the drawing on p. 43). The fit has to be perfect, so dry-assemble the subassemblies, measure the gap and mill the filler apron at that point. Glue the filler apron between the inner and outer aprons, keeping all three aligned with brads or biscuit joints.

The final glue up is best done with the base upside down on a flat table. While the pieces are dry-clamped, check that the hinge will open through its range unimpeded. Then glue up the last two apron-to-leg joints. After the glue-up, pin all the mortise-and-tenon joints with ¼-in.-dia. pegs.

Rule joints

I cut the rule joints that connect the leaves and the fixed top before roughing out the circular shape of the top. I do mill the boards carefully, though, and scrape or plane off the millmarks before cutting the rule joint. I find it easiest to cut the joint on a router table. First cut the roundover on the fixed top with a ½-in. roundover bit. Guide the top against a fence, and make trial cuts on scrapwood. Leave a ⅛-in. fillet at the top of the cut. Then chuck up a ½-in. core-box bit, and cut the leaves to fit the fixed top.

When installing the rule-joint hinges, leave some leeway for the top to expand and contract with variations in humidity. Instead of aiming for a joint that will close entirely on top, offset the hinge barrels ¹⁄₆₄ in. to ¹⁄₃₂ in. toward the leaf.

Once the hinges are in, lay out the top's diameter on its underside. It can be cut out by hand or with a bandsaw or a sabersaw. Scrape and sand the edge to remove the sawmarks, and shape the edge to a slight belly with planes, files and sandpaper. Give the top a final sanding, and attach the base to it with screws driven through slotted holes in screw blocks attached to the inner aprons.

I finished the table with several coats of a tung oil/Danish oil mix. A coat of paste wax was applied after the oil finish was completely dry. Make sure the underside of the top and the inside surfaces of the aprons receive the same amount of finish as the visible surfaces. If you skimp on finish underneath, the table will take on and lose moisture unevenly and could be prone to warping. □

Robert Treanor is a cabinetmaker and teacher in San Francisco.

***Shaping the foot**—Only the lower part of the foot and the pad are shaped on the lathe. To provide good purchase for the live center, leave the leg full-sized above the knee until after turning.*

***Shape and blend the curves of the cabriole legs** with rasps and files. The leg should be round at the ankle and square with rounded corners just below the knee.*

Low Tea Table Highlights Joinery

Sliding dovetails and butterfly keys make strong connections

by C. Michael Vogt

Table assembly

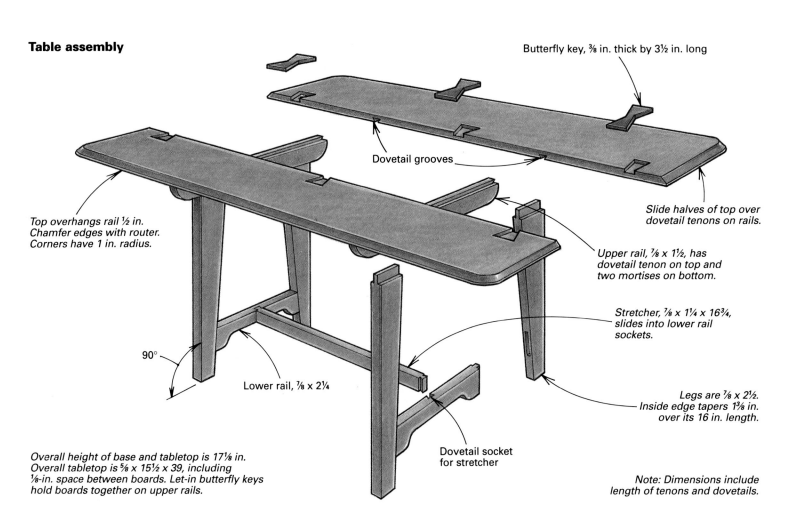

Butterfly key, ⅜ in. thick by 3½ in. long

Dovetail grooves

Slide halves of top over dovetail tenons on rails.

Top overhangs rail ½ in. Chamfer edges with router. Corners have 1 in. radius.

Upper rail, ⅞ x 1½, has dovetail tenon on top and two mortises on bottom.

Stretcher, ⅞ x 1¼ x 16¾, slides into lower rail sockets.

90°

Lower rail, ⅞ x 2¼

Legs are ⅞ x 2½. Inside edge tapers 1⅜ in. over its 16 in. length.

Dovetail socket for stretcher

Overall height of base and tabletop is 17⅛ in. Overall tabletop is ⅝ x 15½ x 39, including ⅛-in. space between boards. Let-in butterfly keys hold boards together on upper rails.

Note: Dimensions include length of tenons and dovetails.

Router setups for sliding dovetails

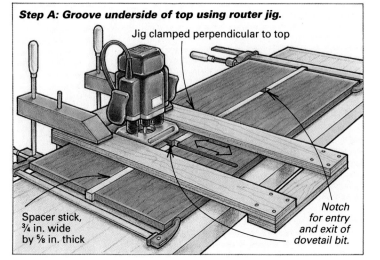

Step A: Groove underside of top using router jig.

Jig clamped perpendicular to top

Spacer stick, ¾ in. wide by ⅝ in. thick

Notch for entry and exit of dovetail bit.

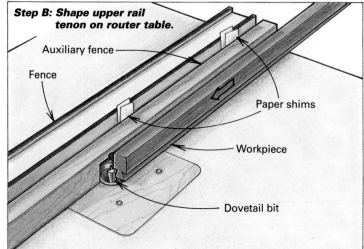

Step B: Shape upper rail tenon on router table.

Auxiliary fence

Fence

Paper shims

Workpiece

Dovetail bit

Drawings: David Dann

I find the dovetail an appealing joint, both aesthetically and structurally. Although its traditional use in carcase and drawer construction is well known, a sliding version of the dovetail can be used to connect furniture components such as tabletops to their bases. I relied on sliding dovetails to join a top to two upper rails in the walnut table shown in the photo at right. And I used a more visible variation of the dovetail, butterfly keys, to connect the halves of the tabletop. The table is quite easy to build, but because its joinery is pre-eminent, the table requires craftsmanship with both machine and hand tools. I'll describe the router setups I used to cut the sliding dovetails, and I'll also explain how I inlaid the table's butterfly keys (see the box on p. 48).

Designing a table for tea

When I made the table for a juried craft show, I knew it would be displayed near Japanese pottery. So when I designed the table, I envisioned it for drinking tea while seated on the floor. I borrowed traditional details, such as sliding dovetails, but I was also influenced by modern work—that of the late George Nakashima. I purposely left a 1/8-in. space between the halves of the top, so I could inlay butterfly keys the way Nakashima did in his altars and tables. The keys are bold and functional. In my table, they join two matching boards; in Nakashima's work, they stabilize checks in large slabs of wood (for examples, see *FWW* #79, p. 99).

Because the table's components and overall form are simple, its material and manufacture are pronounced. I built the original table from walnut (see the photo above), but when built from oak, the table takes on an almost Craftsman-like look. And though this table is small, you can use the same joinery techniques to make larger and more robust pieces. However, if you build a table for heavier use, such as a coffee or end table, I suggest you move the legs closer to the ends of the top to reduce the cantilever and make the table more stable.

Building the base and the tabletop

The tabletop is supported on a base, which is just two end frames (see the drawing on the facing page). Each end frame consists of a pair of legs connected by lower and upper rails. The lower rail has tenons on each end that enter mortises in the sides of the legs; the upper rail has two mortises on its underside that slip over tenons on the tops of the legs. Full-length dovetail tenons on the tops of the upper rails slide into stopped grooves in the underside of the top. Three butterfly keys join the halves of the top and lock them onto the base's sliding dovetails. Finally, a stretcher spans between the two end frames, joining the lower rails.

The elegance of simplicity and craftsmanship—Tico Vogt made this table for a craft show exhibiting Japanese pottery, so he designed the walnut table just 17 in. high for floor-seated tea drinkers. To further reflect Oriental lifestyle, he used simple components and traditional joinery.

Selecting stock—The low tea table is a nice project for bookmatching resawn 8/4 stock for the top. The base looks best made from straight-grained wood, so the components' shapes will be emphasized. After you have resawn stock for the top, let the boards move around with stickers between them for a week so that they will be flat when you work them. Plane the boards a bit over 5/8 in. thick, and crosscut them a few inches longer than their final length. Rip out all the base pieces, and plane them to 7/8 in. thick. Also, saw a few extra 6-in.-long by 1¼-in.-wide pieces for testing the fit of the sliding dovetails.

Legs and rails—It's tempting to use biscuits instead of tenons to join the end frames. However, when I built a biscuited mock-up, I concluded the weaker plate joints compromised the integrity of the project. So go with the mortises and tenons. First saw the top rails to their final length, but wait to saw the curve on their ends until the dovetail tenons have been shaped (see the top photo on p. 49). Next crosscut the legs and bottom rails with enough length for their tenons. Then bandsaw (or taper-rip with a tablesaw and jig) the angled inner faces of the legs, and plane off the sawmarks. Use a tablesaw to cut the end tenons, and then angle the tenon shoulders by hand with a chisel. Waste the mortises with a router, and square them with a chisel. Once you've dry-assembled the joints, bandsaw the profile on the underside of the bottom rails.

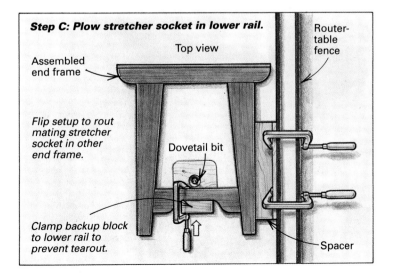

Step C: Plow stretcher socket in lower rail.

Top view

Router-table fence

Assembled end frame

Flip setup to rout mating stretcher socket in other end frame.

Dovetail bit

Clamp backup block to lower rail to prevent tearout.

Spacer

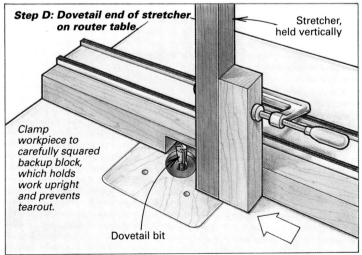

Step D: Dovetail end of stretcher on router table.

Stretcher, held vertically

Clamp workpiece to carefully squared backup block, which holds work upright and prevents tearout.

Dovetail bit

A jig for routing the top's dovetail grooves—To plow the top's dovetail grooves, I relied on a spacer stick and a jig. First make up a ¾-in.-wide spacer as thick and as long as the top with 1-in. notches where the grooves will go (this is the entry point for the router bit). Clamp the two halves of the top around the spacer. Squarely mark off the ends for length, and mark centerlines for the keys. Next transfer your cutoff lines to the underside and measure in from them to layout the centers of the grooves. With a handplane, flatten the boards. Then set up the router jig shown in Step A on p. 46. With a dovetail bit set to ¼ in. deep and dropped into the notch in the spacer, rout a groove in each direction, stopping ⅜ in. from the edges. Lift the router when the bit is over the notch, so you can make the second groove. Also groove a piece of scrap for test-fitting. Finally sand away any fuzzy edges left by the router.

Routing dovetail tenons on the upper rails—A router table is great for shaping dovetail tenons on the upper rails. To get the tenons to fit the tabletop grooves perfectly, use the practice pieces. First make an auxiliary fence (see Step B on p. 46), so you can micro-adjust the cut. Set the bit the same height above the table as the groove is deep. Run each side of a scrap piece, top down, along the auxiliary fence. Then use shims of paper between the fences to fine-tune the width of the dovetail. When the tenon slides snugly into the test groove, use the same router-table settings, and repeat the cut on the actual rails. Test their fit.

To allow for expansion, square the ends, so the tenons are 1/16 in. shorter than the grooves in the top. Then use a chisel to carve a round shoulder on each end. The arc on the tenon ends should match the semicircle of the stopped router groove. Again, sand away any fuzz, and wax the sides of the dovetail tenons. Next rip the spacer board to ⅛ in. wide. Slide the top boards onto the rail tenons, drop in the spacer and clamp the top together. With the rails in place under the top, secure the assembly on the bench, and check for flatness. (I handplaned the boards diagonally to eradicate a small amount of cupping in my top.) Now saw out the butterfly keys, and size and cut their mortises (see the box below).

Assembling the end frames—Once the keys have been fit, take the top apart. Then glue and clamp up the end frames. When the glue is dry and you've scraped and sanded the frames clean, install the top, so you can measure the length of the center stretcher. Measure shoulder to shoulder on the lower rails, and add ½ in. for the ¼-in. dovetail tenon on each end. Next dismantle the top. Place each end frame on the router table, as shown in step C on p. 47, to plow the sliding-dovetail socket on the inside of the lower rail. Use the router table to shape tenons on the ends of the stretcher similar to how you dovetailed the rails. A carefully squared backup block clamped to the stick as you run it vertically past the bit keeps it straight and stable (see Step D on p. 47).

Installing the stretcher and butterfly keys—The real pleasure of building this table comes from assembling the last few joints. First chamfer the bottom edges of the stretcher dovetails. Next put the top back together with the spacer, slide in the frames and glue

Making and inlaying butterfly keys

When making the walnut tabletop shown in the photo at left, I chose rosewood for the butterfly keys. And when I built the table in red oak, I used cherry keys (see the photo at right below). In both examples, I had purposely saved small scraps of contrasting wood for the butterflies.

Bandsawing keys: George Nakashima slightly beveled the edges of his butterflies, but because my table's keys are shallow, I just cut the edges square. First, I make a butterfly pattern and trace its shape as many times as will fit on a scrap block. Second, I bandsaw the block to divide the patterns, which leaves me with stacks of keys. Third, I bandsaw the butterfly shape (see the center photo below). Fourth, I slice off individual keys to roughly ⅜ in. thick. Fifth, I plane and sand away sawmarks from the faces. Finally, I squarely chisel and file the edges to the line. Because the keys vary slightly

Cherry butterflies—Vogt bandsaws a stack of keys from a block of cherry.

1) Scribe the outline of the key with a knife or an awl.

and clamp in the stretcher. Then apply a thin even coat of glue on the mating surfaces of the keys and butterfly mortises. Tap the keys home, and use cauls and clamps to distribute pressure. Although the keys go against the wisdom of no cross-grain construction, I've never had any problems. For extra insurance, you can drive a screw up from the bottom into the center of each butterfly before you allow the table to dry overnight. Because the butterfly mortises are ¹⁄₃₂ in. shy of the key thickness, beltsand or scrape the keys flush to the table surface once the glue has cured.

Finishing touches—Keep the spacer in place while you saw and rout the top to its final shape. (The spacer protects the inner edges from tearout and gives the router bit a continuous surface to bear against.) First scrape the entire table surface, or use a random-orbit sander because they work particularly well for smoothing the crossing grains of the keys and top. Next cut the tabletop to final length using a crosscut box on your tablesaw. Then round the four corners with a sabersaw, and chamfer the top edge all around with a router. (The beveled edge makes the top look thicker, and it's easier on the elbows.) Finally pop out the spacer, and hand-sand all the parts. For a finish, wipe on a mixture of oil and varnish.

A Tokyo furniture-store owner once saw my table at a gallery. He picked it up and examined it closely. Then he placed it on the floor, and kneeling on the top, racked the table back and forth. His nod of approval made all the careful joinery well worthwhile. ☐

C. Michael (Tico) Vogt is a furnituremaker in Saratoga Springs, N.Y.

Rounding off the dovetail tenons—After shaping the upper rails' dovetails on his router table, the author uses a ¹⁄₂-in. straight chisel to trim the ends. Rounding the ends ensures that the dovetail tenons fit the stopped grooves in the underside of the top. Next Vogt will bandsaw the curve marked on the rail.

in size, I number each, so I can match the keys to their butterfly mortises later.

Cutting butterfly mortises: I individually mark out keys rather than use a pattern because even minute differences between key sizes or shapes will be apparent in their fit to the mortises. So I lay a key on a location line on the tabletop, clamp it in place and follow these steps to scribe and mortise the butterfly shape:

1) Using an Exacto knife (or an awl), I carefully scribe the outline of the bottom of the butterfly, making sure the bevel of the knife stays tightly to the key's edge (see the photo at right on the facing page). Then I remove the key, so I can deepen the lines.

2) Using a razor-sharp flat chisel, I carve a shoulder all around the outline, as shown in the photo at left below. The shoulder prevents tearout from the router.

3) Using a plunge router, I waste most of the butterfly cavity to a depth of the thickness of the key less ¹⁄₃₂ in. I work a ¹⁄₄-in. bit as close to the outline as I dare (see the center photo below).

4) Using chisels, I pare the rest of the way to the outline. A ³⁄₄-in. straight chisel works well at squaring the edges (see the photo at right below), and a chisel with its tip ground to a point nicely cleans up the butterfly's corners.

Insetting keys: To inlay the keys, I first number the mortises to match each key. I fit the keys tightly to allow for shrinkage; it should take a bit of force to start them. To help, I chamfer the bottom edges so that they will just ease into the mortises, but I don't drive them into the top just yet. Once I have fit all the keys to their mortises, I set them aside. Later, when I'm assembling the table, I tap the butterflies home with a mallet. —C.M.V.

2) Carve a shoulder around the outline with a chisel.

3) Plunge-rout the mortise with a ¹⁄₄-in. straight bit.

4) Pare to the line, and clean up the corners with chisels.

A Shaker Style Drop-Leaf Table

*Turned legs with
drilled-and-chiseled
mortises*

by Greg Isaak

This single-drop-leaf table was inspired by several original Shaker pieces in New York and Massachusetts. The author modified the legs to reflect his fondness for the designs of Thomas Sheraton.

To cut a mortise with the drill-and-chisel method, the author first bores out most of the waste using a brad-point bit that just barely fits within the layout lines.

I first became interested in Shaker furniture because of some pieces my mother owned. I was drawn to the Shakers' simple, unadorned designs, their restrained, but strong joinery, and their uncompromising insistence on quality. As I examined my family's furniture and studied pieces presented in books and museums, I also became fascinated with the way Shaker designs had been influenced by Federal furniture built in the United States between 1782 and 1815. The ideas of designers like Duncan Phyfe, Robert Adam, Thomas Sheraton and George Hepplewhite can be easily identified in many Shaker originals.

Since I like this diversity of design ideas, it's not surprising that my table, shown finished on the facing page, is not an exact replica of any one piece. Rather, it incorporates the features of several New York and Massachusetts pieces. I based the overall size of the table and the shape of its legs on a New York original, but I modified the turned legs to capture the graceful look of Sheraton furniture. The single drop leaf is from a table at the Hancock Shaker Museum in Massachusetts.

Like its Shaker ancestors, my table is very functional. Its small size and two shallow drawers make it ideal as an occasional table, end table or nightstand. And there is nothing tricky about building the piece; all the work can be done with a few simple tools. Stock preparation is relatively easy because the components are so small. The legs were milled into square blanks, mortised and then turned to shape. After cutting the aprons to size, I tenoned their ends to fit the leg mortises. The top is two edge-glued boards, with a routed rule joint for the drop leaf.

Mortising and turning the legs

I cut the leg mortises with the old drill-and-chisel method. This is one of the simplest methods for cutting mortises if you don't have a horizontal mortising machine, hollow-chisel mortiser or router. A drill press and a chisel or two are the only equipment needed. I started by cutting the stock for the legs to the dimensions given in the drawing on p. 53. To avoid splitting the wood when mortising near the top of the legs or when turning the narrow feet, I cut the square blanks about 1½ in. oversize on each end.

Next, I laid out the mortises and bored out the space between the layout lines using a brad-point bit with a diameter just slightly smaller than the width of the mortise, as shown in the bottom photo on the facing page. If you don't have a correct-size brad-point bit, you could also use a Forstner or spur bit. A fence clamped to the drill-press table helped me align the holes. After boring out as much waste as possible, I squared the mortise walls with a chisel (see the left photo below). Although the side walls can usually be pared with hand pressure alone, you may need a mallet to drive the chisel into the tougher endgrain.

After the mortises were chopped out, the legs were ready to be turned. If you don't have a lathe, you may prefer to use a square-sectioned tapered leg, a characteristic of Hepplewhite design. For stability while turning, I mounted the end that will have the least amount of stock removed, in this case the square top section, on the lathe's headstock, as shown in the photo at right below. Then I measured down each leg to locate several checkpoints: the transition point between the square and turned section; the largest diameter, which is at the midpoint of the turned section; and the diameter of the bottom, as shown in the drawing on p. 53. Basically, my method was to turn the blank to the required diameters at the major checkpoints with either a parting tool or a ½-in. roundnose scraper. Calipers worked well to gauge the diameters. After establishing the checkpoints, I used a roundnose scraper (see the photo at right below) to blend the rest of the leg with the three diameters I had established. (If you don't have a roundnose scraper, you can use a sharp gouge.)

After turning the first leg, I realized that taking additional measurements would help in locating other checkpoints. When I measured my first leg, I found that its diameter was 1⅛ in. at a point 1½ in. from the bottom of the transitional collar, and 1 in. in diameter 14¾ in. below the collar. Establishing these checkpoints, in addition to the original three, not only ensured that all four legs were consistent, but it also sped up the turning process by minimizing guesswork. Next, I smoothed the roughed-out leg with a sharp gouge and a roundnose scraper, and then I lightly sanded the leg. If you work carefully and check the leg with calipers as you turn, all four legs should come out pretty close to the dimensions I've given in the drawing on p. 53. I didn't sand the transitional collar while the piece was on the lathe because I didn't want to soften this crisp detail. Instead, I sanded it by hand after the leg was removed from the lathe, and then I crosscut it to final length.

The ridges left by the drill bit are pared away with a sharp chisel. Hand pressure is usually sufficient to pare the side walls of the mortise, but a mallet is better for squaring up tougher endgrain.

The legs are turned after the mortises are complete. Isaak mounts the top of the leg in the headstock and then uses a scraper to shape the transition between the square top and the rest of the leg.

Case construction

I cut the apron tenons and drawer-rail tenons shown in the drawing by making multiple passes on my tablesaw with the workpiece laid flat on the table and guided by the miter gauge. I made the cuts with a regular sawblade, although you might prefer to mount a dado head on your saw to speed the process. Each of the 6-in.-wide apron tenons is ½ in. thick by ⅝ in. long. The drawer-rail tenons vary in size, as shown in the drawing. The tenons on the top rail are flush with its upper surface, while the tenons on the bottom rail are centered in the ¾-in.-thick stock. The ⅜-in.-thick tenons on the center rail are ½ in. wide by ⅝ in. long.

I was then ready to assemble the table frame. First, I dry-fit the two front legs and drawer rails, and pared the tenons slightly to achieve a good fit. I glued up the front assembly first, making sure that the assembly was square and that the two legs were on the same plane while drying. The clamps may need to be readjusted. Care at this stage is well invested; if the case is twisted or out of square, the drawers will fit poorly. Next, I assembled the two back legs and the back apron. Because of the wide tenons, this assembly should square itself if the mortises have been cut straight.

Now, I notched the left side apron for the pivoting leaf support. I angled the ends of the notch and the support so they would swing past each other easily and blend together without an apparent break when closed. I cut the 45° angles with a dovetail saw, and then I formed the opening by bandsawing away most of the waste. After trimming to the line with a chisel, I cut and fit the matching leaf support. With the support screwed in place, as shown in the drawing, I then planed it until the top surface was flush with the top of the apron. This ensured that the raised leaf would be level with the rest of the tabletop. Be aware that the screw head must be well countersunk to avoid damaging the plane iron. To complete the table frame, I glued the front assembly to the back-legs-and-apron assembly, again making sure that the table was square and true. I assembled the frame upside down on my bench and then measured from corner to corner after applying the clamps. The clamps may need to be adjusted to make the diagonals equal. After the frame was dry, I pinned the tenons with ³⁄₁₆-in.-dia. dowels and sanded them flush. Besides strengthening the frame, the dowels add a nice design detail. To complete the case, I glued on the cleats, which secure the top.

Drawer construction

After assembling the frame, I measured each opening and assembled the drawers to fit with about ¹⁄₁₆-in. clearance on the top and sides. I used half-blind dovetails on the front corners, but made through dovetails on the back because I think these are essential components of high-quality work. In keeping with my affection for the Shakers, I cut the joints by hand. Over the years, I've found handwork satisfying, and it doesn't take much more time than setting up a router and jig, once I get into the swing.

Each drawer bottom is a ³⁄₁₆-in.-thick piece of ash, with its grain running side to side. I glued the bottoms into rabbets in the drawer fronts and fastened the bottoms to the sides with brass brads. Bottoms that float in grooved drawer sides were more common in the Federal period, but my research showed that the Shakers often used nailed-on drawer bottoms for very shallow drawers. Apparently, they felt that the floating panels wasted too much space. The brads flexed enough to allow seasonal wood movement and to prevent the bottom panels from cracking. I turned the pulls shown in the drawing by mounting each one like a small spindle between centers on my lathe. After turning, I trimmed off the waste with a saw, and then I hand-sanded each pull as it was spinning in the Jacobs chuck of my drill press.

The next step was to position the supporting runners to ensure smooth-sliding, level drawers. I screwed the filler blocks in place, as shown in the drawing, clamped the runners for each drawer into position and slid in a drawer. If a drawer slid without binding and its four corners contacted the drawer runner, I screwed in the runners and glued in the drawer stops. Otherwise, I adjusted as needed.

Making the top

I edge-glued two pieces of wood to obtain an 18-in.-wide top. After the top and leaf were squared up and cut to the proper dimensions, I made the rule joint. I milled the top pieces enough oversize so that an offcut was left that I could use for testing router setups for the rule joint.

The rule joint, when done correctly, adds a very attractive visual detail. My method is pretty simple; I used only a ½-in. round-over bit and a ½-in. cove bit. First, I rounded over the edge of the tabletop that will butt the leaf. I made this cut deep enough to leave a ⅛-in. shoulder. Similarly, I made a cove cut on the leaf that was deep enough to leave a ⅛-in. lip that will mate with the tabletop's shoulder cut.

Hinge locations are crucial for a good joint, and so these specially made hinges should be bought before the mating edges are shaped. The hinges are available from Paxton Hardware Ltd., 7818 Bradshaw Road, Upper Falls, Md. 21156; (301) 592-8505, or Lee Valley Tools, 1080 Morrison Drive, Ottawa, Ont., Canada K2H 8K7; (613) 596-0350, and several other supply houses. To ensure that the leaf will move smoothly, the center of the hinge pin must be mortised in line with the shoulder created by the roundover on the tabletop. To locate the center of the hinge pin, I marked down from the shoulder on each edge of the top with a try square and connected the two points with a straightedge on the underside of the top. The hinge pin goes directly on this line or slightly toward the table's edge. If you move the hinge pin's center ¹⁄₃₂ in. toward the leaf, the leaf will fit tightly to the shoulder when the leaf is up, but will gradually draw away from the roundover as it is lowered; this way, parts do not rub, regardless of the season. The hinges can be mortised in with a chisel or router. I used two hinges, each placed about 2½ in. from the end of the joint. (For more information on making a rule joint, see *FWW* #80, pp. 48-52.)

Before assembly, I sanded all parts of the table with 150-grit and 220-grit paper. To make sure everything was smooth and clean before finishing, I resanded again after assembly. I applied six coats of tung oil because I thought this finish would be most in keeping with the oil finishes and thin varnishes that the Shakers used. ☐

Greg Isaak makes period furniture and teaches in LaFox, Ill.

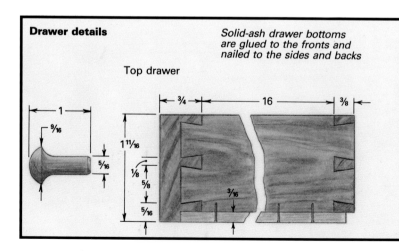

Drawer details

Solid-ash drawer bottoms are glued to the fronts and nailed to the sides and backs

Top drawer

Photos except where noted: Dick Burrows; drawings: Lee Hov

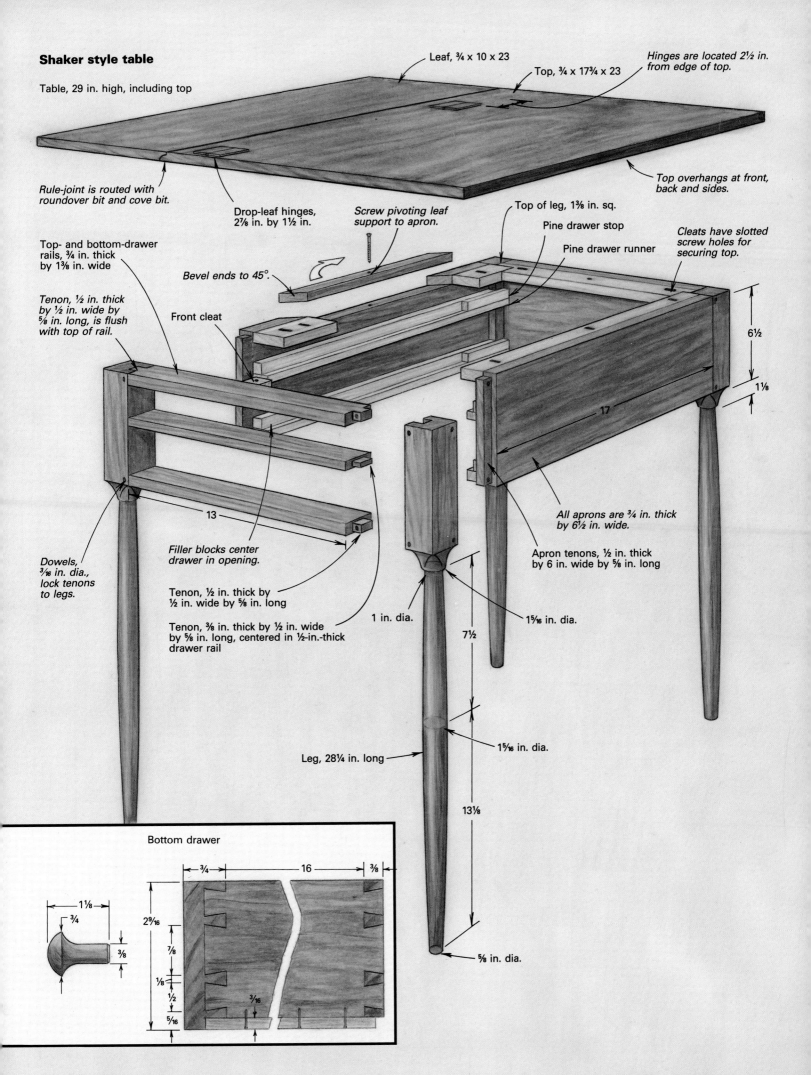

Shaker style table

Table, 29 in. high, including top

Leaf, ¾ x 10 x 23

Top, ¾ x 17¾ x 23

Hinges are located 2½ in. from edge of top.

Top overhangs at front, back and sides.

Rule-joint is routed with roundover bit and cove bit.

Drop-leaf hinges, 2⅞ in. by 1½ in.

Screw pivoting leaf support to apron.

Top of leg, 1⅜ in. sq.

Pine drawer stop

Pine drawer runner

Cleats have slotted screw holes for securing top.

Top- and bottom-drawer rails, ¾ in. thick by 1⅜ in. wide

Tenon, ½ in. thick by ½ in. wide by ⅝ in. long, is flush with top of rail.

Bevel ends to 45°.

Front cleat

6½

1⅛

17

Dowels, ³⁄₁₆ in. dia., lock tenons to legs.

13

Filler blocks center drawer in opening.

Tenon, ½ in. thick by ½ in. wide by ⅝ in. long

Tenon, ⅜ in. thick by ½ in. wide by ⅝ in. long, centered in ½-in.-thick drawer rail

All aprons are ¾ in. thick by 6½ in. wide.

Apron tenons, ½ in. thick by 6 in. wide by ⅝ in. long

1 in. dia.

1⁵⁄₁₆ in. dia.

7½

1⁵⁄₁₆ in. dia.

Leg, 28¼ in. long

13⅛

⅝ in. dia.

Bottom drawer

1⅛

¾

⅜

¾

16

⅜

2⁹⁄₁₆

⅞

⅛

½

⁵⁄₁₆

³⁄₁₆

From *Fine Woodworking* (September 1991) 90:90-93

Twin aprons, tapered legs, edge chamfers and sculpted joinery details *enhance these otherwise simple, clean-lined hall tables. Loose tenons in mortises milled in both the aprons and legs join the base together.*

Refining Table Design with Details

Twin aprons, sculpted joints and chamfers

by Ross Day

From *Fine Woodworking* (November 1991) 91:72-75

W ith a successful piece of furniture, the closer you get, the more interesting details there are to discover. This was a point stressed by my teacher, James Krenov. I kept that thought in mind when I was designing a table a couple of years ago. I wanted something different from the typical arrangement of a simple apron and tapered legs supporting the top, so I came up with a few variations to enhance the design. First, I split the wide apron into two thinner members, connected midspan with small supporting posts. To add visual intrigue, I joined these twin aprons to the legs at raised-and-chamfered mortise sockets, and chamfered most edges on the aprons, legs and top. Finally, I beveled the tapered legs almost diamond shaped in cross section and allowed their ends to come within ³⁄₆₄ in. of an inset top that has ebony string inlay, which leads your eye around and through the corner chamfers and the reveals under the top. These design details can be seen in the tables shown at left.

While I was pleased with the look of these details and the way they kept a simple table from resembling a featureless production piece, I wanted a table that could be produced in multiples. Fortunately, I came up with a combination of hand and machine operations for the joinery and details that kept the process efficient enough for limited production pieces and that resulted in work that was up to the standards of the best one-off furniture. The method has been so successful that I've incorporated these details into a number of other tables and casework pieces, including the coffee table and stereo cabinet shown in the photo at right. I don't always employ all of these details; in some cases, I've used just the raised-and-chamfered joint with a single apron, as shown on the nightstand in the bottom, right photo on p. 57. On other pieces, I've doubled up the supporting posts between the twin aprons, for both strength and visual interest.

The legs and twin aprons are constructed and joined as shown in the drawing. Both the legs and the ends of the aprons are mortised and joined together with loose tenons. The raised-and-chamfered area is sculpted at the top of the legs after mortising. This detail is created by routing with a Dremel tool mounted in a router-type base and hand-chiseling using an angled block as a guide. I'll take you through the process of making one of my leg-and-apron assemblies for a simple table; you can alter the forms and dimensions to suit the type of furniture or cabinet you wish to build. The process includes cutting out and mortising the legs and aprons, chamfering, final assembly and fitting the top.

Beveling and mortising the legs

After selecting stock that's thick and wide enough for the leg profile I have in mind, I joint and mill the stock square and cut each leg to final length. Then I lay the four legs on my bench, decide how they'll be paired and which ends will be up or down, and mark each leg with a cabinetmaker's pyramid. This allows me to keep track of each leg's orientation during subsequent operations, and it prevents me from having three left-hand legs. Next, I bevel each leg's two outward-facing surfaces on the tablesaw with the blade at 75°. (For some furniture, I bevel the legs at 85° instead.) Note that these are straight cuts; the tapers are made on the two inner faces later. Finally, I check to make sure the two inside faces are square, and I make any necessary adjustments with a handplane.

I mark out the two pairs of mortises for the twin aprons at the top of each leg, locating them as shown in the drawing. I arrange them so that the upper apron will be below the end of the leg by the thickness of the top. This allows the top of the leg to show, and further enhances its diamond-shaped profile. Next, I plane the outside faces of each leg to eliminate the sawmarks, making sure to keep the surfaces straight and even.

Day's frame joinery and detailing enhance his custom work, including the white oak coffee table and stereo cabinet shown here. Both pieces feature twin aprons and pairs of connecting posts that span between them. He combined hand and machine operations so that the process wasn't so labor-intensive.

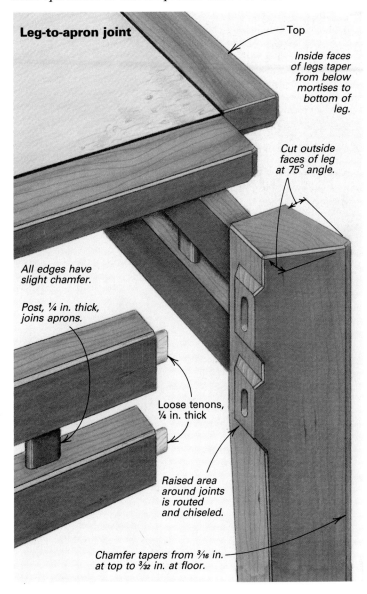

Leg-to-apron joint

Top

Inside faces of legs taper from below mortises to bottom of leg.

Cut outside faces of leg at 75° angle.

All edges have slight chamfer.

Post, ¼ in. thick, joins aprons.

Loose tenons, ¼ in. thick

Raised area around joints is routed and chiseled.

Chamfer tapers from ³⁄₁₆ in. at top to ³⁄₃₂ in. at floor.

Day's shopmade horizontal mortiser chops mortises in the ends of the aprons and the sides of the legs. He prefers to work free-hand, gauging each mortise's depth by a line drawn on the table.

The raised areas around the joints are routed using a Dremel tool fitted with a special router base. A small-diameter end mill removes the waste around each joint prior to chamfering.

I cut all the mortises using a horizontal mortising table, shown in the photo above left. This shopmade machine uses a mandrel fitted with a drill-type chuck to a fixed shopmade plywood framework. A ½-HP, 1,735-RPM motor underneath the table, which holds the work, supplies power via a V-belt drive. To make the mortises, I mount a ¼-in.-dia. four-flute end mill in the arbor chuck. By using this type of end mill to make shallow passes back and forth, I feel confident mortising without any fences or hold-downs. You *must*, however, use a fence and hold-down if you mortise with a router and regular straight bit; otherwise, the high-speed bit might grab the part and pull your hand into harm's way. You may also do the mortising with hand tools. I make the length of each mortise ⅜ in. less than the width of its corresponding apron member. All the mortises in the legs are about ⅝ in. deep; I put a pencil mark on the horizontal mortiser's table as a depth guide.

Mortising the twin aprons for loose tenons

Next, I mill the twin apron members from ¾-in.-thick stock, ripping the lower one a little narrower (about ⅛ in.) than the upper one. Because I mortise both legs and aprons and join them together with loose tenons, the apron stock is crosscut to exact length. Now, I cut the mortises in the ends of the aprons to receive the loose tenons, centering the mortises with regard to both width and thickness. To keep any minor discrepancies that creep in during mortising consistent, I hold the outside face (marked earlier) of each apron member down on the mortising table. At this time, I also lay out and mortise for the short posts that connect the twin aprons. Depending on the length of the apron, I'll use either one post midspan or two located at visually pleasing intervals. I make the posts the same thickness as the loose tenons (¼ in.) so that I can use the same mortising bit and setup, and also so that I can cut the posts at the same time I cut the tenon stock.

I make the tenon stock by first ripping ¼-in.-thick rock maple strips to the width of a leg-to-apron mortise. Then, using a ⅛-in.-radius roundover bit, I rout all four edges of the strips. Finally, I cut the individual loose tenons to length (about 1⅛ in. in this case) on the radial-arm saw. The tenons can then be glued into their mortises on the ends of the aprons. I also rip a shorter, narrower strip (from the primary wood of the table or case) for the posts, round over the strip's edges and cut the posts to length.

Chamfering around the mortises

I dry-assemble the legs to the aprons, carefully driving the tenons into their sockets. I make sure that the outside face of each apron

fits flush to the angled face of the leg; I plane or scrape any discrepancies. Then I scribe the end profile of each apron onto the leg. These lines provide the layout for the chamfers where each apron joins the leg. Another set of layout lines, marked around each set of apron profile lines, shows about where the chamfers will end (see the photo above right). I then use a Dremel tool fitted with a special router base and a ⅛-in.-dia. end mill to remove waste just outside the second set of layout lines, as shown in the photo above right. I like the end mill because I can rout freehand without worrying about the bit grabbing and taking off. I leave stock at the tops of the legs until they have been tapered.

Now I use a sharp chisel to cut the chamfers. First, I clamp a wood block that's been cut at a 42° angle to the leg on the workbench and use the block as a shooting board to guide the chisel during chamfering (see the top, left photo on the facing page). I cut three chamfers around each mortise, but I leave the ones below the lower aprons until after the legs are tapered. At this time, I decide on the degree of taper for the legs. I mark the tapers, which should start just below the bottom edge where the lower-apron chamfer will be. Because the tapers stop at the chamfers, it's best to make this stopped cut on the bandsaw. With the bandsaw table tilted, I saw the taper on one side of each leg and tape the waste piece back on the leg to keep it level while the other taper is being cut. Then I return the bandsaw table to square and saw the remaining tapers (see the top, right photo on the facing page). I remove the sawmarks with a small handplane held skewed to cut as close to the chamfers as possible. I finish cleaning up the tapers by scraping the surfaces smooth. Now, I reclamp the angled block and chop the bottom chamfers so that they meet the tapers cleanly. Any sawmarks or chisel marks that remain around the chamfers can be cleaned up with a handplane, scraper or file.

After rechecking the fit of the aprons to the legs, I disassemble all parts and sand them down to 220-grit, cleaning up any remaining defects. Next, I run small chamfers, each only about 1/16 in. wide, on all the edges of the aprons, using a 45° bit fitted in my router table. I chamfer the edges of the legs using a handplane instead of a router because the legs' angled faces don't allow the piloted bit to work correctly. In places where the handplane can't reach, such as around the apron-joint chamfers, I finish the detailing with a small file. Handplaning also allows for some subtle variation. I diminish the chamfer on the outside edge of the leg (see the bottom, right photo on the facing page), where the angled faces meet, from almost 3/16 in. wide at the top to less than ⅛ in. at the bottom. This accentuates the taper of the leg.

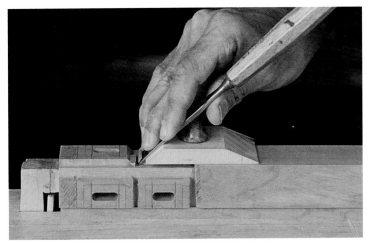

To guide the chisel during chamfering, the author uses a shooting board, a wood block that's been cut at a 42° angle, clamped to the leg.

The taper on each leg is bandsawn after the mortises are chopped. The scrap from the taper cut on one side of a leg has been taped on to level the leg while the taper is cut on its other side.

Filing between mortise sockets (above) is one of the final steps to complete the chamfered details before the table frame halves are glued together.

Although this nightstand features a single apron, the piece (right) still employs the same raised-and-chamfered mortise sockets as in Day's other tables.

Photo: Chris Eden

Assembling the frame and fitting the top

Before final assembly of the frame, I finish-sand all the parts to 400-grit. I also prefinish the inside surfaces of the aprons and the posts, as these areas are hard to get to after assembly. I prefer a shellac finish, which I mix myself using flake shellac thinned at least 3-to-1 with denatured alcohol.

I begin assembling the frame by gluing each pair of aprons together with their posts. I apply glue sparingly in each post mortise, to avoid having to scrape excess squeeze-out. I use spacer blocks between the aprons to keep the apron members parallel during gluing. I also use clamping blocks on the top and bottom, for even pressure.

Next, I glue the apron assemblies to the legs, working in pairs. First I do the two long sides of the table or case. To apply even pressure to the joints, I made angled clamping blocks from scrap hardwood cut at an angle to match the legs' profile and lined with thin cardboard. When the assemblies are dry, I lay each faceup on my workbench and carefully file the chamfers on the edge of the legs in the area between the mortise sockets, which are between the aprons (see the bottom, left photo). Now I glue up the remaining short apron assemblies to complete the base and finish up by filing the detailing between the short side aprons.

The top, which is designed to be flush with the ends of the legs, is constructed from a veneered-plywood center panel with four trim strips glued to the edges. These strips create a space at each corner that fits around the end of each leg (see the bottom, right photo). For the center panel, I glue ³/₃₂-in.-thick veneers to both sides of ½-in.-thick Baltic-birch plywood, and then cut the panel to width, minus the width of two trim strips. Next, I glue the strips on the long edges of the panel and crosscut it to length before I fit and glue on the short strips. Then I rout and glue in the ebony string inlay at the seam between the panel and strips, and clean up the top with a handplane and scraper. I fit the top onto the assembled base, trimming as necessary and taking care to keep the reveals around each leg equal. Then I finish-sand the top and the ends of the legs. I chamfer all edges of the top with a router, as I did on the aprons, and I touch up the chamfer's inside corners with a file. Finally, I apply two coats of shellac, followed by two coats of clear lacquer for moisture protection. □

Ross Day builds furniture and cabinets in Seattle, Wash. His hall tables were included in the 1990 Krenov and Friends show at Pritam and Eames Gallery in New York (see FWW #91, pp. 94-97).

Making an End Table
Multicolor laminates accent a design

by Tage Frid

I believe wood looks best in its unadorned, natural form, and the more you embellish it, the more you detract from its beauty. So when designing the end table shown below, my goal was to make a simple piece that would be strong, yet appear light, and include subtle details that entice you to look closer.

As shown in figure 1 on p. 60, the 22-in.-high table is based on straight, crisp lines and sharp corners. The sense of lightness is strengthened by the legs, which taper to half their square dimension from top to bottom. And the angled joinery required to fit the legs to the aprons isn't difficult. You can mortise the legs with a router and jig, and cut the apron's angled tenon shoulders with a tablesaw.

At first glance the table appears to be made entirely of cherry; but a narrow rabbet in each leg's outside corner reveals that the legs are actually three different woods: layers of cherry and maple laminated to a black walnut core, which appears as a thin line in the rabbet's inside corner. The various parts of the table also relate to each other well. The leg rabbets are $\frac{5}{16}$ in. square, the top overhangs the frame only $\frac{1}{4}$ in. and the apron is set back from the face of the leg less than $\frac{1}{8}$ in., the thickness of the outer cherry laminate. Don't let the simplicity lull you into carelessness. Because of

the crisp lines, an error will stick out like a sore thumb. Everything must be shaped meticulously. To achieve this precision, first make a full-size drawing to help you work out proportions and measure angles and dimensions. For this table, I drew an elevation of two legs and one apron and a plan view of two aprons and one leg.

As I made my drawings, I considered construction and assembly details. For example, notice that the tenons don't meet in a miter (see the detail in figure 1). If they did, the leg would be weak with so little wood between the tenon ends and the rabbet. Also, the apron's $\frac{3}{8}$-in.-thick tenons are offset with a $\frac{5}{16}$-in. shoulder on the outside and a $\frac{1}{16}$-in. shoulder on the inside, to position the tenon as close as possible to the middle of the leg for strength. By using haunched tenons the full width of the apron, the top of the leg is stronger and you needn't clamp the mortise sides to the tenon cheeks when gluing. Finally, I left a $\frac{1}{16}$-in. space between the end of the tenon and the bottom of the mortise for excess glue that could compress and split the top of the leg during assembly.

Preparing stock—After I made the drawings, I developed the bill of materials on p. 61 listing the necessary angles and dimensions. Initially, leave everything about 1 in. longer than called for and trim later. Also note that the bill of materials recommends some pieces be left oversize to simplify assembly; the plywood edge facing, or edgebanding, for instance, is easier to apply if it's a bit wider than the thickness of the plywood it's glued to.

Begin building the legs by gluing, one at a time, the maple laminates and then the cherry laminates to the black walnut. Spread the glue sparingly and evenly. As shown in the left photo on the facing page, you can glue and clamp laminates on two legs at the same time if you sandwich the laminates between the walnut. If you spread the glue neatly, you won't need wax paper between the laminates to keep them from sticking to each other. By beginning with oversize, $1\frac{5}{8}$-in.-square walnut leg stock, you can clamp directly to the wood without pads, because clamp-dented wood will be ripped away later. Use three clamps, applying pressure from the middle clamp first and wiping away excess glue with a damp rag. If you wait until the glue is dry and then chisel it off, you can dull your tools or chip away enough wood to make the leg look as if mice gnawed it.

After the glue has cured, saw or plane and scrape the protruding laminate edges flush with the leg stock. You can remove this excess with a smoothing plane, but I rip it on the tablesaw after fitting a $\frac{3}{4}$x$1\frac{1}{2}$x18 auxiliary fence to the rip fence. Because of the low height of the auxiliary fence, the laminate doesn't interfere with the accuracy of the cut. The walnut core bears against the fence and the laminate overhangs it while you rip the excess from the leg's other side, as shown in the top, right photo on the facing page. When ripping the excess from the first maple laminate, set the auxiliary fence

The lines of the author's end table are straight, the corners sharp and crisp, and the parts proportional to one another. The legs are thin strips of cherry and maple laminated to a walnut core, visible in the rabbet on the leg's corners.

From *Fine Woodworking* (May 1990) 82:52-55

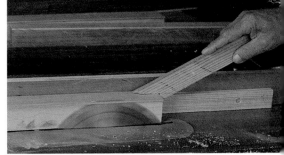

Frid clamps one laminate on each of two legs at once by sandwiching the laminates between the stout walnut. Clamp pads aren't necessary because the inside of the legs will be cut away when they are tapered.

1⅝ in. from the blade. If you use a hollow-ground blade for these narrow rip cuts, the wood won't tear and the surface will almost be planer smooth. I finish the surface with a sharp cabinet scraper before gluing on another laminate. Remember to move the fence away from the blade as additional laminates are glued to the leg.

Cutting the leg mortises—After all the laminates are glued in place, each leg will be 1⅞ in. square and must be ripped on the inside surface and finished 1¾ in. square before mortising. I use a plunge router and the jig shown in the bottom, right photo above to mortise the legs to accept the haunched tenons. The jig is a three-sided box in which the leg is positioned against a stop, shimmed to height and clamped on one side. The router's fence bears against one side of the jig, and the length of the mortise is determined by stops set on the other side of the jig to limit router base travel. For more on the mortise jig, see *Fine Woodworking on Joinery* (The Taunton Press, 1985).

My square-base plunge router has three depth settings. I use one for a ⁵⁄₁₆-in.-deep mortise for the haunch and one for a ¹³⁄₁₆-in.-deep mortise for the main part of the tenon. After positioning the leg and setting the jig's stops for 2-in.-long mortises, I gradually plunge a ⅜-in. straight bit into all the legs until I've reached the haunch depth. Then, I reset the stops for the 1⁹⁄₁₆-in.-long tenon and gradually plunge to the tenon depth. Since the mortise is offset to one side of the leg, turn the leg end for end and reset the jig to cut the mortises on their opposite side. After routing each mortise, I square the corners with a chisel and mallet, and then slightly undercut each one to receive the angled tenon end.

Next, rip the full-length taper in the leg on the tablesaw with the plywood jig shown in figure 2 on p. 61. The jig should hold the leg

snugly as you taper it from 1¾ in. square at the top to ⅞ in. square at the bottom, which is large enough not to cut into carpet or dent a wooden floor. Cut the same amount from each of the leg's two inside surfaces, but leave the dimensions slightly heavy so each surface can be trued on the jointer.

Lastly, rabbet the outside corner of each leg to reveal the laminates. I remove most of the waste by ripping the rabbet slightly smaller than shown on the drawing. Then, I finish the rabbet to ⁵⁄₁₆ in. square with a straight bit in a table-mounted router. Since most of the waste was removed on the tablesaw, the router will leave surfaces that only need light sanding. Be careful not to round over the corners of the rabbet when sanding.

Making the aprons—The apron ends and shoulders are angled to fit the leg's full-length taper with some simple tablesaw setups. Before cutting the aprons to length, you should mark an X on their best side. Then, measure the angle between the leg and the apron and the aprons' length (including tenons) from the drawing. I measure the angle with a sliding bevel and duplicate it between the miter gauge and the blade, and then crosscut one end of each apron. By clamping a stop to the gauge, you can cut duplicate lengths of the two long aprons before resetting the stop to cut the short ones.

To cut the tenon cheeks, I use a jig made of two pieces of plywood with a piece of wood, the thickness of the saw fence, sandwiched in between (see the top photo on p. 61). The plywood edges slide on the table, and the jig is guided by the fence. To cut the cheeks, I clamp the apron to the jig so the angled end of the apron is flat on the table, set the blade height at ¾ in., square to the table, and locate the fence to leave the proper-size offset tenon. For more about this tenon jig, see my book, *Tage Frid Teaches Wood-*

Fig. 1: End table

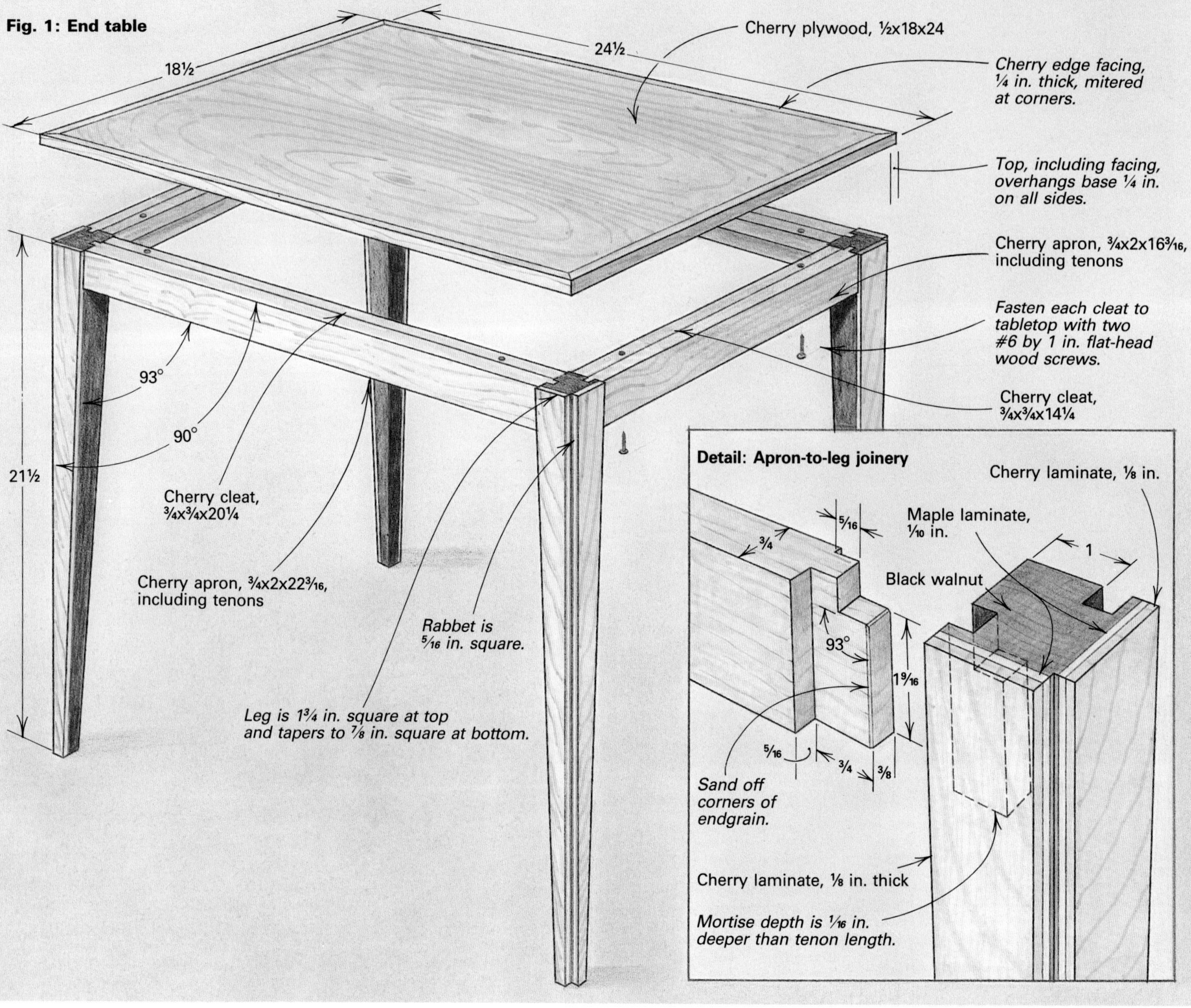
18½
24½
Cherry plywood, ½x18x24
Cherry edge facing, ¼ in. thick, mitered at corners.
Top, including facing, overhangs base ¼ in. on all sides.
Cherry apron, ¾x2x16 3/16, including tenons
Fasten each cleat to tabletop with two #6 by 1 in. flat-head wood screws.
Cherry cleat, ¾x¾x14¼
93°
90°
21½
Cherry cleat, ¾x¾x20¼
Cherry apron, ¾x2x22 3/16, including tenons
Rabbet is 5/16 in. square.
Leg is 1¾ in. square at top and tapers to ⅞ in. square at bottom.
Detail: Apron-to-leg joinery
Cherry laminate, ⅛ in.
5/16
Maple laminate, 1/10 in.
¾
1
Black walnut
93°
1 9/16
5/16
¾
⅜
Sand off corners of endgrain.
Cherry laminate, ⅛ in. thick
Mortise depth is 1/16 in. deeper than tenon length.

working, Book 1: Joinery (The Taunton Press, 1979), p. 131.

To cut the shoulders, remove the tenon jig and use the miter gauge previously set for the shoulder's angle, based on the leg's taper. Clamp a 1x2x6 block to the rip fence about 6 in. in front of the blade and position the fence for a ¾-in.-long tenon by measuring between the blade and the block. Using the block as an end stop provides clearance between the blade and rip fence to prevent the cutoff from getting trapped and kicking back.

When cutting the tenon, butt the end of the rail against the block and then grip the rail tightly to the miter gauge fence as you make the cut. Set the blade height at 1/16 in. for the inside shoulder and test the cut on a scrap to ensure the shoulder is parallel to the rail's end. Because of the offset tenon and the opposing angles on opposite ends of the apron, you will have to cut the two right-hand, 1/16-in. shoulders, reverse the miter gauge angle and cut the left-hand, 1/16-in. shoulders. Then you can raise the blade for the 5/16-in.-deep shoulder, make the left-hand cuts and again reverse the miter gauge angle to make the right-hand cuts. I avoid having to change the miter gauge angle, which can lead to inaccuracy, by using two gauges preset to the same but opposing angles. Then I can just interchange miter gauges for either a left- or right-hand cut.

I bandsaw the tenon's haunch by clamping a fence 7/16 in. from the outside of the blade and a stop 7/16 in. behind the blade's cutting edge. Before assembly, pare a 1/16-in. bevel on the end of the tenon, so it's easier to push home in the mortise.

Sand everything before frame assembly. Since the leg stands off the face of the apron a little less than ⅛ in., the leg's line is distinct from bottom to top and presanding is possible. Lightly sand with 180-grit paper just enough to dull the edge so it won't cut your finger.

Assembling the frame—Before assembly, scrape and sand the inside of the four legs and the front and bottom of the aprons. Don't try to glue the entire frame in one operation or you'll have a difficult time squaring it. Glue the short aprons to two of the legs first, making sure each apron's thickest shoulder is on the outside of the leg. Apply glue sparingly only to the outside corners of the mortise and on the front part of the tenon cheeks; there's no need to put any on the end of the tenon. As you press the parts together by hand, the glue will spread evenly on the tenon cheeks and the sides of the mortise. If the tenons must be forced, pare off any burnished high spots. You need only one clamp (with pads), set parallel to the apron, to hold the assembly together.

The frame must be square in order for the table's four legs to be flat on the floor at the same time. I check for squareness with the bevel gauge, previously set to the inside angle between the leg and apron, and a framing square, for the 90° outside angle. If the frame

Drawings: Vince Babak

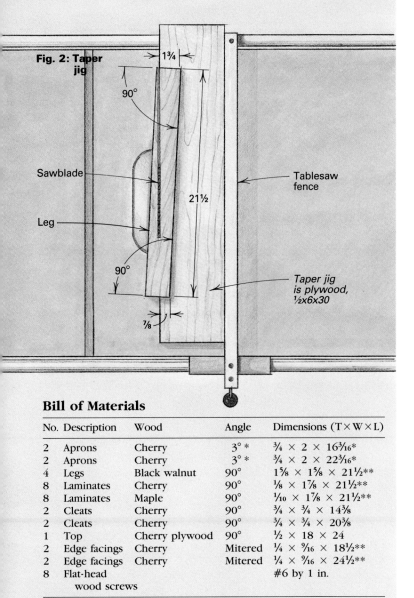

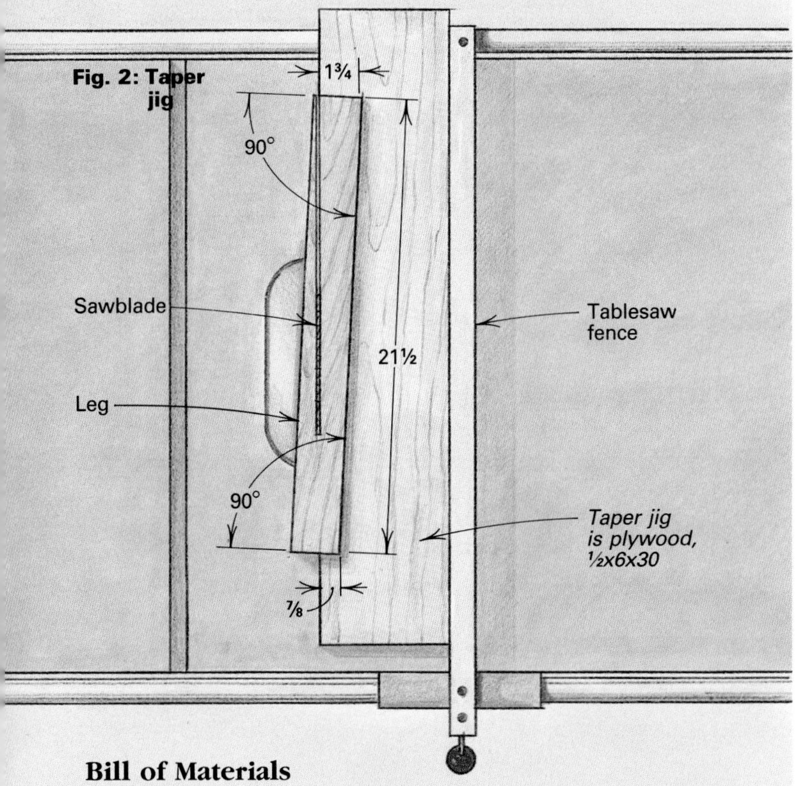
Fig. 2: Taper jig
1¾
90°
Sawblade
Tablesaw fence
21½
Leg
90°
Taper jig is plywood, ½x6x30
⅞

Bill of Materials

No.	Description	Wood	Angle	Dimensions (T×W×L)
2	Aprons	Cherry	3° *	¾ × 2 × 16 3/16*
2	Aprons	Cherry	3° *	¾ × 2 × 22 3/16*
4	Legs	Black walnut	90°	1⅝ × 1⅝ × 21½**
8	Laminates	Cherry	90°	⅛ × 1⅞ × 21½**
8	Laminates	Maple	90°	1/10 × 1⅞ × 21½**
2	Cleats	Cherry	90°	¾ × ¾ × 14⅜
2	Cleats	Cherry	90°	¾ × ¾ × 20⅜
1	Top	Cherry plywood	90°	½ × 18 × 24
2	Edge facings	Cherry	Mitered	¼ × 9/16 × 18½**
2	Edge facings	Cherry	Mitered	¼ × 9/16 × 24½**
8	Flat-head wood screws			#6 by 1 in.

* Angles and lengths copied from full-size drawings for accuracy.
** Ripped wider than their finish dimension for easier alignment during assembly.

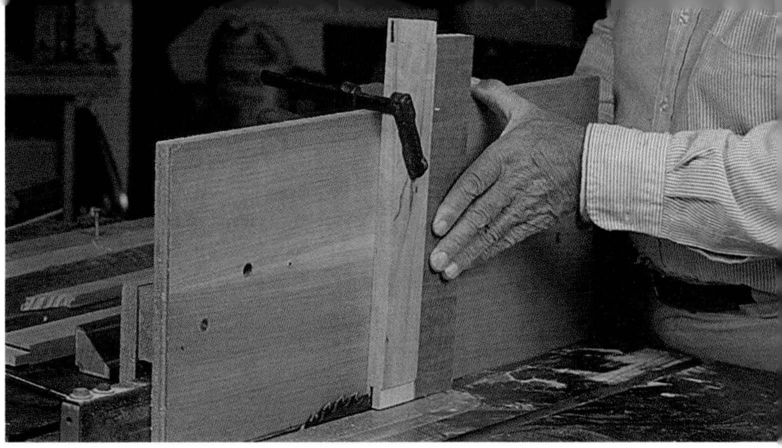

Apron tenons are cut with a plywood jig that is guided by the saw fence. The jig holds the apron so that its end runs flat against the saw table.

Frid guides a modified router around the table's top and bottom surfaces to flush-trim excess facing. A piece of ¾-in. plywood is fastened to the router base and the ½-in.-dia. straight bit's flat end is nearly flush with the plywood base.

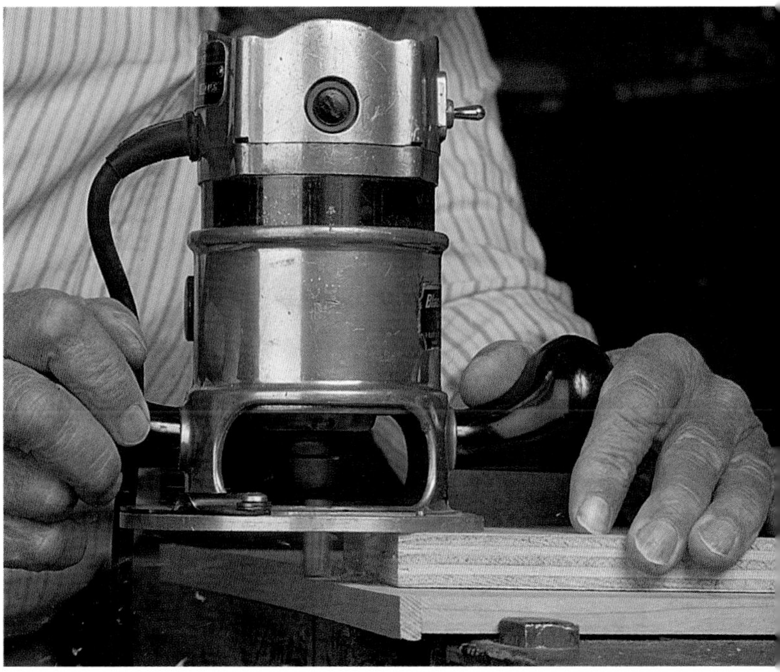

isn't square, adjust the direction of the clamp's pressure by slightly moving one or both of its ends. Before setting the glued subassemblies aside to dry, check that the legs are parallel and the outside diagonals are equal.

After the glue is set in the subassemblies, complete the frame by gluing the subassemblies to the long aprons. Again, you only need one clamp per side, but you may need one across the top to adjust the frame square as you look at it from above. Recheck that the legs are parallel and their diagonals, as well as those of the top, are equal.

Before you fasten the top in place, block-plane or belt-sand the tops of the legs, if they extend above the aprons. If you plane them, pare the inside top corners away so they don't tear out as you plane in from the outer edges of the frame. Finally, glue the cleats to the inside and the top of the aprons, as shown in figure 1.

Finishing and fastening on the top—Since the edges of the cherry plywood tabletop aren't attractive, I cover them with cherry edge facings. Dry-clamp the four facing pieces to the outside of the plywood, to ensure that the mitered ends fit well, as shown in figure 1. Remove two opposite pieces, apply glue to their joining surfaces, but not to the miters, and clamp them to the plywood's edges until the glue sets. Then, remove the other two facing pieces, apply glue to all their joining surfaces (including the miters) and glue them in place, tightly aligning the miters. If you want to avoid miters, you can butt-joint the facings as I did.

Although you could use a smoothing plane, scraper and sandpaper to dress the facings flush with the top and bottom plywood surfaces, I use a simple router modification, shown in the bottom photo above. Fasten one end of a piece of ¾-in. plywood, about 6 in. wide by 12 in. long, to the router base so that its edge is set back about ½ in. from a ½-in.-dia. straight bit. Adjust the bit's flat end flush with or slightly recessed from the plywood base. When you guide the router around the surfaces, the bit will flush-trim the excess facing. Finish-sand so the cherry facing appears as one with the cherry plywood.

All surfaces are sanded to remove machining marks and two coats of Watco Danish Oil Finish (available from Minwax Co., 102 Chestnut Ridge Plaza, Montvale, N.J. 07645) are applied.

Finally, attach the frame to the top with two #6 by 1-in. flat-head wood screws through each cleat. Since the screws penetrate only ¼ in. into the top, a small-diameter screw with more threads per inch holds best. Lay the top, finished-side down, on a soft blanket and center the frame on its underside. Be careful not to countersink the heads when boring for or driving the screws, or the screw point might penetrate the tabletop's finished surface. □

Tage Frid is a Contributing Editor to FWW.

Convertible Furniture
Tables designed to lead dual lives

by Edward R. Monteith

Some pieces of furniture literally work. The tambour of a rolltop desk, or even a rocking chair, allows—or perhaps even demands—human interaction. Similarly, but in a more subtle manner, the game table, shown in the photos on the facing page, and the spinet desk on p. 65 are hard workers. Both perform double duty and do so gracefully, but unlike a rocker or a rolltop, they hide their alter egos. Perhaps the element of surprise is partially responsible for my satisfaction in owning them; when visitors comment on my hall tables, they're fascinated and drawn in by the transformations that occur. Designing and building these tables was satisfying as well. In describing them, I'll provide you with the critical concepts and relationships that make these pieces of furniture work, so you can build similar pieces that suit your particular needs.

An expanding game table

Annoyed for years by a card table that swayed like a tall pine in a gale, I had often considered building a sturdier model. In addition, I was fed up with having to burrow through an overstuffed coat closet to drag out my old folding table. And I wanted a table that provided more playing surface than standard models but didn't dominate my living room.

During a visit with friends, an 18th-century Dutch game table caught my eye. Its rails folded on two sides, allowing it to transform from a full-size card table into an attractive side or occasional table that's only half as large. Even though the Dutch table was more than 200 years old and the hardware was somewhat worn and loose, it was still remarkably sturdy. I decided to try my hand at building a similar table. Rather than using reproduction hardware, I substituted contemporary, precision hardware (for a far sturdier table), and I adjusted the size to fit my needs. Since that first effort, I've built two more of these tables (see the photos on the facing page). The actual construction was relatively straightforward, but the design required a bit of thought.

Dividing up the folding rails—The most critical aspect of the design was determining the lengths of the various pieces of the folding rails. Figure 1 (see the facing page) illustrates the requirements for the folding rails. I found it easiest to work backward from the desired final dimensions of the tabletop. On the basis of comparison with existing card tables, I decided to build my table 34 in. sq. when open and half that width closed. A 2¼-in. overhang all around gave me a base that's 29½ in. sq. when open and folds to 12½ in. when closed. I arrived at these numbers unscientifically; the table's proportions when closed pleased my eye, and I knew it would provide plenty of space when open for cards, tea and such.

Having established these dimensions, I simply subtracted 9 in., the distance between legs when the table is closed, from 26 in., the length of the front and back rails between the legs. This gave me 17 in. as the correct overall length for the *exposed* portions of the two remaining pieces of each folding rail when the table is open (see figure 1). However, this is only the exposed overall dimension. A half-lap notch cut into the back rail piece and the corresponding notch cut into the middle rail piece hide the folded rails when the table is closed up and help stiffen the back-to-middle rail-piece joint when open. For the

table to close properly, these notches must be long enough to accommodate the thickness of the two folding rail pieces and the front back flap hinge when folded (see figure 1). For my table, I cut the notches 2¼ in. long, which gave me a little play. Adding this 2¼ in. to the 17 in. gave me a total of 19¼ in. for the middle and front rail pieces on each side.

At this point, common sense might tell you simply to halve that number to give you the proper length for each of the remaining pieces of rail. You wouldn't be far off the mark. I've found, though, that cutting the front rail ⅛ in. longer than the middle piece prevents the folding rails from binding in the corner. This is because the back flap hinge isn't mortised into the front leg and spacer block, so the end of the front rail piece must extend past the center point of the hinge pin, if the rail is to butt up snugly against the leg (see the drawing at right). Therefore, the front rail piece must be ⅛ in. longer (the approximate width of a hinge leaf), if it and the middle rail piece are to fold parallel to the front rail and not bind.

Milling the parts and installing the hinges—Once I'd worked out these relationships, I felt comfortable beginning construction. I cut the leg blanks to 1¾ in. sq. by about 28 in. long, which left me an inch for trimming the legs to final length and removing chuck marks from the top ends after I'd turned them. I turned the legs and trimmed them to length. Then I cut the ½-in. sliding-dovetail mortises for the fixed front and back rails (and for the fixed back end of the folding rails) on my router table using wooden stop blocks and running a test cut on a piece of scrap first.

From *Fine Woodworking* (March 1992) 93:68-71

A 200-year-old Dutch table was the model for the author's interpretation, shown above and at right. An ingenious folding-rail system allows the table to do double duty as a simple hall table most of the time and as a game table when the need arises.

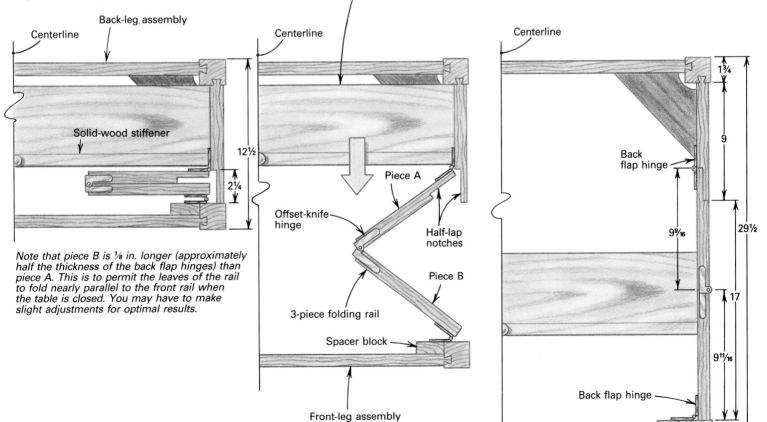

Fig. 1: Folding card/side table

Plywood spreader slides into dado near bottom of rails to lock folding rails open.

Centerline

Back-leg assembly

Centerline

Centerline

Solid-wood stiffener

12½

2¼

Offset-knife hinge

Piece A

Half-lap notches

Piece B

3-piece folding rail

Spacer block

Front-leg assembly

Back flap hinge

Back flap hinge

1¾

9

9⁹⁄₁₆

17

9¹¹⁄₁₆

29½

Note that piece B is ⅛ in. longer (approximately half the thickness of the back flap hinges) than piece A. This is to permit the leaves of the rail to fold nearly parallel to the front rail when the table is closed. You may have to make slight adjustments for optimal results.

Photos: Sandor Nagyszalanczy

When milling the rail stock, I left it slightly wide so that I could trim away any tearout along the edge that might result from routing the sliding dovetails. I then selected and routed the face side of all my sliding dovetails. I reset the fence for the other half of each dovetail, checked the cut on a piece of scrap and made some minor adjustments to get a good, snug fit in the dovetail mortises in the legs. Satisfied with my cut, I routed the back side of the dovetails on all rails. Before cutting the two folding rails into three pieces each, I routed dadoes near their bottom inside edges to accommodate the ¼-in. plywood spreader that slides forward and locks the rails open. I then cut each folding rail into three pieces, as described above, and marked them so that the grain on the rails of the assembled piece would be nearly continuous.

Proper hinge installation is as essential as is determining the requisite lengths of the folding rail pieces. I routed mortises for the offset-knife hinges that join the front and middle section on my router table, and then I cut the half-lap notches on the back and middle rail pieces. After installing the offset-knife hinges into the mortises, I mounted the back flap hinges on the overlapping back and middle rail pieces. It is essential that this hinge is mounted with its pin perpendicular to the top edge of the rail, so the rail won't bind and so the tabletop will sit flat.

Next, I glued and clamped the leg-to-rail dovetails. After they dried, I inserted the ¼-in. plywood spreader into the dado near the bottom of the rails and screwed the front pieces of rail to the front legs and to a spacer block. Again, it's very important that the hinge pins be perpendicular to the rails. After assembling the base, I cut and installed diagonal corner braces to keep the corners rigid.

Because I've found it easier to work with narrow boards when drilling deep mortises (like those required for the three Soss hinges I used to connect the two leaves of this tabletop), I ripped the innermost board of each leaf to about 3 in. wide and routed the mortises for the hinges before gluing up the leaves. Two hinges might have been adequate, but the third hinge should help prevent the leaves from warping. Once the hinges were installed, I glued up both leaves and finish-sanded them. The tabletop is attached to the base with a screw

through each of the diagonal corner braces. The screw holes should be elongated to allow for cross-grain movement.

A spinet desk goes undercover

The first true spinet desks were made for school use in the 1830s by fitting cast-iron cabriole legs to melodeon cabinets (boxes which contained the innards of an organ-like instrument). The desk I used as a model was made at a later date, though, and is a simple box with a front panel hinged to a folding top. Turned wooden legs are attached to the box's bottom with hanger bolts, and the interior of the box contains a slide-out writing surface and pigeonholes for paper storage. Time has taken its toll on this piece, leaving it a bit wobbly, but the desk's ability to transform from utilitarian writing desk to demure hall table captivated and inspired me (see the photos on the facing page).

I wanted to build a similar piece that retained the style and character of the original, but was more stable. I accomplished this by using sliding dovetails (as on the game table) for all leg-to-rail joints except for the front fascia piece, which I tenoned into mortises in the front legs (shown in figure 2 on the facing page). I also wanted a larger writing surface that would be more suitable for adults, so I increased all dimensions of the piece proportionally. The resulting piece is a simple, yet elegant desk, and the writing surface (and any attendant mess) can be hidden in a moment by pushing it in and then folding the top down.

Assembling the desk—The drawing on the facing page shows the desk's construction and the relationship of the parts. I first glued and clamped the back rail and legs and the front fascia and legs together; I let them dry, and then glued the front and back assemblies together with the side rails. Next, I screwed the cleats that support the writing surface all around the inside of the box. The cleats are flush with the top surface of the front fascia and the side cleats are notched to fit around the legs.

To fill the gap between the side rails and the inner surface of the legs, I glued and screwed L-shaped guide pieces (one piece of wood routed out) to the side rails. The guide's vertical arm comes just flush with the inside edge of the legs, and the hori-

zontal arm extends beyond the legs to form a pocket between itself and the side cleats so that the writing surface can slide freely. These guides also support the removable pigeonhole assembly. I constructed the assembly from ⅜-in. stock and designed it to accommodate standard writing paper and envelopes as well as to provide miscellaneous storage. With the pigeonhole assembly in place on the writing surface guides, I measured for filler blocks on either side and for the top cleats, through which I screwed the back leaf of the folding top. The filler blocks and top cleats were screwed to the side rails through elongated holes to allow for wood movement.

I'd glued up the writing surface ahead of time so that it would be ready to trim to size when it came time to assemble the desk. I used a glue joint tongue-and-groove bit to rout the ends of the boards and the end caps, but I only glued the end caps to the main field of the writing surface in the middle, to allow for expansion and contraction. Now, with the box assembled and the guide pieces installed, I trimmed the writing surface to fit neatly between the front legs and to set back far enough to allow the false drawer front to close flush with the fascia. Two short dowels glued into the bottom of the writing surface, as shown in the drawing on the facing page, act as stops, and a brass sliding-door pull is mortised into the top. To fill the space between the pigeonhole assembly and the writing surface, I glued and screwed a narrow filler piece (about 1½ in. wide) to the writing surface so that it would protrude about an inch beyond the pigeonholes when fully open.

The top consists of two equal-width leaves joined with Soss hinges, like the top of the game table. To mount the top, I ran screws up through the top cleats at either side of the box and into the back leaf. Then, with the top closed, I marked the underside of the front leaf for the false drawer front, cut the front panel to fit and attached it to the front leaf with a piano hinge.

Ed Monteith is a hobbyist woodworker who lives in Pebble Beach, Cal. All the hardware used in the expanding game table and in the spinet desk was purchased from Woodcraft, 210 Wood County Industrial Park, PO Box 1686, Parkersburg, W. Va. 26102-1686; (800) 225-1153.

Fig. 2: Spinet desk/hall table

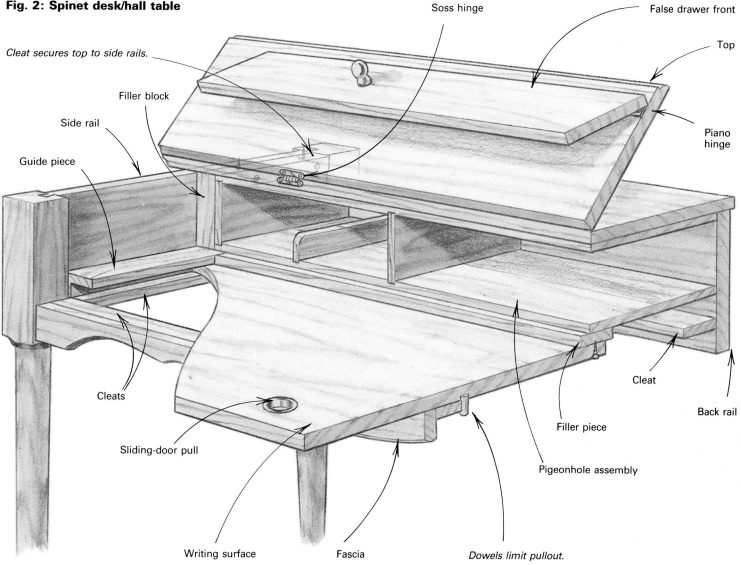

Soss hinge

False drawer front

Top

Cleat secures top to side rails.

Filler block

Side rail

Guide piece

Piano hinge

Cleats

Sliding-door pull

Writing surface

Fascia

Dowels limit pullout.

Pigeonhole assembly

Filler piece

Cleat

Back rail

With the cover up, *it's a work station; with the cover down, it's a simple and unobtrusive table. This combination hall table/spinet desk helps to maintain order in the author's house. Although the design is based on an old school desk, Monteith sized the piece for himself, increasing all dimensions proportionally. The pigeonholes, too, were adapted for modern use to fit standard envelopes and stationery.*

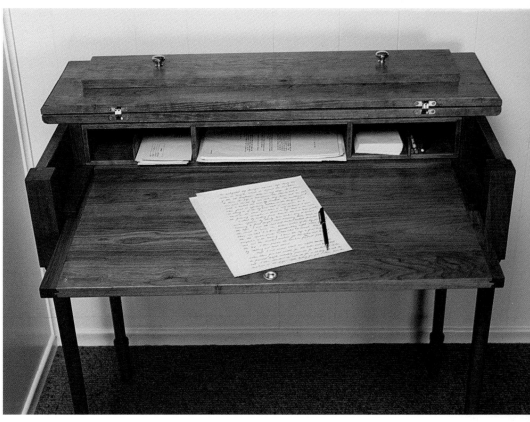

A Semielliptical Table
Veneering laminated aprons and inlaying ebony

by Bill Clinton

Many of my designs are developed from photographs and drawings of historical furniture. The table shown in the photo on p. 69, for example, is based on 18th-century English and American semicircular or semielliptical pier tables, which were generally set against a wall between windows in a dining or sitting room. The legs on many of these early tables were fluted and embellished with elaborate marquetry, which I found a little overwhelming. I decided to simplify my mahogany table and support it with turned legs that gently taper to thin ebony feet. The semielliptical top is veneered with quilted mahogany and decorated with ebony string inlay. I also added a small white dot of tagua nut vegetable ivory to the turned ebony drawer knobs.

In building tables, I use the top as a guide for sizing the base and for developing jigs or full-size drawings, and so I began by drawing a pattern of the tabletop with a shop-built ellipse tracing machine. This machine is also needed to trace patterns for the forms used to laminate the curved front aprons. I simplified the base construction by joining the curved aprons to the turned legs with loose tenons and by cutting all the mortises with a router and jig. Then I adapted my router to the ellipse machine to trim the tabletop edges and to cut a concentric groove for the string inlay.

Drawing an ellipse—An ellipse is an attractive shape, but drawing one can be frustrating, especially if you use the traditional "pin and string." I developed my own system based on the ellipse tracing machine in the 18th-century Dominy workshops. That machine was simply a beam trammel with three points: one scribe and two pivots. Each pivot slides in one of two wood tracks that cross at a right angle in the center of a baseplate. The pivots on my machine (the router version is shown in the bottom, right photo on p. 68) are screwed to shaped blocks that slide in dovetailed tracks. The size and shape of the ellipse being drawn can be changed by varying the lengths of the beam and tracks and the location of the pivots.

To use the machine, you need to know the ellipse's width (the minor axis) and length (the major axis) and to locate the center of the machine base at the point where these two perpendicular centerlines cross in the middle of the ellipse. I laid out the tabletop pattern in the drawing on a 1/4x20x56 piece of plywood by marking one-half of the ellipse's 36-in.-long minor axis perpendicular to and intersecting the center of its 48-in.-long major axis. After aligning the tracks with the ellipse axes, I temporarily screwed the tracks to the plywood. The points are adjusted by setting the scribe 18 in. (half the ellipse width) from the first pivot, which slides in the major axis track; and setting the second pivot, which slides in

the minor axis track, 24 in. (half the ellipse length) from the scribe. Clamp the three points to the beam before tracing the half-ellipse.

Before bandsawing the half-ellipse, I drew a full-size plan of the table's framework on the plywood. First, with the ellipse machine still set up, draw the concentric 3/4-in.-thick front apron and drawer front 1 in. inside the top's perimeter. To do this, simply move and reclamp the scribe, without changing the pivot points. I then removed the ellipse machine, so I wouldn't have to work around it, and drew drawer supports and guides, back apron, stretchers, and leg tops with their mortises and loose tenons; that way I could take lengths and angles directly from the plan when machining the parts. To make paper patterns for the drawer-front- and two apron-laminating forms, I reattached the ellipse machine to the plywood and used it to draw the inside edges of the curved parts on separate sheets of paper. Extend the lines beyond the length of each part and then trace the crosscuts from the drawing on the plywood underneath.

Making and mortising the curved front—I glued up seven laminates plus a face veneer for the two 3/4-in.-thick front aprons and the drawer front, and clamped each assembly between laminated plywood forms, like the one in the top, left photo on p. 68. The drawer-front form is made by gluing up a 5 1/4x5x21 stack of plywood, rubber cementing a paper pattern on top and bandsawing the form in half along the pattern line. The apron forms are made the same way, except their initial plywood stack is 5 1/4x6 1/2x23. Note: each form is extra thick and long on both ends to ensure that the edges of the laminations are clamped adequately.

After the laminations dry overnight, transfer the marks from the paper pattern to the part, which can then be removed from the form, jointed and cut to the dimensions in the drawing. As shown, the end of the apron that joins the front leg is crosscut perpendicular to the tangent of the apron curve. This is easy to do on the tablesaw (shown in the top, right photo on p. 68). Set the blade perpendicular to the table and place the apron's convex side flat on the table (the tangent). After aligning the blade with the cut mark taken from the pattern, clamp the apron to the miter gauge, insert a curved support block under the workpiece and clamp the block to the gauge before making the cut. Repeat the procedure for the same joint on the other apron. The angle on the apron end that joins the rear leg is 5° less; so for these cuts, use the same miter gauge techniques as before, but angle the blade 5° toward the apron. You can make test cuts in the scrap you previously ripped from the apron edge and check the angle by laying it on the full-size drawing. The same procedure is used to cut the ends

Photos: Gary Weisenburger; drawings: Kathleen Rushton

A semielliptical table

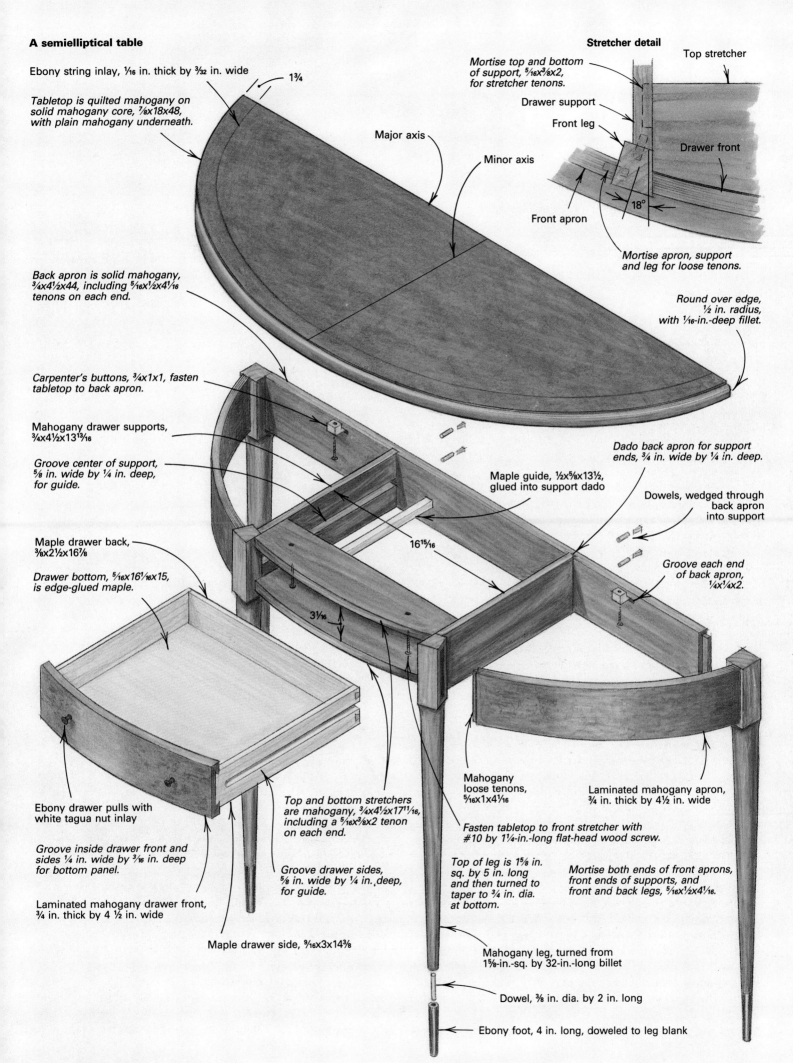

Ebony string inlay, 1/16 in. thick by 3/32 in. wide

Tabletop is quilted mahogany on solid mahogany core, 7/8x18x48, with plain mahogany underneath.

1 3/4

Stretcher detail

Mortise top and bottom of support, 5/16x3/8x2, for stretcher tenons.

Top stretcher

Drawer support

Front leg

Drawer front

18°

Major axis

Minor axis

Front apron

Mortise apron, support and leg for loose tenons.

Back apron is solid mahogany, 3/4x4 1/2x44, including 5/16x1/2x4 1/16 tenons on each end.

Round over edge, 1/2 in. radius, with 1/16-in.-deep fillet.

Carpenter's buttons, 3/4x1x1, fasten tabletop to back apron.

Mahogany drawer supports, 3/4x4 1/2x13 13/16

Groove center of support, 5/8 in. wide by 1/4 in. deep, for guide.

Dado back apron for support ends, 3/4 in. wide by 1/4 in. deep.

Maple guide, 1/2x5/8x13 1/2, glued into support dado

Dowels, wedged through back apron into support

Maple drawer back, 3/8x2 1/2x16 7/8

Drawer bottom, 5/16x16 1/16x15, is edge-glued maple.

16 15/16

Groove each end of back apron, 1/4x1/4x2.

3 1/16

Ebony drawer pulls with white tagua nut inlay

Groove inside drawer front and sides 1/4 in. wide by 3/16 in. deep for bottom panel.

Top and bottom stretchers are mahogany, 3/4x4 1/2x17 11/16, including a 5/16x3/8x2 tenon on each end.

Groove drawer sides, 5/8 in. wide by 1/4 in. deep, for guide.

Mahogany loose tenons, 5/16x1x4 1/16

Laminated mahogany apron, 3/4 in. thick by 4 1/2 in. wide

Laminated mahogany drawer front, 3/4 in. thick by 4 1/2 in. wide

Maple drawer side, 9/16x3x14 3/8

Fasten tabletop to front stretcher with #10 by 1 1/4-in.-long flat-head wood screw.

Top of leg is 1 5/8 in. sq. by 5 in. long and then turned to taper to 3/4 in. dia. at bottom.

Mortise both ends of front aprons, front ends of supports, and front and back legs, 5/16x1/2x4 1/16.

Mahogany leg, turned from 1 5/8-in.-sq. by 32-in.-long billet

Dowel, 3/8 in. dia. by 2 in. long

Ebony foot, 4 in. long, doweled to leg blank

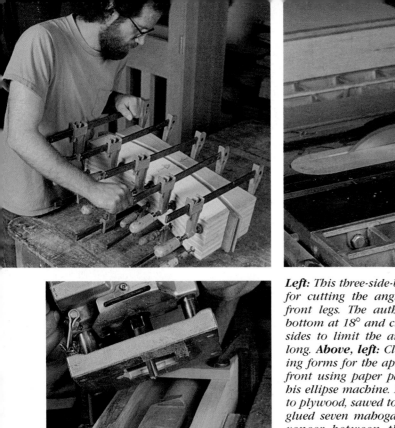

Left: *This three-side-box router jig is ideal for cutting the angle in the top of the front legs. The author grooved the jig's bottom at 18° and clamped a stop on the sides to limit the angled face to 4½ in. long.* **Above, left:** *Clinton made laminating forms for the aprons and this drawer front using paper patterns he drew with his ellipse machine. He glued the patterns to plywood, sawed to the pattern line, and glued seven mahogany laminations plus veneer between the clamped forms.* **Above, right:** *The author crosscuts the curved apron by setting its cut-off mark on the table, which is tangent to the curve at that point, and aligning the mark with the blade.* **Right:** *Clinton adapted his router to a flat beam on the ellipse machine to trim the edge of the tabletop and to rout a groove for the ebony string inlay, shown here.*

of the drawer front at 18°, as shown in the drawing.

I cut 5/16x1/2x4 1/16 mortises in both ends of the curved aprons with a table-mounted router and a 5/16-in.-dia. straight bit. Since the apron ends that join the front legs were crosscut with their convex sides on the saw table, you can plunge-cut the mortise on that end by guiding the same face against a perpendicular fence on the router table. To mortise the apron ends angled 5°, I tilted the fence 5° so the end would be flat on the router table. Although I gauged mortise length by starting and stopping the cut on pencil marks on the fence, you can do this by clamping stop blocks to the fence.

Making and mortising the legs—The 32-in.-long mahogany legs taper from 1 5/8-in.-sq. tops to 3/4-in.-dia. ebony feet, which I doweled to the legs before turning them. After turning the legs, I routed mortises for the loose tenons that join the aprons and drawer supports using a three-side-box mortising jig. Each leg's square top is clamped in the box and the router base runs on the box's upright sides between two stop blocks. (For more on this jig, see Tage Frid's article in *FWW on Joinery*, The Taunton Press, 63 S. Main St., PO Box 5506, Newtown, Conn. 06470-5506.) As shown in the drawing, one side of the square top of the front legs must be angled 18° to accommodate the drawer. You can bandsaw this angle, but I routed it with another three-side jig, shown in the bottom, left photo. I grooved the jig's bottom at 18° and secured the leg by driving screws through the jig bottom and inconspicuously into the leg mortise. Guide the router base on the jig's top edges and set the straight bit's cutting depth to leave the leg's front face 1 5/8 in. wide.

Making the straight parts—Following the dimensions in the drawing, cut the remaining parts, including the two stretchers,

which link the front legs and act as a drawer stop; the back apron; loose tenons; the pair of drawer supports and guides; and the drawer sides, back and bottom. The front of each stretcher is curved by marking out the shape from the drawer-front laminating form, and then bandsawing and planing to the line.

The stretchers have 5/16x3/8x2 integral tenons on their ends. To cut them, I adjusted my table-mounted router so a 5/16-in.-dia. straight bit would protrude 7/32 in. (the width of the shoulder above the table) and set the fence 1/16 in. from the bit. I then routed both faces, holding the work flat on the table while running the end against the fence, and bandsawed the excess width from the outer edge to make a 2-in.-wide tenon. To cut the 5/16x1/2x4 1/16 integral tenons on the back apron's ends, I moved the fence 3/16 in. from the bit and repeated the process, this time routing all four sides for a 7/32-in.-wide shoulder all around. Before removing the bit, rout the mortises in the angled front of the drawer supports. I guided each support against an 18° angled fence following the method used to mortise the angled apron ends. Also, rout the 5/16-in.-wide mortises near the top and bottom edge of each support for the stretchers.

The drawers are next. I set up my router with a ball-bearing-guided slot cutter to groove the inside of the drawer front and sides 3/16 in. deep to accept the bottom's 1/4-in.-thick rabbeted edges. Don't groove the narrower drawer back, since the bottom is slid under the back and screwed to it. The slot-cutting bit can also now be used to groove the back apron for cabinetmaker's buttons, which will fasten the top to the base.

The drawer slides on 1/2x5/8x13 1/2 guides, which are glued into each support's groove. I set up the tablesaw with a dado blade to machine a 5/8-in.-wide by 1/4-in.-deep groove in each support and in the outside of each drawer side. I also dadoed a 3/4-in.-wide by 1/4-in.-deep groove across the back apron where the drawer supports join it.

To hide the drawer-front laminations, I glued strips of mahogany on the edges. Then I hand-cut the half-blind and through dovetails on the front and back corners (you could also rout them) and glued up the drawer.

Assembling the base – Before assembling the various sections of the base, I sanded the legs and aprons to 220-grit. Then I glued and clamped the rear legs to the back apron, and assembled the stretchers to the drawer supports. When those assemblies were dry, I glued them together. Next, the drawer supports were fit in the dadoes in the back apron. After the glue dried, I reinforced the dadoes with wedged dowels. The last step was the trickiest: attaching the curved aprons and front legs. This is one of those times when you should take the phone off the hook. After a dry run, I glued all the mortises and loose tenons together and put a few band clamps around the assembly. I also added pipe clamps from front to back to secure the front legs against the ends of the supports. While the base is drying, you can glue up the solid mahogany core for the tabletop and then let the two assemblies set overnight.

Making the top – The core of the veneered tabletop is solid mahogany, assembled with several pieces of $\frac{7}{8}$-in.-thick stock. The rough blank should be at least $19\frac{1}{2}$ in. wide, to provide a waste strip for screwing down the ellipse machine and router attachment. Allow the glue to dry for 24 hours and then plane the glue-up to $\frac{13}{16}$ in. thick; this core, plus the quilted mahogany veneer on top and plain mahogany veneer on the bottom, yields a $\frac{7}{8}$-in.-thick top. In gluing the veneers, I rolled a liberal coat of yellow glue on the core only, since moisture in the glue could cause the veneers to curl up, or worse, stick to the roller and shatter. Since I don't have a veneer press, I clamped each veneer on the substrate with a 20-in.-wide by 48-in.-long curved caul (plywood fastened to a sturdy, slightly curved frame). The curve ensures adequate pressure in the center of the tabletop. After the veneer had dried for about 20 minutes, I removed the clamps to make sure it was completely glued down. If some areas don't bond, you can sponge them with water to reactivate the glue and reclamp the caul. But if you wait much longer than 20 minutes, the glue may be too dry to be reactivated.

After lightly scraping the veneer to remove any glue, I traced the tabletop's semielliptical perimeter from the plywood pattern. Align the pattern's straight back edge (the ellipse's major axis) parallel to and 1 in. from the edge of the veneer. Then bandsaw the top's perimeter to within $\frac{1}{8}$ in. of the pattern line, but don't cut the back edge. Also, trace the minor axis perpendicular to and in the center of the major axis, pressing lightly so you can sand away the line.

To trim the curved edge and rout the groove for the string inlay, I adapted my router to the ellipse machine. I replaced the original beam with a wider $\frac{1}{2}$x3x24 beam, as shown in the bottom, right photo on the facing page. I fastened the dovetail pivot blocks through slots in the beam with screws and wing nuts, so the pivots are adjustable. And I replaced the scribe with my router and a $\frac{1}{2}$-in.-dia. straight bit, to trim the table's edge. To make the router adjustable, I screwed an aluminum plate to the top of its base and fastened the plate to the underside of the beam with screws and wing nuts.

To use the router ellipse machine, align its tracks on the tabletop's axes and screw the major axis track to the top's back waste. Rout to the line in two passes, but remove only $\frac{1}{16}$ in. on the second pass, for a smooth edge. On the first pass, set the bit to cut $18\frac{1}{16}$ in. from the first pivot, which slides in the major axis track, and $24\frac{1}{16}$ in. from the second pivot, which slides in the minor axis track.

Now rout the concentric groove for the string inlay. Replace the $\frac{1}{2}$-in. bit with a $\frac{1}{16}$-in. straight bit, set to cut $\frac{3}{32}$ in. deep. Reset the

Clinton built this pier table from a mahogany core, veneered the top, aprons and drawer front with quilted mahogany, and inlaid the top with a string of ebony. The feet are ebony as are the drawer pulls, which he decorated with vegetable ivory plugs.

router (without altering either pivot position) so the bit will be $16\frac{1}{4}$ in. from the major axis pivot. The inlay is ripped from $\frac{1}{16}$-in.-thick by $\frac{3}{32}$-in.-wide ebony. After coating the pieces with glue, I hammered them into the groove, butting the mitered ends together. After the glue dried, I scraped the inlay flush with the veneered surface. To finish the top, remove the ellipse jig, rip the 1-in.-wide waste from the back edge and rout the curved edge of the table with a $\frac{1}{2}$-in. roundover bit, leaving a $\frac{1}{16}$-in.-deep fillet on top. I fastened the top to the base with two wood screws through either end of the top stretcher and with cabinetmaker's buttons on each end of the back apron, as shown in the drawing.

Applying the finish – After assembling the frame and tabletop, I raised the wood grain with a damp sponge, resanded everything, and applied tung oil. Brush on the first coat, let it set and wipe it off. When the first coat was dry, I sanded with 400-grit and then applied four more coats, sanding in between with 600-grit. Finally, after a light buffing with 0000 steel wool, I applied Watco Satin Wax. For a tougher, more moisture-resistant finish, you could use a mixture of one-third each oil, varnish and turpentine.

Finally, I turned two ebony drawer pulls with tenons, and drilled and plugged them with tagua nut. You can make the vegetable ivory plugs on a drill press with a plug cutter by holding the nut between clamp jaws. I drilled the center of the pulls by spinning them in a Jacobs chuck in the lathe headstock while I advanced a drill bit in a tailstock chuck. Glue the tagua into the pulls and sand off the excess plug. Then drill holes in the drawer front and glue the pulls in place. □

Bill Clinton is a furnituremaker in Bozeman, Mont.

Building a Tea Cart

A simple method for making spoked wheels

by John Dunham

Fig. 1: Tea cart

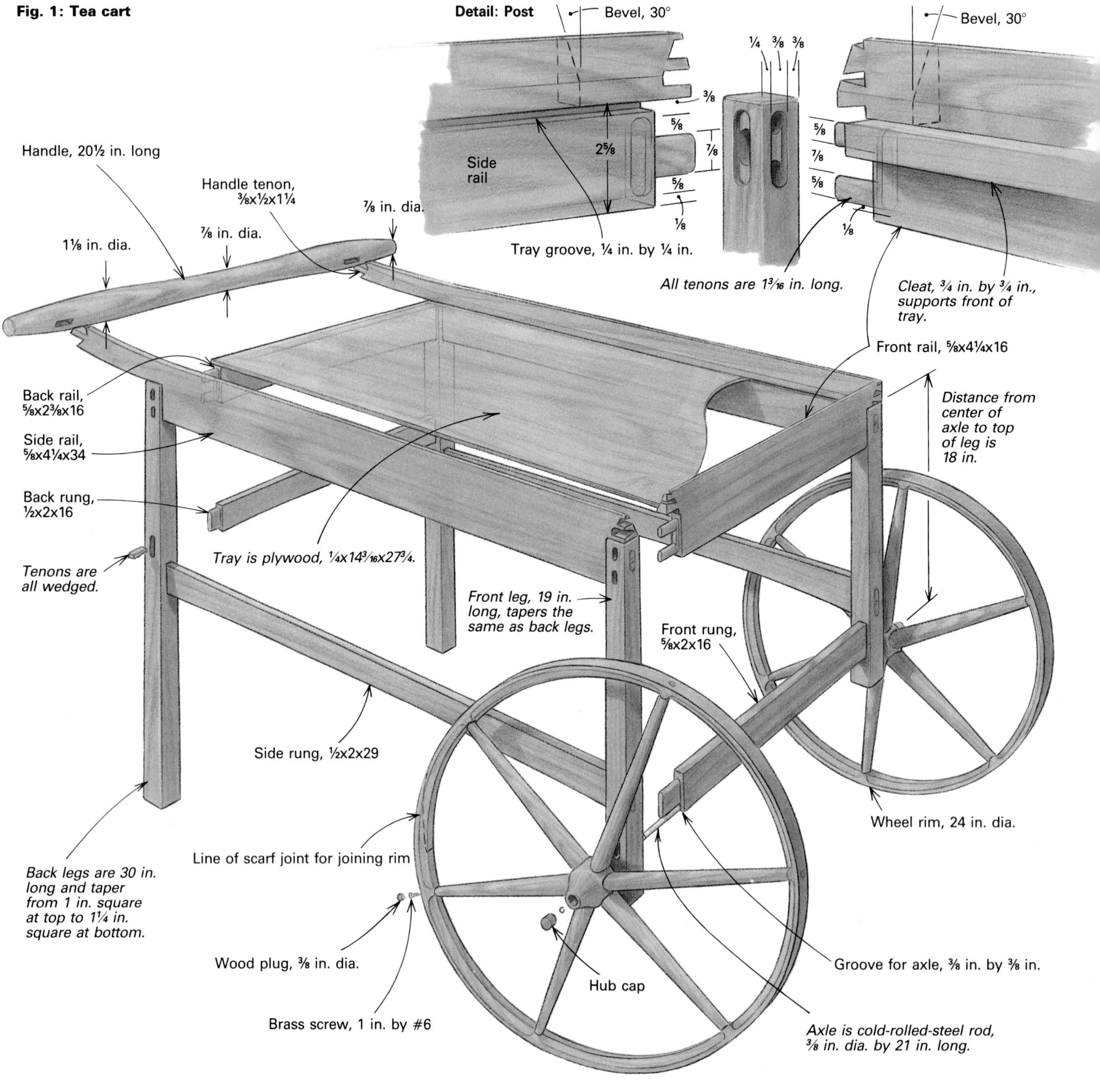

Detail: Post
Bevel, 30°
Bevel, 30°
¼ ⅜ ⅜
⅜
⅝
⅞
⅝
⅛
2⅝
Side rail
⅝
⅞
⅝
⅛
Tray groove, ¼ in. by ¼ in.
All tenons are 1³⁄₁₆ in. long.
Cleat, ¾ in. by ¾ in., supports front of tray.
Handle, 20½ in. long
Handle tenon, ⅜x½x1¼
⅞ in. dia.
1⅛ in. dia.
⅞ in. dia.
Front rail, ⅝x4¼x16
Back rail, ⅝x2⅜x16
Side rail, ⅝x4¼x34
Distance from center of axle to top of leg is 18 in.
Back rung, ½x2x16
Tenons are all wedged.
Tray is plywood, ¼x14³⁄₁₆x27¾.
Front leg, 19 in. long, tapers the same as back legs.
Front rung, ⅝x2x16
Side rung, ½x2x29
Wheel rim, 24 in. dia.
Back legs are 30 in. long and taper from 1 in. square at top to 1¼ in. square at bottom.
Line of scarf joint for joining rim
Wood plug, ⅜ in. dia.
Hub cap
Groove for axle, ⅜ in. by ⅜ in.
Brass screw, 1 in. by #6
Axle is cold-rolled-steel rod, ⅜ in. dia. by 21 in. long.

From *Fine Woodworking* (May 1990) 82:40-45

A tea cart has been a regular attraction in my booth at craft fairs for the past 10 years. Even though it isn't as essential as a table and chairs in a dining room, it's always been a good seller. People are fascinated by the cart's mobility and intrigued by the possibility of simplifying the daily task of setting and clearing a table. The tea cart in the photo at right is lightweight, but strong, and the large diameter of its wheels enables it to pass easily over thresholds and carpets.

The cart itself is basically a small table with both legs at one end cut off just below the cross rung. The steel axle, which is housed within the cross rung, does not rotate. Instead, each hub is fitted with a pair of shopmade brass bushings that turn very smoothly on the axle. Although I steam-bend the wheel rims when working with woods that bend well, like oak, ash or walnut, rims can also be made by laminating thin strips together around a circular form. The bent rim stock is wrapped around the spokes, screws are run through it into the ends of the spokes and the screw holes are then plugged. The loose ends of the rim are bandsawn at an angle and glued together in a long scarf joint to close the wheel's circumference.

Before building the tea cart, you might want to consider a few options that can add to the utility of the basic cart shown in the photo at right. A shallow drawer can be installed below the handle by screwing guides to the side rails and reducing the width of the back rail to accommodate the drawer front. If you want more surface area than the tray provides, a lower shelf can be added by gluing cleats to the side rungs to support it. I recommend ¼-in.-thick tempered glass for this lower shelf because a wood shelf makes the cart look too heavy. Another option is lining a portion of the tray's surface with ceramic tile.

Cart joinery—The cart's frame consists of four tapered legs, four upper rails that form the tray's sides and ends, four lower rungs and the handle. For the oak cart shown in the photo above, I began with ¾-in. stock, ripping and crosscutting the rails and rungs to size and planing them to the dimensions given in figure 1 on the facing page. Notice that the front rung is slightly thicker than the other rungs to accommodate the axle. You'll need a 7-in. by 30-in. piece of ⁶⁄₄ stock for the handle and legs. Even though the front legs will eventually be cut off just below the front rung, you should make four full-length legs so you can taper them all on the same tablesaw jig. If you cut the legs from a 7-in.-wide board and reverse the stock in the jig after each cut, you'll have enough stock left over for the handle.

The leg-taper jig, shown in figure 2 at right, will let you rip and plane 30-in.-long legs that taper from 1 in. square at the top to 1¼ in. square at the bottom. To make the jig, begin with a 1x2x32 board and lay out and bandsaw the taper as shown in figure 2. Fine-tune the tapered surface with a handplane or jointer and then glue a ½-in. by 1-in. stop on the flat end of the jig.

To cut the tapered legs, place the jig on edge on the saw table and up against the rip fence. The fence should be adjusted to leave about 1⅛ in. between the jig and the sawblade just in front of the jig's stop. Now, pull the jig back so there's room to lay your leg stock flat on the table in front of the blade with its end against the stop and its jointed edge firmly against the jig. Hold the jig and stock against the fence and rip the first leg. The operation is repeated with the stock reversed end for end after each pass, until you have four legs tapered on one side. Then, roll each leg 90° and taper all four legs on an adjacent side. To clean up the sawmarks and to plane the legs to their final size, place them on the jig with the sawn side up and run them through the planer, stop end first. Plane each leg on both adjacent sides until the small end is 1 in. square. The two front legs can now be crosscut to 19 in. long. Tilt

This basic oak tea cart is as much fun to build as it is to own. The large spoked wheels present a unique challenge to the builder and the finished cart adds a functional touch of class to any dining room.

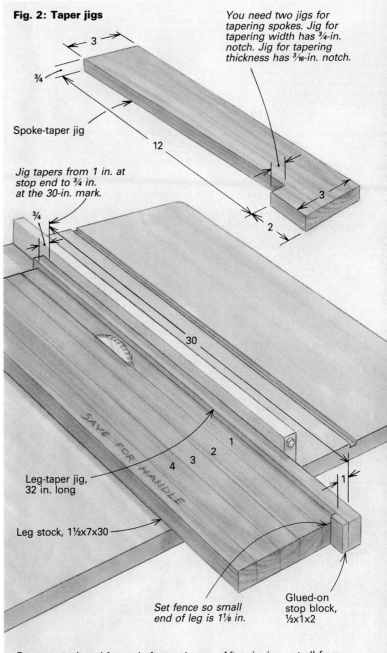

Fig. 2: Taper jigs

You need two jigs for tapering spokes. Jig for tapering width has ¾-in. notch. Jig for tapering thickness has ³⁄₁₆-in. notch.

3

¾

12

Spoke-taper jig

3

2

Jig tapers from 1 in. at stop end to ¾ in. at the 30-in. mark.

¾

30

SAVE FOR HANDLE

Leg-taper jig, 32 in. long

4   3   2   1

Leg stock, 1½x7x30

1

Set fence so small end of leg is 1⅛ in.

Glued-on stop block, ½x1x2

Reverse stock end for end after each pass. After ripping out all four legs in this manner, use the jig to taper each leg on an adjacent side.

Photo this page: Bob Hansson; drawings: Bob La Pointe

the blade used for crosscutting just a tad so that the end of the leg is cut square with the centerline and not just with the tapered side.

The rails and rungs are joined to the legs with through, wedged tenons all around. In addition, the front corners of the tray portion of the rails are also dovetailed together (see figure 1 on p. 70). On the first cart I built, the one in the photo on the previous page, I made the side and front rails wide enough to include the tray sides, and then I ripped each rail into two pieces even with the top of the legs. This made it possible to lay out and cut the tenons on the rails separately from the dovetails on the tray sides. Then I edge-glued the rails and tray sides back together before gluing up the cart frame. This simplified the joinery, but I was unhappy with the visible glueline. So now, instead of ripping the rail stock into separate rails and tray sides, I leave the rails their full 4¼ in. width. Then, I bandsaw the rail tenons, handle supports and dovetail pins on the side rails, and finish them up by hand with a chisel. Although this complicates fitting and cutting both the rail tenons and the tray dovetails, I think it's worth the trouble to preserve the smooth, unbroken surface on the side of the rails.

Whether you rip the rail/tray sides before joinery or attempt the one-piece method, the mortises for the upper rail tenons are laid out on the two adjacent sides as shown in the post detail in figure 1. The adjacent mortises are then cut on different sides of the lines so the intersecting tenons will miss each other. I originally designed haunch tenons for the side rails to resist any tendency for the rails to twist. After building the piece, I decided the haunches weren't necessary because there is enough support with the handle at one end and the dovetails at the other. However, I still use the haunch tenons on the rails because it's easier and faster to chisel a clean shoulder if the haunch remains.

I use a ⅜-in.-dia. end mill in my drill press to cut the mortises. A fence clamped to the drill-press table registers the mortises side to side and a featherboard holds the pieces firmly against the fence. I drill overlapping holes to clear out most of the mortise and then slide the piece sideways along the fence to smooth the sides. Of course a table-mounted router or a plunge router with templates can also be used for mortising.

When all the mortises are complete, the tenons are cut to fit them. As I mentioned earlier, if the rails and tray sides are left in one piece, the tenons on the side and front rails must be band-

After fitting the rail tenons to the leg mortises, Dunham draws around the dovetail pins on the side rail to mark out the tails on the tray portion of the front rail. The depths of the pins must be adjusted along a 30° angle to fit tightly to the bevel that he'll plane on the inside edge of the front rail after marking and cutting the tails. The side rail is beveled before the pins are cut.

sawn and fitted by hand. The rung tenons and those on the narrow upper rail that runs beneath the tray at the handle end can be cut on the tablesaw. I use a small carving gouge that has a ⅜-in.-dia. arc to round the tenons to fit the arc of the mortise ends and then individually check the fit of each tenon to its mortise.

Joining the tray—When the rail and rung tenons are done, you can turn your attention to the upper portion of the rails that form the tray sides. Before sawing out the dovetail pins on the front ends of the side rails, I plane a 30° bevel on the inside edges, as shown in the post detail in figure 1. This bevel makes a nice detail where the tray sides meet at the front corners and lightens the tray visually, but it is yet another complication for making the dovetails. You might want to avoid the dovetails entirely and miter the tray corners instead. I wouldn't blame you. But if you continue with the dovetails, you will have to vary the pin depth on the side rails to accommodate the 30° angle that you will later plane on the front rail (see the detail in figure 1). First, cut the pins on the side rails, assemble the front rail and front legs, and mark for the tails as shown in the photo below. Then, cut the tails to fit, and bevel the inside of the front rail to match the angle for the pin.

Now you can rout the ¼-in. by ¼-in. groove on the inside of the side rails for the tray. I use ¼-in. veneered plywood for the tray, which I slide into the grooves after gluing up the cart frame. A narrow cleat is glued to the front rail to support that end of the tray and a strip of hardwood is glued on to cap the back edge.

The last step in forming the tray sides is to shape the handle extensions. First bandsaw the gentle curve along the top edges of the sides and then bandsaw the ends of the extensions to receive the handle. As shown in figure 1 on p. 70, the ends of the extensions are cut out to wrap partway around the 1⅛-in.-dia. handle, and a ⅜-in. by ½-in. tenon protrudes from the extension through the handle and is wedged like the other tenons. Turn the handle to the dimensions shown in figure 1. I recommend waiting until the cart frame is glued up before marking and drilling the mortises that join the handle to the extensions to ensure that the back of the frame pulls tightly together. These mortises are cut on the drill press like the others, except the round handle is clamped into a V-block to keep it from turning.

Because I usually make a number of carts for each show, I've devised a shaper jig for curving the tops and bottoms of the rungs. But for a single cart, the rungs can be easily shaped by hand with a spokeshave, compass plane or rasp. The bottom of the thicker front rung is left straight and a ⅜-in. by ⅜-in. slot is routed in it to house the axle. Break the edges of the rungs and legs with a ⅛-in.-radius roundover bit and sand all the parts before assembly.

The axle is a ⅜-in.-dia. by 21-in.-long cold-rolled-steel rod. It extends through the front rung mortises in the legs and is locked in place when these tightly fitting joints are assembled. The hubs are secured to the axle with snap rings, which are available at most hardware and auto-parts stores. Before the cart frame is assembled, the axle is cut to length and its ends are slightly beveled and grooved to receive the snap rings. In determining precise axle length, you must consider the distance between the snap-ring groove and the end of the axle, as well as the hub size, leg thickness and distance between the front legs. Adjust your axle's length if any of these critical dimensions vary from those in figure 1. To make the snap-ring grooves, I place one end of the axle in a Jacob's chuck mounted on the headstock of my wood lathe and the other end in the shallow cup of the tailstock center with its center point removed. The cup happens to be just the right diameter for the axle and about ³⁄₃₂ in. deep. This depth seemed to be a good distance from the end for the snap-ring grooves, so I use the rim of the center cup as a guide for cutting the groove with a hacksaw. I lubricate the cup with a little grease, and with the lathe turning the axle at low speed, I hold the hacksaw blade against the cup's rim and cut about a $\frac{1}{32}$-in.-deep groove. Test the groove to be sure the snap ring fits and then reverse the axle and groove the other end.

Now, you're ready to glue up the cart frame. Assemble the end frames first and then split the endgrain of the tenons with a $\frac{3}{8}$-in. chisel and drive in a wedge dabbed with glue. Glue up the front rung with the axle in place and centered so that the snap-ring grooves are equidistant from the outside faces of both legs. Trim and sand the tenons flush with the legs on the end frames, and then glue up the sides and trim and sand those tenons. The top ends of the legs now interrupt the groove for the tray, so chisel the grooves through the legs so the plywood tray can slide all the way to the front rail. Secure the tray at the front rail by gluing it to the cleat that's also glued to the front rail.

Making the hubs and spokes—Building the wheels is not as difficult as it looks. I make the hexagonal hubs first, and then shape the spokes and glue their tenons into the hubs. The spokes are then trimmed to length on the bandsaw with a circle-cutting fixture, as shown in the top photo on the following page. Next, the narrow wheel rims are steam-bent, wrapped around the spokes and screwed into the end of each spoke.

To make the hubs, set the tablesaw blade to 30° and rip the corners off a $2x2\frac{5}{16}x7$ block to form a regular hexagon. Locate the centers of both ends and mount the block between centers on the lathe. Turn both hubs from the blank to the shape shown in figure 3 above, right. Remove the hub stock from the lathe and bandsaw the hubs apart. Next, a Jacobs chuck with a 1-in.-dia. Forstner bit is mounted in the headstock of the lathe. Now, mount each hub between the tailstock center and the center of the Forstner bit. With the hub suspended between centers, advance the tailstock center with the hand screw and drill a $\frac{1}{2}$-in.-deep hole in the round end of each hub. Then, change bits and drill a $\frac{7}{16}$-in.-dia. hole all the way through each hub. Now, remove the hub from the lathe and with a $\frac{1}{2}$-in.-dia. bit in the drill press, enlarge both ends of the $\frac{7}{16}$-in.-deep hole to $\frac{3}{8}$ in. deep to accommodate the brass bushings (see figure 3).

Metal bushings ensure that the cart will roll smoothly for a long time. A steel axle with wood bushings just won't do; if the wooden hub expands, it will lock onto the axle, and if the hub shrinks, the wheel will become floppy. I make brass bushings by boring a $\frac{3}{8}$-in.-dia. hole in the center of a $\frac{1}{2}$-in.-dia. round brass rod. To bore out the rod, mount Jacobs chucks on both the headstock and tailstock of the lathe. Chuck a 2-in.-long piece of brass rod in the headstock chuck and a $\frac{3}{8}$-in. bit in the tailstock chuck, and then with the rod turning at low speed, slowly advance the tailstock to drill through the rod. Then, with the rod still spinning at low speed, saw off $\frac{3}{8}$-in.-long sections with a hacksaw: two for each hub, four for each cart. Epoxy the bushings into the hubs and when the epoxy dries, run a $\frac{3}{8}$-in. drill bit through the bushing's center to remove any squeeze-out. Squeeze-out on the bottom of the 1-in. hole can be cleaned up with the 1-in. Forstner bit.

Although the spokes are eventually rounded over and shaped with a handplane, I start out by tapering them in both thickness and width on the tablesaw. Because the amount of taper is different in each dimension, you'll need two spoke-taper jigs (see figure 2 on p. 71). A 1x8x12 board will yield six tapered spoke blanks, so you'll need one board this size for each wheel. Begin with the jig that has the $\frac{3}{4}$-in.-deep notch and adjust the rip fence so the blanks are tapered from $\frac{3}{4}$ in. at one end to $1\frac{1}{2}$ in. at the other end. Rip the individual tapered blanks by reversing the workpiece end for end after each cut, just as you did with the legs. Next, joint one

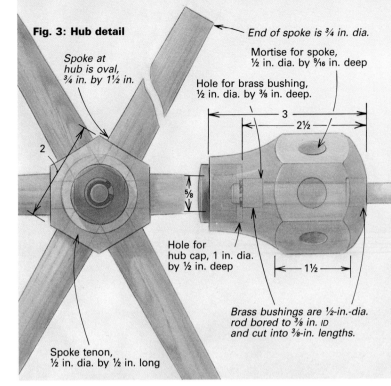

Fig. 3: Hub detail

End of spoke is $\frac{3}{4}$ in. dia.

Spoke at hub is oval, $\frac{3}{4}$ in. by $1\frac{1}{2}$ in.

Mortise for spoke, $\frac{1}{2}$ in. dia. by $\frac{9}{16}$ in. deep

Hole for brass bushing, $\frac{1}{2}$ in. dia. by $\frac{3}{8}$ in. deep.

Hole for hub cap, 1 in. dia. by $\frac{1}{2}$ in. deep

Brass bushings are $\frac{1}{2}$-in.-dia. rod bored to $\frac{3}{8}$ in. ID and cut into $\frac{3}{8}$-in. lengths.

Spoke tenon, $\frac{1}{2}$ in. dia. by $\frac{1}{2}$ in. long

This clamping fixture holds the spokes tightly, yet allows them to be quickly rotated, to speed up the process of handplaning the spokes so that they taper from oval at one end to round at the other.

edge of each blank and run this edge down on the saw table as you use the jig with the $\frac{3}{16}$-in. notch to taper the blank thickness. Adjust the fence to taper the spokes from 1 in. to $\frac{13}{16}$ in.

Find the center of both ends of each blank and, one by one, mount them between centers on the lathe and turn a $\frac{1}{2}$-in.-dia. by $\frac{1}{2}$-in.-long tenon on the large end of all 12 spokes. Before removing each spoke from the lathe, rough-turn the spoke just enough to be sure the tenon will be dead center after the spoke is final shaped. The wide end, with the tenon, is shaped to a nice oval that tapers smoothly to a $\frac{3}{4}$-in.-dia. circle at the other end. The spokes can be left on the lathe and shaped with a spokeshave if the headstock can be locked so it won't turn. I made the fixture in the photo above to clamp to the bench and hold the spokes so I can handplane them to shape.

After shaping and sanding the spokes, they are glued into the hub. Locate the centers of the flat surfaces on the hub and then drill a $\frac{1}{2}$-in.-dia. mortise, $\frac{9}{16}$ in. deep, in each face to receive the spokes' tenons. Glue two spokes at a time, spanning across both spokes and the hub with a pipe clamp. After all six spokes are glued into the hub, I use the bandsaw circle-cutting setup

The spokes are trimmed to length after they're glued into the hub. The drill bit, which acts as the pivot point, must be aligned with the bandsaw blade and centered exactly 11⅜ in. from the blade for the wheel to be 24 in. in diameter when the rim is wrapped around the spokes.

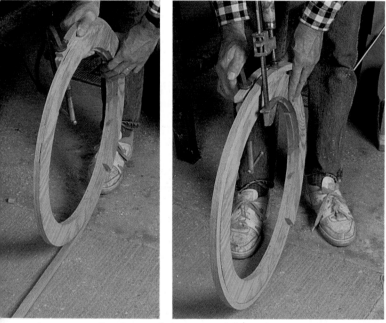

As soon as the rim stock is removed from the steam box, one end is clamped to the "spiral" form, as shown at left. Then, the rim is rolled up onto the form and its other end is clamped so that the ends overlap at least 6 in., as shown at right.

shown in the top photo above to trim them to length. Drill a ⅜-in.-dia. hole in a scrap block and, for a 24-in.-dia. wheel, clamp the block to the bandsaw table so that the hole's center is 11⅜ in. from the blade, measured 90° from the blade's cutting line. Place a ⅜-in.-dia. drill bit in the scrap block's hole to mount the hub, and clamp a shim near the blade to support the small end of the spokes. Then, turn on the bandsaw and rotate the hub to trim the spokes.

Making the wheel rims—Oak steam-bends well, and I use steam-bent parts in other pieces of furniture that I make on a regular basis, so it was natural for me to use this technique for the wheels' rims. Of course, with woods that don't steam-bend very well, like mahogany or cherry, you could start with slightly thicker wheel stock, resaw it into three or four thin strips and laminate them back together over a form. However, steam-bending has the advantages of no messy edges to clean up and no gluelines. I've had good luck steam-bending oak, ash, beech and walnut, in that order.

No matter which bending method you use, you'll need a plywood form, the same diameter as the trimmed spokes, to bend the rim stock around. The ends of the rim stock must run past each

other at least 6 in. on the form to allow for the scarf joint that closes the rim's circumference. Instead of doubling up the form to make it wide enough for the ends to run past each other, I make a kind of spiral form. I bandsaw a 2-in.-wide, 22¾-in.-OD ring from a scrap of ¾-in.-thick plywood. Then, I cut about a 4-in.-long section out of this ring and glue quarter sections of another 2-in.-wide, 22¾-in.-dia. ring on opposite sides of the original ring, so that the quarter sections overlap at the gap. This forces the original ring into a spring-like shape, as you can see in the two bottom photos.

Now you're ready to steam the rim stock. You'll need 7 ft. of clear straight-grain stock, ⅝ in. thick and ¾ in. wide, for each rim. Rip an extra rim strip for each cart you're building in case one breaks when bending. My steaming box is very low tech: I screwed together a 7-ft.-long by 5-in.-square wooden box, left open at both ends, and sawed a 4-in.-square hole in the middle of the bottom. A row of dowels, inserted from side to side, creates a rack to hold the part being steamed off the bottom of the box. I place the box on top of an electric fry pan full of water so the steam will enter the box through the 4-in. hole. Scrap boards cover the portions of the frying pan that aren't covered by the steam box, making it easy to check and replenish the water level when necessary. When the water is rapidly boiling, I put the rim stock in the box, plug the ends with cloths to keep most of the steam in and wait about 45 minutes.

When the pieces are removed from the steam box, you must work smoothly and quickly because as the wood cools and dries out, it loses its flexibility. Have your form and a couple of C-clamps ready. Remove the rim stock from the box and clamp one end to the "beginning" of the spiral form as shown in the left, bottom photo. Quickly turn the form so the steamed wood is on the floor, and roll the rim onto the form, pressing firmly on the floor as you go. When you get around to where the clamp hits the floor, pull the free end of the rim stock up by hand and clamp it to the form so it overlaps the first end (see the right, bottom photo). Now, place another length of rim stock in the steam box, replenish the water and wait 45 minutes. When the second rim is ready to be bent, unclamp the first rim from the form and clamp its over-lapping portions side by side to maintain the circle. This frees up the form for bending the second rim. Repeat the steaming and bending processes until you have all the rims you need and then let them dry overnight.

To support the hub-and-spoke assembly while attaching the rim, clamp the axle in a bench vise. Then, hold the rim so the scarf joint that closes the circle will fall between two spokes and screw the rim to one of the spokes opposite the joint. To do this, first bore a ⅜-in.-dia. hole about ⅛ in. deep for a wood plug, and then bore a ⅛-in.-dia. hole through the rim for a 1-in.-long, #6 brass wood-screw shank; finally, while holding the rim in position against the spoke, bore a 1/16-in.-dia. pilot hole into the end of the spoke. Now that the rim is located on the hub-and-spoke assembly, you can continue around the rim boring holes and screwing the rim to each of the spokes, except the one nearest the rim's joint.

With this one spoke still unattached, remove the wheel from the axle so you can lay out the rim's scarf joint. First, let the loose portion of the rim overlap alongside the attached portion and use C-clamps at both ends of the rim to clamp it into the proper arc, as shown in the top, left photo on the facing page. Next, measure 6 in. along the rim's circumference and divide this into four equal 1½-in. sections. All five lines should now be transferred down the sides of the rims with a square. Then, still working on the rim's sides, divide the centerline in half and the lines on the right and left of the centerline in quarters. Now, begin at the inside edge of the rim and draw a diagonal across to the outside edge by con-

Before the rim is screwed to the last spoke, the rim's ends are clamped as shown above and lines are transferred down both sides as references for laying out the scarf joint.

Dunham bandsaws close to the scarf joint line: above the line on one end and below the line on the other. Then, he will smooth the scarf joint's mating surfaces with a rasp.

After the last spoke is screwed to the rim, Dunham glues and clamps the scarf joint with scrap blocks sawn to fit the inside and outside arcs. Once the dried glue is cleaned up, the wheel is ready to roll.

necting the appropriate points along the lines (see the top, left photo above). Turn the wheel over and draw a similar diagonal on the other side of the rim's overlap.

After laying out for the scarf joint, remove the clamps and bandsaw close to the diagonal lines: above the line on one overlap and below the line on the other (see the bottom, left photo above). With a rasp, clean up the mating surfaces until they clamp together without a gap and then screw the rim to the last spoke. The scarf joint is glued together and clamped with pieces of scrapwood bandsawn to the rim's inner and outer arcs to distribute the clamping pressure as shown in the right photo above. After the glue is completely dry, scrape and sand the sides of the rim so the joint can't be detected.

The wheels are now complete except for plugging the screw holes in the rim and some final detailing. I bevel the rim's inside edges on the router table with a 45° pilot-bearing router bit, taking care not to nick the spokes. Then I use carving tools and files to shape the transitions where the spokes meet the rim and hub (see figure 1 on p. 70). Before mounting the wheels on the cart, I finish them and the assembled cart with several coats of Danish oil.

When the wheels are mounted on the ends of the axle, you should be able to see the snap-ring groove. If you can't, remove the wheel and drill the 1-in. hole a little deeper. You can get a pair of snap-ring pliers at any auto-parts store, but for the convenience of my customers who usually have to assemble their tea cart after removing the parts from a shipping carton, I include a shopmade tool for putting on the snap rings. The tool is simply a ¾-in.-square length of hardwood with an axle-size, ⅜-in.-dia. hole drilled in one end. To mount the wheels, lay the cart on one side, place the wheel on the axle and balance a snap ring on the axle's slightly beveled end. Then, use the tool to press the snap ring onto the axle until it fits in the groove. Turn the cart over and mount the other wheel the same way. To cover the axle and cap the hubs, I turn tapered plugs to fit in the 1-in. holes and then drill a ⅝-in. hole, about ¼ in. deep, in one end to make room for the axle. □

John Dunham does restoration work for Sotheby's in Claverack, N.Y., and builds custom furniture out of his own shop in Glens Falls, N.Y.

Coffee Table Is Spare and Sturdy

Loose tenons simplify joinery

by Lars Mikkelsen

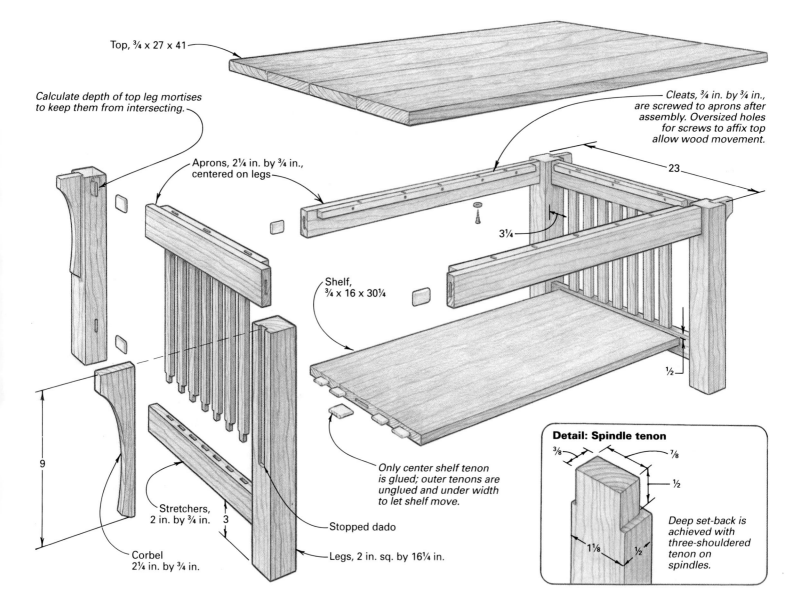

Top, ¾ x 27 x 41

Calculate depth of top leg mortises to keep them from intersecting.

Cleats, ¾ in. by ¾ in., are screwed to aprons after assembly. Oversized holes for screws to affix top allow wood movement.

Aprons, 2¼ in. by ¾ in., centered on legs

23

3¼

Shelf, ¾ x 16 x 30¼

½

9

Only center shelf tenon is glued; outer tenons are unglued and under width to let shelf move.

Stretchers, 2 in. by ¾ in.

3

Corbel 2¼ in. by ¾ in.

Stopped dado

Legs, 2 in. sq. by 16¼ in.

Detail: Spindle tenon

⅜   ⅞

½

1⅛   ½

Deep set-back is achieved with three-shouldered tenon on spindles.

Ever since I started building furniture, I've taken pleasure in making the many different components in a piece and seeing them all fit together like pieces of a puzzle. As I progressed as a craftsman, the joints got better and more complex, and my enjoyment of the process increased. But making a lot of tight-fitting joints can be quite time-consuming and expensive, and most of my clients have tight budgets. They have come to me because they want something more than they can get in the department store, but they can't necessarily afford to have me spend a lot of time doing greatly detailed work. I often have to find ways to compromise while still aiming to produce beautiful furni-

ture of sound construction. I look for ways to simplify, to use what tools and materials I can afford and to make limited resources grant handsome returns.

I recently had a challenge of this kind when a client approached me about making a coffee table. Together we settled on a basic table in the Craftsman vein (see the photo on the facing page) and a carefully trimmed budget for the job. Two hallmarks of Craftsman furniture are pinned through-mortises and legs coopered or veneered so quartersawn grain shows all around. But I decided to leave them out of my table, substituting the simplicity of loose-tenon joinery and solid-wood construction (see the drawing).

Drawing: Heather Lambert

Laying out lumber

I went looking for about 30 bd. ft. of quartersawn white oak. What I found was a few very rough boards that had turned quite black. After the first pass through my planer, I could see that the wood was not white oak. I was disappointed, but I kept on planing. What emerged was beautiful red oak of a variety I had never seen before. I decided it would suit my purpose well.

With the freshly planed boards arrayed on my outfeed table, I studied the grain and color to decide where the boards would be used to their best advantage. First I selected the boards for the top. These should be picked not only for their beauty but also with an eye toward having even color and straight grain along the edges, so they match well when joined together.

I needed four pieces for the top. I first crosscut them a few inches over length and arranged them as they would be joined. Next I marked a triangle across all four, so I could easily orient them. Then I arranged and marked the shelf boards and cut them to rough length.

Simplicity simplified—Lars Mikkelsen picked the functional Craftsman style for this low table and pared it down to its essence.

I don't have a jointer, but with short boards like these, I can get good glue joints by ripping them a few times on the tablesaw, taking off about ¹⁄₁₆ in. with each pass and checking them for fit after each cut. For longer stock or waney-edged pieces, I clamp a straightedge to the board and joint it with a flush-trimming router bit.

Flat top

I glued up the top and shelf with pipe clamps, using ¾-in. dowels laid parallel to the boards as clamping blocks, as shown in the top left photo on p. 78. The dowels concentrate the pressure right in the center of the stock and minimize the clamps' tendency to tweak the boards up or down. I keep a stock of dowels of various diameters set aside for this purpose. I find it much easier to grab a pair of the correct size than to hunt down scrap or make up pressure blocks to the thickness of the workpiece each time.

After the glue had set, I beltsanded the slabs. I run my sander diagonally to flatten glued-up panels, feeling for the high spots and concentrating on them to attain a nice, flat surface. I start with a 100-grit belt, first sanding diagonally and then with the grain. Then I change to a 120-grit belt and sand with the grain only. People often complain that a belt sander is hard to control and easy to gouge with, but I have developed a good working relationship with my 3-in. by 21-in. Makita. With practice, you can gain the touch required to flatten a wide surface.

When the beltsanding is finished, I switch to a random-orbit sander and work through the grits, starting with 120 and moving on to 180 and 220. Then I hand-sand with a block and 220-grit paper to remove any slight swirl marks the random orbit may have left. On a relatively forgiving wood like oak, this step is my last, but with something hard and close-grained like cherry, I might finish up with 320-grit paper. Someone once asked me when you know you've sanded enough, and I told him, "You know you never have." There's always more you could do, but it's important to work methodically and take everything to the same level of finish. Instead of beltsanding, you could use handplanes to flatten the top and shelf or rent time on a big thickness sander.

Panels this wide cry out for a panel saw of some kind when it comes to crosscutting, but I don't have one. Instead, I clamp a crosscutting fixture square to the sides and cut one end with a hand-held trim saw, which is a small circular saw. When I had one end straight and square, I made the second cut on the tablesaw about ¼ in. longer than needed. Then I flipped the top around to make a finish cut on the trim-sawn end. I laid out the width so the two outside boards were roughly equal and ripped both sides. Using this method, I got good tablesaw cuts on all four sides with no tearout. A few strokes with a block plane were all that was needed to clean up the edges.

Building up leg stock

I glued up the blanks for the legs by sandwiching a piece of ½-in. stock between two ¾-in. pieces. I normally make legs from single sticks, but in this case, I couldn't obtain thick enough stock when I needed it. I took a lot of care with these laminations, matching the layers for color as well as grain orientation. When I was done, the joints were barely perceptible even under close examination. I ripped the twelve pieces for the leg blanks ¼ in. oversized in width and 5 in. oversized in length. The extra width gave me some leeway for slippage during the glue-up and for the final ripping to width. The extra length ensured that any snipe left by the planer in final thicknessing could be cut off.

I arranged the legs carefully, so matching grain would show on each side of the table. Then I held them together, and across the top end grain of the four pieces, I drew a single triangle. This quick marking method makes it easy to establish the orientation of a part at any point in the construction process.

Joinery

Loose tenoning is the method I use most often for making structural joints because it is strong and straightforward. Also called a splined mortise or floating tenon joint, the loose tenon joint is simply a pair of mating mortises with an independent tenon to span them. With a mortising fixture like mine, as shown in the bottom left photo on p. 78, the joints are easy to make. (For details on the construction and use of my jig, see *FWW* #92, p. 55.) Of course, you could also make the mortises by hand, on a router table or with a hollow-chisel mortising setup.

I make loose tenons from the same material as the table, so all seasonal movement will be the same. Just make sure the grain runs the length of the loose tenon. For this table, with 1-in.-wide mortises, I first ripped long strips ¹⁵⁄₁₆ in. wide and ⁷⁄₁₆ in. thick. Then I thickness-planed them to exact size, checking them every pass or two in a sample mortise until I got that wonderful feeler-gauge fit. If you have to use strength to pull the spline from the mortise, the fit's too tight; if there's no resistance, it's too loose. Making the tenons ¹⁄₁₆ in. undersized in width leaves room for ex-

Dowels deliver clamping pressure at the center of the board (right), and they keep the glue-up flat. The author keeps dowels of various diameters for gluing different thickness stock.

Offset tenons create a deep set-back. For the gallery of spindles on narrow stock, the author offset the tenons, leaving out one shoulder (above).

Loose tenons need clean mortises—Plunge-routing on a fixture like this shopmade one (left) produces crisp, uniform mortises for the loose tenons.

cess glue and also gives you some welcome lateral adjustment in the glue-up. I rounded over the tenon edges on the router table and then cut them to length—⅛ in. shorter than the combined depth of the two mortises.

With all but the shelf and spindle joints cut, I dry-assembled the table. At this point, I measured between the stretchers to find the length of the shelf. This dimension could be calculated, but because even a slight misplacement of a mortise or variation in the thickness of the stretcher could throw everything off, I find it better to measure the length once everything else has been done.

I cut the shelf to size in the same way that I cut the top. It is attached to the stretchers with loose tenons, but only the center tenon is glued. The outer tenons, cut narrow by ⅛ in. and left loose, give the shelf room to move with changes in humidity while supporting it firmly.

The spindles are too small for loose tenons, so I tenoned their ends and cut mating square mortises in the stretchers and aprons. As I played around with the placement of the spindles, I decided that a ¼-in. set-back from the outside edge of the stretchers and aprons gave it the feeling I wanted. It's surprising what a difference ⅛ in. can make in places like this. If you pull the spindles up to the edge of the rails, you create a flat surface; if you push them in a bit, suddenly the spindles impart a feeling of structure and strength. Given the thickness of the stock I had, this decision meant cutting tenons with no shoulder on the outside face, as shown in the photo at right above. I could have used thicker material for the aprons and stretchers, but none was readily available. So to get the job done and to keep my expenses down, I worked with what I had. I cut the tenons with a dado set on the radial-arm saw.

I chopped mortises for the spindles on the drill press with a ⅜-in. mortising chisel. I wanted the mortises to be ¾ in. by ⅜ in., so I made a ⅜-in. spacer block, which I placed in front of a stop block on the fence. Once the stop block was clamped down at the right spot, I could make a mortise in two quick chops, one with the spacer block and one without. The sides of the mortises required a little cleanup with a chisel, but the ends, which are severed end grain and provide no glue surface, I left rough.

Corbels

With all the other parts milled and joints cut, I turned to the corbels. These curved supports, borrowed from architecture, are one of the elements that distinguish Craftsman furniture. In this case, they're not structurally significant, but like the deep set-back of the spindles, they lend the piece a sense of weight and solidity. Because I'd left out other decorative details, I wanted to get these right.

I started by making a template. I drew what I felt was a pleasing shape for the corbels on a ½-in. piece of plywood and cut it out with a jigsaw. To fair the curve and rid it of sawmarks, I used a technique I learned from a friend with boatbuilding experience. I folded sandpaper around a ¹⁄₁₆-in.-thick sliver of wood, as shown in the top photo below. The sliver conforms to the curve, riding over low spots and cutting the high spots. If the initial cut is reasonably true, this quickly produces a perfectly fair curve. Then I used the piece of plywood as a template to shape the corbels. I first jigsawed the corbels a bit too large and then nailed the template to them with a couple of brads placed in the edge that would be let into the leg. By running the template against a flush-trimming bit in the router table (see the bottom photo below), I quickly produced identical copies.

The corbels fit into the leg with a stopped dado, which I cut on the tablesaw using a stacked dado blade. I set the fence to position the dado in the center of the leg and clamped a stop block to the fence so that the cut would stop exactly where the corbels end. When the leg hit the stop block, I turned the saw off, waited for the blade to stop and removed the leg. It is quite easy to finish the stopped dado with a chisel.

Assembly

The corbels were the last parts I made. When they were finished, my favorite moment had arrived—the time for dry-assembly. If all the joints are just right, dry-assembly is a joy to do as everything snaps together and holds tightly without clamps. In this case, I could lift the whole assembly by one leg without anything coming apart. This little act gave me a thrill and impressed my client, who happened to have stopped by my shop at just that moment.

Before final assembly, I block-sanded everything and eased all the edges. Some sanding will always be needed after glue-up, but it is easier to do the bulk of it beforehand when all the pieces lie flat and all their faces are easy to reach.

I did the assembly in stages, first gluing up each end and later linking them together. I started the glue-up by fitting one set of spindles into their stretcher and apron mortises. As soon as these joints were pulled tight, I glued the apron and stretcher to the legs. It's important to square this subassembly by measuring the diagonals with a tape. And I made sure the legs ended up in the same plane by sighting across them. By gluing all this in one operation, I prevented the possibility of having a skewed spindle assembly that would not fit neatly into the legs.

When the glue dried, I glued the two side aprons and the shelf between the end frames. I did this on a flat surface, checking the diagonals

again to make sure the table ended up square and making certain all four legs were solidly on the surface. Sometimes a clamp or two must be skewed a bit to achieve this and to ensure the table will not rock later on.

I attached the top with cleats screwed solidly to the apron. To accommodate seasonal movement of the top, I drilled oversized holes up through the cleats and pulled the top tight with pan-head screws fitted with washers.

The finishing touch

For the finish, I applied three coats of Antique Minwax. I rubbed in the final coat with fine steel wool and immediately wiped it off, leaving a beautifully smooth finish that, with occasional reoiling, will only get more beautiful with time.

This table was my first effort in the Craftsman style. I had originally suggested this style to my client because I felt that it would fit the decor and because it stands up so well to heavy use. But while building the table, I came to appreciate the honesty with which design and construction are related in Craftsman work. There is no unnecessary ornamentation—sound structural components make the design. □

Lars Mikkelsen is a furnituremaker in Santa Margarita, Calif.

***Shaping corbels**—The author takes down the high spots on the corbel template's jigsawn curve with sandpaper backed by a flexible stick (above).*

***Corbel copies**—A plywood template on the router table (left) is used to flush-trim the corbels.*

Building a Gate-Leg Card Table

Tackling curved rails and inlaid legs

by Frank M. Pittman

Tapered legs with fine inlays, curved rails and light proportions give this gate-leg card table a delicate look. A knuckle joint built into the rear apron allows the left rear leg to swing back and support the flip top when fully opened. The deep reddish-brown color of the 50-year-old air-dried cherry used for the top and legs blends perfectly with the mahogany crotch veneer on the curved rails.

About 10 years ago I promised my wife I would build her a card table. Needless to say, after a decade of watching me "research" the problem, she had almost given up hope, and so she was especially delighted when I presented the gate-leg card table shown at left.

Tables such as these, with tapered legs and string inlay, are often attributed to the 18th-century furniture designer George Hepplewhite, but my research suggests that this association may not be entirely accurate. Hepplewhite's principle claim to fame is a book of furniture designs, *The Cabinet-Maker and Upholsterer's Guide,* published by his wife Alice in 1788, two years after his death. And although the tables illustrated in this book have the same light proportions and similarly tapered legs, none have the same balance of uncluttered lines and graceful curves that enhance the table shown here. Fortunately, I can avoid attributing the table's design to a particular style by crediting a former teacher of mine, Walter B. Nalbach, with its inspiration. Nalbach built a pair of tables similar to this in the 1930s, and with his permission I measured them and incorporated a few minor design changes of my own, such as running the string inlay on all four faces of each leg and inlaying the bell flowers on two faces of each leg instead of just one (see the photo at left).

My table is from cherry, with crotch mahogany veneer on the aprons. The legs require 6 bd. ft. of ⁸/₄ stock, which is enough for the table's four legs plus one extra for checking the tool setups for the many machining operations involved with the inlays. The top requires 11 bd. ft. of well-matched ⁴/₄ stock. You'll also need an additional 2 bd. ft. of ⁴/₄ cherry for the back apron, which is actually a three-part construction that includes an inner apron dovetailed into the side aprons and the two-part knuckle-joint gate-leg mechanism that supports the hinged top when open. The cherry apron beads can be made from leg or top scraps. The front and side aprons are stack-laminated poplar, bandsawn to shape and then veneered. I used about 10 bd. ft. of ³/₄-in.-thick poplar for the laminated blanks.

Because of the curved aprons and the intricacies of the inlays, the first step in building this table is to make full-scale drawings to work out the details in actual size. You'll need patterns for the curved parts anyway, and so you might as well prepare them ahead of time. In addition, if you buy the oval flower inlays and the banding that trims the lower leg as I did, you should have them on hand before beginning the project. I got my inlays from Constantine, 2050 Eastchester Road, Bronx, N.Y. 10461; the banding is catalog #B3 and the ovals are #IW562. Stringing is traditionally made from holly, maple or satinwood. I was lucky enough to have a piece of ⁴/₄ satinwood, which I sawed into ¹/₁₆-in.-wide inlay strips.

Legs, banding and stringing—Begin by ripping the five 1¹¹/₁₆-in.-sq. leg blanks from the ⁸/₄ stock. Crosscut the blanks to finished

Fig. 1: Gate-leg card table

Detail: Top view and patterns for curves

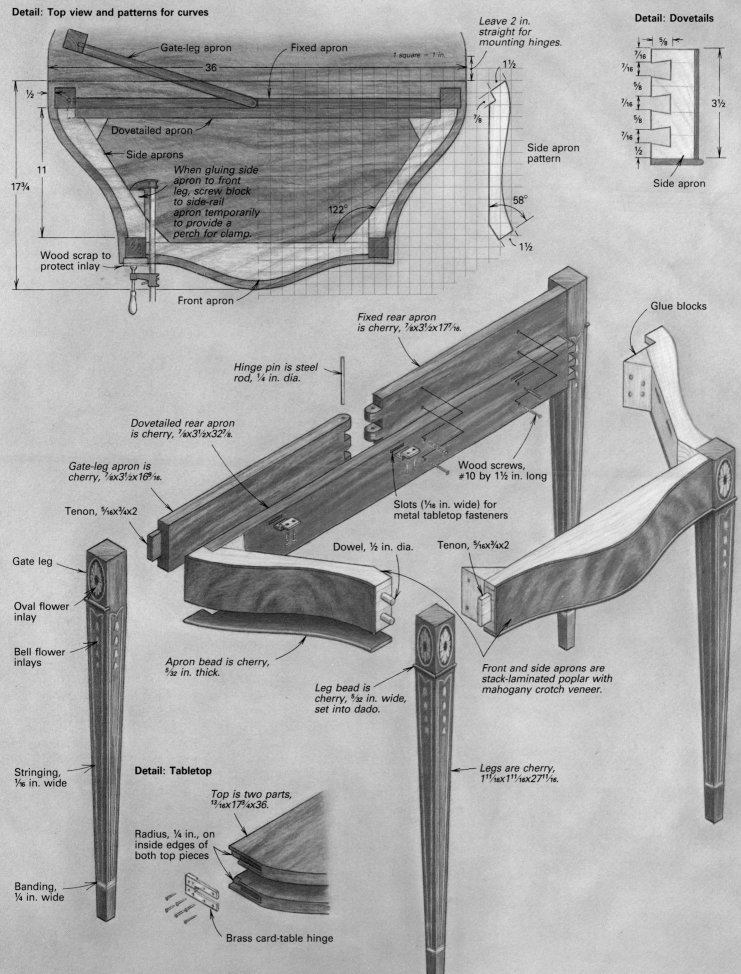

Leave 2 in. straight for mounting hinges.

Gate-leg apron

Fixed apron

1 square = 1 in.

36

1½

½

7⁄8

Side apron pattern

11

17¾

Dovetailed apron

Side aprons

When gluing side apron to front leg, screw block to side-rail apron temporarily to provide a perch for clamp.

58°

122°

1½

Wood scrap to protect inlay

Front apron

Detail: Dovetails

5⁄8

7⁄16

7⁄16

5⁄8

7⁄16

5⁄8

7⁄16

½

3½

Side apron

Fixed rear apron is cherry, ⅞x3½x17⁷⁄₁₆.

Hinge pin is steel rod, ¼ in. dia.

Dovetailed rear apron is cherry, ⅞x3½x32⅞.

Glue blocks

Gate-leg apron is cherry, ⅞x3½x16⁹⁄₁₆.

Wood screws, #10 by 1½ in. long

Tenon, 5⁄16x¾x2

Slots (1⁄16 in. wide) for metal tabletop fasteners

Gate leg

Oval flower inlay

Dowel, ½ in. dia.

Tenon, 5⁄16x¾x2

Bell flower inlays

Apron bead is cherry, 5⁄32 in. thick.

Front and side aprons are stack-laminated poplar with mahogany crotch veneer.

Leg bead is cherry, 5⁄32 in. wide, set into dado.

Stringing, 1⁄16 in. wide

Detail: Tabletop

Top is two parts, 13⁄16x17¾x36.

Radius, ¼ in., on inside edges of both top pieces

Legs are cherry, 1¹¹⁄₁₆x1¹¹⁄₁₆x27¹¹⁄₁₆.

Banding, ¼ in. wide

Brass card-table hinge

length, and then taper each side using a jig that holds the leg at a slight angle as it's passed through the tablesaw. As you can see in figure 2 on the facing page, the taper begins 4 in. below the top of each leg and extends to its base, which is only ⅝ in. sq. After tapering, each leg requires five separate operations to cut the grooves for the inlays. The legs must also be mortised to receive the apron tenons and dadoed for the lower apron bead that runs across the legs, but it's best to do these operations after constructing and veneering the aprons to ensure these joints are located properly.

You should cut the banding grooves around the bottom of the legs first because they make handy stops for the long stringing grooves that you will cut next. This bit of wisdom comes from hindsight; I cut the stringing grooves first, as you can see in the photo below. But more importantly, the photo shows how I routed the banding grooves on the tapered legs with the aid of a miter gauge, even though the router table had no miter gauge slot; I simply ran the gauge's bar along the table's front edge with the router table fence clamped parallel to the front edge to locate the grooves. I set the miter gauge angle to compensate for the legs' taper by making test cuts on the fifth leg and measuring up squarely from the bottom of the leg until the groove ran parallel to the bottom.

I made the long, straight grooves for the stringing with a Dremel tool fitted with a router-base attachment and guide. My dentist helped me acquire a few carbide dental burrs (Pennwalt #559, from Health Co International, 1 Field Lane, Orchard Ridge Corporate Park, Brewster, N.Y. 10509; 914-277-4074), which I used to cut the ¹⁄₁₆-in.-wide grooves. (See *FWW* #83, pp. 62-64 for more on this method.) To cut the ¾-in.-radius grooves at the top of the stringing pattern, I made a ⅛-in.-thick Plexiglas fixture that has a ⅛-in.-dia. hole in the center of each of the arcs (see the top photo at right on the facing page). A pivot pin screwed through the router-attachment base is inserted into each center hole in turn and the Dremel tool is pivoted to cut the arcs. I used a pair of dividers with a dowel taped to one leg to locate the fixture on the surface to be inlaid, as shown in the top photo at left on the facing page. When the fixture was aligned so the arcs began at the ends of the straight stringing grooves and met at the centerline of the leg, I clamped

the fixture to the leg and cut the grooves.

After cutting the banding and stringing grooves, I ripped out the thin satinwood strips. When I got around to fitting the curved stringing sections, I discovered that satinwood is too brittle to bend well, and so I had to soak the stringing in water for several minutes and then bend it over a hot pipe mounted on a soldering iron. The soaking and heating had to be repeated several times to achieve the desired bend, and even then I broke several pieces. I cut and fit all the stringing for one leg surface at a time, including miters at the corners, and then glued the pieces in right away so I wouldn't lose them. The stringing expands slightly when it absorbs glue; so you should press the pieces into the glue-filled grooves as quickly as possible. The expansion holds the pieces so tightly that there is no need to clamp the stringing. After all the stringing is applied, I glued the banding strips into their grooves at the base of the legs. Before inlaying the flowers, I sanded the stringing and banding flush using 100-grit paper on a sanding block.

Flower inlays—My table required eight sets of satinwood bell flowers. Each set has four flowers that diminish in size from top to bottom, and so I needed 32 flowers in all. To streamline the process of cutting out the flowers, I glued up a stack of nine pieces of satinwood veneer with a piece of paper between each layer so the stack could be easily separated later. The ninth layer gave me an extra set of flowers just in case. Then I made a photocopy of the full-size inlay drawing and glued it to the top of the veneer stack. After cutting out the flowers with a scroll saw, I sanded and filed each stack to final shape and then inserted a sharp knife (you could also use a razor blade) on the paper glueline to pop the veneer layers apart (see the bottom photo on the facing page).

Inlaying the 32 separate flowers isn't difficult, but it is slow work. It's not something you can whip out in a couple of hours; so realize up front that you have to take your time. To begin, place one of the large flowers carefully on the centerline of the leg and trace around it with a sharp pencil; do one flower at a time. I use my Dremel tool with a router base to clear out most of the wood, and then I clean out the tight corners and final fit each flower with a knife and a small chisel. For both the routing and the final fitting, I use a lighted magnifying glass (the kind that clamps to a tabletop and that jewelers often use). I've found that if I'm satisfied with the way an inlay looks through the magnifying glass, it really looks great without magnification. Fit one flower at a time and then glue it in place with a clamp and waxed-paper-covered block. By the time you've inlaid one flower on each leg, the first leg will be dry enough to unclamp so you can inlay its next flower. The six oval inlays at the top of the legs are fitted the same way as the flowers.

After all the inlaying is complete, finish-sand the legs through 220-grit. Make sure that all traces of dried glue have been sanded away. I thought I had done a thorough sanding job, but when I sprayed on the first coat of lacquer, several glue smears showed up and I had to resand all of these areas. You can locate dried glue before finishing by wetting the wood's surface with water: glue residue will show up as light-colored areas.

Veneered front and side aprons—The front and side apron blanks are made by stack laminating ¾-in.-thick yellow poplar to the following sizes: one 3½x4½x21½ front apron; and two 3½x3½x15 side aprons. Use the gridded drawings of the front and side aprons in the detail in figure 1 on the previous page to make full-size templates for laying out the curves on each blank. When you bandsaw the curves keep the cuts as clean as possible, because the waste part of each apron will be used to clamp the veneer to the apron. Sand or scrape out any slight irregularities in the apron

The author routs the banding groove in a leg by running the miter gauge bar along the router table's front edge. The router-table fence, which locates the cut, is clamped parallel to the table's front edge.

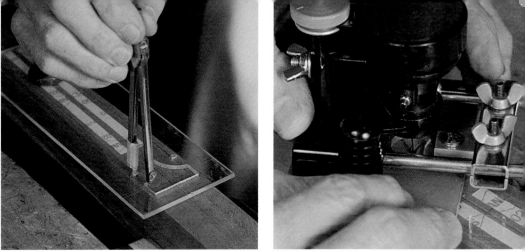

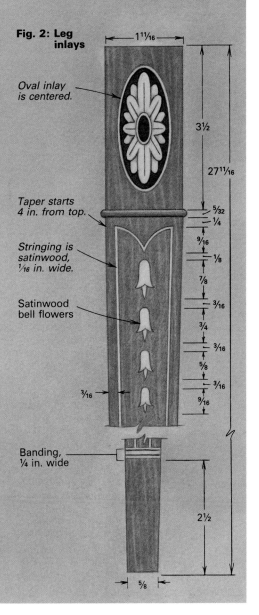

Fig. 2: Leg inlays

1¹¹⁄₁₆

Oval inlay is centered.

3½

27¹¹⁄₁₆

Taper starts 4 in. from top.

5⁄32
¼
9⁄16

Stringing is satinwood, ¹⁄₁₆ in. wide.

⅛

7⁄8

Satinwood bell flowers

3⁄16
¾
3⁄16
5⁄8
3⁄16
9⁄16

3⁄16

Banding, ¼ in. wide

2½

5⁄8

Left: Pittman uses a set of dividers with a dowel taped onto one leg to locate the plastic template for cutting the curved stringing grooves. Right: The arc is cut with a Dremel tool fitted with a screw that is inserted in one of the template's holes. The screw allows the bit to be pivoted through the ³⁄₄-in.-dia. arc.

To make the flower inlays, the author glued up a stack of veneers with paper between each layer, cut the flowers from the stack and then separated the inlays with the tip of a knife.

curve, and then screw temporary blocks to each end of the waste portion of the apron blank to ensure perfect alignment when clamping the veneer. I recommend using backed veneer if you can find it because it is much easier to handle than single-ply crotch mahogany. I bought book-matched crotch mahogany veneer backed with poplar veneer from Cummings Veneer Co., Box 49, New Albany, Ind. 47150. Cut the veneer so it overhangs about ¼ in. on both edges of the blank. Then glue the veneer to the outer face of the apron, clamp the waste half of the blank over the veneer with C-clamps and let it dry overnight. The next day, unclamp the aprons and trim the overhanging veneer with a sharp knife.

As you can see in the detail in figure 1, the ends of each side apron must be trimmed to length at a 58° angle from the straight back side. Because of the difficulty of cutting tenons on these an-gled ends, the side aprons are doweled into the front legs. In addi-tion, a notch must be cut at the back end of each side apron to square off an area to receive the dovetailed rear apron. Make the 58° parallel end cuts using the miter gauge on the tablesaw and with the blade tilted 32° from its usual 90° position. Then lower the blade and make the 58° cut on the inner face of the side apron to form the notch that will house the rear apron. Return the blade to its square position and complete the notch by standing the apron on its back end and supporting it with the miter gauge. After notching both side aprons, raise the blade and trim the front ends of both side aprons in a similar manner, with the aprons

standing on their front ends, to form a flat area to join with the glue blocks, as shown.

The tenons that join the front apron to the legs must be cut in two steps because of the curve on the apron's face. Trim the apron to length first, allowing for the ¾-in.-long tenons. Then, on the tablesaw, cut the tenon shoulder and cheek on the apron's back side with its flat side down. The apron can't be flipped over and run facedown because of the curve and so the top shoulder and cheek must be cut from above with the radial-arm saw. I made the tenons ⁵⁄₁₆ in. thick and centered them on the apron's squared-off ends.

When locating the mortises and the dowel holes in the front legs, keep in mind that the aprons are set back ⅛ in. from the corner of those legs. I bored the ½-in.-dia. dowel holes in the front ends of the side aprons on the drill press by clamping a wood hand screw to the back end of the apron to provide a "foot" to stand it up vertically on the drill-press table. Then I used another hand screw as a leg to support the upper portion of the angled apron. I inserted commercial dowel centers into the holes to locate the mating holes in the legs. To complete the front legs, locate and cut ⁵⁄₃₂-in.-wide by ³⁄₁₆-in.-deep dadoes on the outside surfaces of each leg to receive the bead that runs around the bottom of the aprons.

Rear aprons—The three-part rear apron consists of a long inner apron dovetailed to the side aprons, and two short aprons that are tenoned into the rear legs and joined at the middle with a knuckle joint, or wooden hinge. The apron that's joined to the fixed rear leg is screwed and glued to the long dovetailed apron, while the other is tenoned to the gate leg and allowed to pivot to support the tabletop when the flap top is open.

To determine the length of the dovetailed apron, dry-assemble the front legs with the front and side aprons, and then while holding the joints together tightly, measure the exact distance between the notches in the back ends of the side aprons; don't forget to add the length of the dovetails. The detail in figure 1 on p. 81 shows the layout for the hand-cut dovetails I used on my table.

When making the two-part outer rear apron, don't cut the parts to exact length; leave each about 2 in. too long until after you've cut and fit the hinge. There's no reason to be intimidated by the idea of making a wooden hinge. Simply lay out the interlocking fingers directly on both hinge parts and mark the areas to be cut. Set the tablesaw blade at the same height as the thickness of the parts, and while holding the workpiece vertically and supported by the miter gauge (fitted with an auxiliary fence), make repeated cuts to remove the waste.

Before rounding over the corners to form the knuckles, put the two parts of the hinge together and use the drill press to bore the $\frac{1}{4}$-in.-dia. hole for the steel hinge pin, as shown in the photo below. Drill clear through the hinge assembly so you can easily remove the pin when trial-fitting. You'll trap the pin at final assembly by gluing a dowel plug in the bottom of the hole. After drilling the hole, take the hinge apart and use a disc or edge sander to round over the corners that form the hinge's barrel; replace the pin and make sure the gate-leg apron swings through 90°, even when the fixed apron is held tightly to the dovetailed rear apron.

When the hinge is complete, cut both parts of the hinged apron to length, allowing $\frac{3}{4}$ in. at each end for the leg tenons. Instead of centering the rear leg tenons as on the front apron, I made them flush with the back surface of the aprons to give the mortise a larger setback in the gate leg. Finally, locate and cut a mortise in each rear leg so that the hinged apron's inside face is flush with the face of the leg.

The hinge-pin hole is drilled through the two-part rear apron after an end-to-end finger joint is cut on the two parts, but before the vertical corners are rounded over to form the hinge barrel.

The front and side aprons can now be finish-sanded to 220-grit in preparation for assembly. However, before gluing up the table base, use the front and side aprons as patterns for bandsawing the $\frac{5}{32}$-in.-thick cherry that is glued to the bottom of the aprons to form the bead. Make sure the front edges will protrude about $\frac{1}{8}$ in. and round over these edges with a finger plane or small-radius router bit. Also, round over some of the scrap from the curved pieces to make the short sections of bead for the legs.

Gluing up the base and attaching the top—Because of the unusual construction of the base, I glued it up in several steps. First, I glued the two hinged aprons to the rear legs and the side aprons to the front legs. In order to clamp the side aprons, I had to screw blocks to the inside of the aprons temporarily, as shown in the detail in figure 1 on p. 81. After the side apron/front leg assemblies were dry, I glued the front apron and the dovetailed back apron in place. Then I cut, fit and screwed in the corner glue blocks. Next, I glued and screwed the fixed rear apron/leg assembly to the dovetailed apron and attached the gate-leg assembly by inserting the hinge pin into the knuckle joint (after plugging the bottom of the hole with a short dowel). Finally, I glued the apron beads in place, and fitted the small leg beads into the dadoes and glued them in place.

As you can see in figure 1, I used metal clips to secure my tabletop to the aprons. These tabletop fasteners, which hold the solid top to the aprons while still allowing it to expand or contract, are available from most woodworking mail-order companies and in some hardware stores. With the table standing on all four legs, it's easy to rout the slots with a $\frac{1}{16}$-in.-wide, winged slot-cutting bit; of course, you need to buy the clips first so you know how far the slots should be from the upper edge of the aprons.

Construction of the two-part tabletop is very straightforward. The $\frac{4}{4}$ stock is planed to $\frac{13}{16}$ in. thick and then glued up to make two pieces about 20 in. wide by 37 in. long. When these top blanks are dry, the glue squeeze-out is scraped from the joints and the mating (hinged) edge of each blank is cleaned up on the jointer. Then apply double-faced tape to the surface of one blank, and place the other blank on top, taking great care to perfectly align the mating edges. The top's shape is then drawn on the upper surface from a full-scale pattern and both pieces are bandsawn out at the same time. With the two tabletop halves still stuck together, sand the sawn edges to finished shape. Then you can separate the two halves and use a router with a $\frac{1}{4}$-in.-radius bit to round over the inside mating edge of both top pieces to provide clearance when the top is opened and closed.

I bought my card-table hinges from Wise Co., 6503 St. Claude Ave., Arabi, La. 70032 (catalog #H05A). I had to grind down a $\frac{1}{2}$-in.-wide high-speed steel router bit to cut the $\frac{15}{32}$-in.-wide mortises in the edges of the tabletops to receive the hinge leaves. I recommend that you use steel screws for fitting the hinges initially and then replace them with brass screws at final assembly. At this point, you can place the assembled top on the base, screw the tabletop fasteners to its underside and check that the top and gate leg both open and close as they should.

Finally, disassemble the tabletop from the base and the hinges from the tops and apply the finish. I used spray lacquer, rubbing between coats with 400-grit paper and smoothing the final coat with 0000 steel wool to produce a satin sheen. □

Frank Pittman teaches furniture design and construction, as well as wood technology and guitarmaking, at Western Kentucky University in Bowling Green. The Cabinet-Maker and Upholsterer's Guide, *by George Hepplewhite, is available from Dover Publications Inc., 31 E. 2nd St., Mineola, N.Y. 11501.*

Working Green Wood

From raw logs, chairs that will stand the test of time

by Harriet Hodges

A shaving horse is ideal for green woodworking. Other holding devices will work satisfactorily, but with the shaving horse, you can flip the workpiece around instantly and repeatedly so that you're nearly always cutting with the grain.

Green woodworking delights our desire for thrift and speed. In a few days, you can fashion a chair from the forest. The tools are few, the techniques simple and the work satisfying. Green wood is simply wood that's still in possession of most of the moisture it had when it was a tree. This moisture makes the wood much softer and more responsive so that working it is pure delight. It's also a lot easier: The froe, drawknife, spokeshave, brace and auger bit—the main tools of the green woodworker—all respond much better to wood that is not yet dry and brittle. To use these tools on green wood is to understand how simple cutting tools are meant to respond. While still wet, hickory peels like a carrot. Dry, it rings like stone.

Why bother, though? Machine tools have taken much of the labor and difficulty out of working dried woods. But there are several reasons why a woodworker at the end of the 20th century should be interested in a technology that's more than 1,000 years old, and they all hark back to the essential nature of wood itself. A woodworker uses a drawknife to dimension green stock to follow the plane of one of the tree's growth rings. That maintains long, continuous fibers. These bundles of long fibers are strong: Because there are no severed bundles (short grain), there's no danger of any portion of a drawknifed spindle, for example, shearing or springing under stress. A Windsor chair, belying its delicate lines, can take a terrific beating (see the photo on p. 86).

Another reason green woodworking has endured is that phenomenally strong joints are possible. Green-wood joinery takes advantage of the high moisture content of freshly felled trees (or well-preserved tree sections, more on this later) and of the fact that wood shrinks much more in the tangential plane than in the radial plane (see figure 2 on p. 88). Wet-dry joinery takes a stretch-

Photos except where noted: Vincent Laurence

***Windsors are the ultimate expression of the green-wood-working tradition.** They're tough, resilient chairs, making up in engineering what they lack in mass. Shaved components with long, continuous fibers; wet-dry joinery that mechanically locks the various parts; and choosing specific woods for specific uses all contribute to the chairs' great strength.*

Windsor chairs I build professionally. It's an elemental process, from felling a tree and bucking it into lengths, to riving blanks for the various parts and squaring up those blanks with a drawknife, to shaping the parts and attending to the joinery. Then a bit of sanding, a couple of coats of milk paint, and you have a unified, elegant whole, a strong, handsome chair that will last for generations.

The best way to learn the basics of green woodworking is to take a course with a good teacher. The hands-on experience will give you the confidence to dive in. I learned most of what I know from Curtis Buchanan in a class I took five years ago and a private tutorial a year later. But if you can't afford a class or don't have the time, you can still learn the process on your own. The craft is forgiving, and you need no jigs, just good eyes and hands.

Getting logs

The first thing you need to do is get some stock. Fortunately, this is simple and cheap in most parts of the country. You want logs. Look in the local paper for a firewood dealer or check the yellow pages for a sawmill nearby. Or if you live in a rural area and have a truck, many farmers will let you cut your own for a lot less than you'd pay even a firewood dealer. If you're going to cut down your own trees, look for perfectly straight boles with no limbs. Make sure there aren't any bark striations or irregularities revealing twisted grain or buried knots. If your project involves bending, you'll do best to get a hickory, white-oak or red-oak log. Other trees that bend well are beech, birch and ash. Sugar maple is ideal for many purposes, particularly for turned legs (it takes crisp, sharp detailing), but beech, red maple, birch, walnut, cherry, almost any North American hardwood, is fine.

Your log should be freshly cut—no more than a week old. After that, checking starts, and you lose useable stock. Logs should be crosscut to no longer than 5 to 6 ft. for easy handling, though there are exceptions. A settee, which has the longest bent member of common Windsor designs, requires nearly 7 ft. for the rough back blank. I've also found that trees in the neighborhood of 12 to 14 in. dia. are just about right. Smaller trees can also yield good stock, but often, by the time you rive (split) off the sapwood and the pith, neither of which is particularly desirable, you will get no more than one blank from each pie-slice shaped wedge that you split out, which makes it kind of a waste. At the other end of the spectrum, a great hickory tree came down last year when Hurricane Hugo blew through our neck of the woods. At nearly 30-in. across, there's plenty of useable wood, but moving sections around is all but impossible.

For stock that won't be bent, I crosscut bolts, or short log sections, fairly close to their final length as spindles or legs or whatever. For your bending stock, you want no more than 15 growth rings to the inch; eight is about ideal. This may seem counterintuitive, but for ring-porous hardwoods (oak, ash, hickory—all your best bending woods), the greater the ring density, the higher

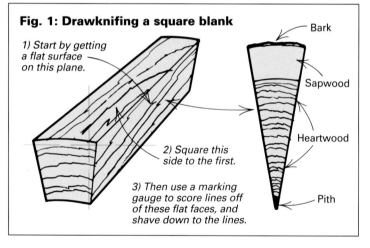

Fig. 1: Drawknifing a square blank

1) Start by getting a flat surface on this plane.

Bark

Sapwood

Heartwood

2) Square this side to the first.

3) Then use a marking gauge to score lines off of these flat faces, and shave down to the lines.

Pith

er or spindle, dries it for a short while in a makeshift kiln and then inserts its tenoned ends, properly oriented, into properly situated mortises in the still wet legs or seat. This kind of joinery relies more on the nature of wood than on the strength of the glue for its longevity. As the two parts reach equilibrium in moisture content, the joint becomes tighter. A dry tenon in a wet mortise is a joint for the ages.

Another advantage of working green wood is the ease with which it can be bent (for a primer on steam-bending, see *FWW* #107, p. 62). Green wood bends readily as long as your bending stock is free of defects. That's because it hasn't had the chance to dry out, and kiln drying hasn't baked the wood and set the lignin.

One of the most satisfying aspects of green woodworking for me is to take what many would consider no more than firewood—logs in their raw form—and make of it something as refined as the

PREPARING GREEN STOCK

Green-woodworking stock is cheap and easy to prepare (top left). *Log sections can be split out by driving a wedge into the end and then leapfrogging wedges in the crack that opens on the sections' inner face.*

A froe and club work well to separate sapwood from heartwood (bottom left). *Although the sapwood can be used, its moisture content differs from the heartwood, which could result in uneven or unpredictable shrinkage.*

A forked log, called a brake, holds a wedge-shaped section upright (far right) *while the author removes bark, sapwood and pith and rives the section into rough chair-part blanks.*

the proportion of weak, large-pored earlywood to overall tissue.

Bending wood must be virtually perfect: If the first log you split for bending doesn't split easily into quarters to reveal perfectly straight grain, try another log. You can always use sections of the first log between defects for shorter pieces. Just don't kid yourself about bending flawed stock. Bending perfect wood is quick and easy. Bending stock with even a pin knot usually turns out to be a waste of all the effort you put into shaping the bending blank.

Preparing green stock from logs to square blanks

The absolute minimum in tools is a steel maul and three wedges, but a froe and club work well on smaller stock and will make the job more pleasant. Starting with a log, you position a wedge with one hand at the center of the log and strike it. Follow the split back with other wedges, leapfrogging them as one loosens the other. Then repeat with each half, quarter and so on, starting the splits at the log ends (see the top left photo).

When your log is down to manageable pie-slice shaped wedges, move one to a brake (a propped-up horizontal portion of a forked tree), as shown in the photo at right, or brace one end against another tree. The nice thing about the brake is it holds a pie-shaped piece well. Mark the end of each piece to be rived just where you intend to make divisions. Always mark divisions and begin splits from the smaller end of a log section; that way, if it wanders, you won't end up with a piece that's too small (see the photo at right). If you need a 1-in.-sq. piece for a chair back, try for 1½-in.-sq. pieces until you can do that consistently and have a good feel for how a log will split. Be generous in your divisions. I've ruined a lot of pieces trying to make one perfectly good, but slightly oversized, blank into two that were "just right." Make extras of everything.

Always try to halve each section, and then halve again and so on. By keeping the mass on each side of a division equal, the split runs truer. You can correct a split somewhat, but it's not a precise science. If you're using a froe and a brake, for instance, and your split begins to run to one side, you can exert pressure on the thicker side and possibly force a correction. With a maul and wedge, your only recourse is to flip the stock and start again from the other end as soon as you see a split start to drift.

You're interested in heartwood only. Bark and pith are obviously out, but even sapwood's tricky. You can use it, but its moisture content is so much different from heartwood that it's usually more of a pain than it's worth. To remove bark and sapwood, I usually wait until I'm down to a pie-slice shaped wedge to froe it off (see the bottom left photo). The pith generally gets discarded with the small triangular section I discard from a final split.

I take rough blanks to the shaving horse (see the photo on p. 85), although other holding devices such as a bench vise would also work. I begin drawknifing, bevel down, in the radial plane, shaping a flat side perpendicular to the growth rings (see figure 1 on p. 86). Sight down stock frequently, and correct wind, or twist, as necessary. Then flip stock to an adjacent side, and square it to the first, being careful to follow the line of one growth ring. When in doubt, study the piece from the side, marking the ring line you're trying to follow. Reverse stock as necessary so that you're cutting with the grain as much as possible. Once adjacent sides are square and true, score down from those faces with a marking gauge to mark your needed dimension. The dimension chosen must allow for shrinkage. For a chair back-bow that must be ¾ in. dry, I square to about $^{13}/_{16}$ in. Square to your marked lines, and your piece is ready for drying or bending if you're going to make a

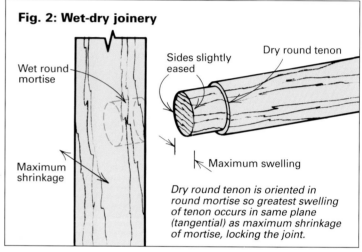

*A **drive plate helps size tenons precisely.** Simply a thick piece of precisely machined steel, the drive plate helps to match tenons exactly to the auger bit used to drill the socket mortises. Such precise joinery ensures the longevity of the final product.*

Fig. 2: Wet-dry joinery

Wet round mortise

Sides slightly eased

Dry round tenon

Maximum shrinkage

Maximum swelling

Dry round tenon is oriented in round mortise so greatest swelling of tenon occurs in same plane (tangential) as maximum shrinkage of mortise, locking the joint.

stool or rustic chair with square members. For Windsors and other pieces requiring round members, you have a bit more work.

The closer to a perfect square you produce, the more nearly perfect your round. A perfect round bends perfectly. A round begins as a square, which is turned into an octagon and then rounded. To turn squares into octagons, remove corners with a drawknife. Then just spokeshave the high points off to get a round. A concave-sole spokeshave is particularly handy here.

Stock that you're not going to be using right away needs to be stored properly if it's to stay green. Minimally, stock should always be stored out of the sun, but ideally, it should be kept immersed in water. I keep blanks in a pond by my house, but even a trough would do the job. Log halves and smaller sections also can be stored heart side down on damp ground, out of the sun and covered with a tarp. Stock that you intend to bend requires more care in this regard than wood that will be used for straight parts.

Joining green-wood components

Green-wood joinery techniques take advantage of wood's tendency to dry predominantly in the tangential plane, or roughly parallel to the growth rings. Bone-dry tenons (0 to 5% moisture) are created from the green stock by drying the shaved components, generally stretchers and spindles, in a kiln for 48 hours or so. My makeshift kiln consists of scored, foil-faced building insulation folded into a box, with wooden ends and a light bulb for a heating element. The dry tenons are then sized to a very tight fit in the tangential plane, eased slightly in the radial plane to prevent splitting out the socket mortise, and inserted into mortises drilled in moist, green wood (15 to 20% moisture). As the tenon picks up moisture from the surrounding wood, glue and air, the tenon

swells in the tangential plane, locking itself permanently in place. One important caveat: A tenoned member that will also have a mortise drilled in it needs to have the mortise area protected from drying. An aluminum-foil wrap works well.

Glue in this joint acts initially to reintroduce water to an artificially dry tenon, and then it acts as a barrier to overly quick moisture exchange, protecting the wood from drastic changes. The glue is actually of secondary importance to the strength of the joint, though; it's primarily a mechanical bond.

These joints depend on close tolerances for optimum strength. A less-than-perfect joint won't usually relegate a chair to the scrap pile, but the sturdiest, most long-lived chairs will be those with perfect joints. For that reason, I had a machinist make a drive plate for me. It's nothing fancy, just a ¼-in.-thick sheet of ground steel with holes bored in it at precisely ⅜ in., ½ in. and ⅝ in. and above and below each of these in ¹⁄₆₄ in. increments (see the photo above). That way, I can size my tenons to the auger bit I use for the socket mortises, thereby ensuring a perfect fit. The incremental steps also allow me to take a roughly shaved spindle and gradually work it down to exactly the dimension I need by driving it to depth in successively smaller holes. Any metalworking shop should be able to make one of these plates.

A word of caution: Some woods react better to being driven than others, especially in small diameters. I've had good luck with hickory mostly and with an occasional piece of red oak, but you should take your time and get the spindles as close to tolerance as possible before driving them. □

Harriet Hodges raises sheep and harvests chair wood on a Craig County, Va., farm. She is also the indexer for Fine Woodworking.

Bowback Windsor Step by Step
Green woodworking lends its strength to this classic design

by Harriet Hodges

T he rewards of building Windsor chairs are sweet indeed. From logs, I create objects of beauty and utility, strong but graceful, steeped in tradition and destined to last generations (see the photo at right). The process isn't difficult as long as you take it step by step.

Preparation

Before you start to make a bowback (or any other style) Windsor, you have to get green wood, preferably in whole log form. Split out, square and then round blanks for the back-bow, spindles, legs and stretchers. I use sugar maple for legs and spindles, pine or basswood for the seat and hickory for the back-bow.

You'll need to make a crude kiln to dry the tenons that go into wet mortises: Wet-dry joinery gives Windsors their characteristic strength. A cube of folded foil-faced insulation with a light bulb inside and plywood ends works well for me. Shape your spindles (see figure 6 on p. 94 for dimensions), and dry them for at least 24 hours. If you don't want to build a kiln, you can put the spindles in a gas oven with a pilot for 48 hours.

Drilling and shaping the seat

Using the seat pattern from figure 2 on p. 91, scale the pattern onto a piece of cardboard or heavy paper. Now set the blank on the bench, heart side down, and trace the pattern on it. Mark the centers of spindle, back-bow and depth holes. Mark leg centers on the top for reference in carving. You want to leave a lot of material around the legs for strength. Mark spindle sight lines (see figure 2). They will be used later to help drill the spindle mortises at the correct angles.

Cut the front profile of the seat, but leave the back waste intact so you'll have corners to clamp. Then set the pattern on the bottom, lining it up at the front and marking leg centers for drilling. Also, transfer the sight marks for the legs from the pattern (marks FL and

Strength belying its delicacy is the hallmark of a Windsor chair, a trait it derives from the wet-dry joinery and the long, unbroken grain of the drawknifed, not sawn, pieces. The Windsor's classic good looks fit in almost anywhere.

RL in figure 2), and then draw sight lines, as shown. Next mark the centerline of the gutter, which defines where the seat carving begins and the plateau for the back ends.

Start drilling with the center spindle mortise. Set a bevel gauge to 8° back from perpendicular, and center its blade on the sight line. Use a ½-in. auger bit, and set a depth stop for 1½ in. Drill with a mirror set to the side of the bit and bevel gauge, so you can sight both angles at once (see the photo on p. 90). After the center spindle, drill in pairs, one mortise to each side of center. Change the bevel gauge's angle setting for each pair. Use a ⅜-in. bit to drill the back-bow mortises.

Turn test tapers now to match your reamer (see figure 5 on p. 93). The reamer tapers leg and back-bow mortises. Ream the back-bow holes from the top until the test taper protrudes below. Check angles repeatedly, aligning the center of the test taper, the blade of a try square and the sight line to get one angle right in one plane. Use the bevel gauge to check the angle in the other plane (see the bottom photo on p. 91).

The first step in shaping the seat is to carve the gutter. Carving a crisp gutter requires a scalpel-sharp veiner (a carving tool that cuts a V-groove), see figure 1 on p. 90. Before you start removing more seat material, draw contour lines along the front of the seat and the forward part of the sides (see figure 2 on p. 91). Bore depth holes to ⅞ in. with a Forstner bit. Then have at it with an adze, inshave or large gouge. Proceed evenly, from the middle of the inner circle in figure 2, aiming for a shallow bowl that gradually deepens and widens. Bring in area A. Drawknife the front, spokeshaving when close to the line. Round the seat

DRILLING AND SHAPING THE SEAT

Aligning brace and bit in two planes isn't difficult, but it takes practice. Hodges positions a bevel gauge along the sight line she'd marked previously for each spindle mortise. By keeping her bit in line with the bevel gauge in front of it and checking the mirror to make sure the bit remains parallel to the gauge, she can bore all the spindle mortises in about 10 minutes.

Fig. 1: Carving the gutter

Veiner

Use a sharp veiner to carve a crisp gutter before shaping the seat.

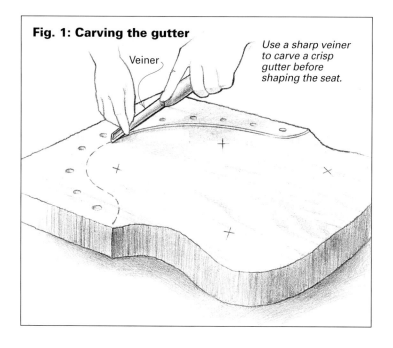

over slightly below the gutter. Undercut the underside at the front deeply, tapering into the areas under the gutter edge. Finish up with scrapers on the top, leaving the bottom spokeshaved. Saw the waste off the back.

The side S-curves are difficult, undulating in two planes, perpendicular to the floor at the back and twisting subtly. Use rasps and files as necessary. Look for symmetry between the two sides and for fluidity (see the top photo on the facing page).

Once you've shaped the seat, turn it over and bore leg holes, using the same mirror technique as the spindle holes. Ream them from the bottom until the test taper protrudes slightly all the way around, testing frequently for angles with the test taper.

Preparing legs and stretchers

I chose simple bamboo-style turnings for this chair. Bamboo turnings can be done with a gouge and just the tip of a skew, which is good news if you haven't done much turning. Note the positions of the bamboo nodes in figure 3 on p. 92. Be sure to sand the legs while they're still on the lathe.

Once you've turned the legs, lap them to mate with their mortises. Mark a heavy line down the reamed hole with a soft pencil. Twist the leg in the hole, re-chuck it and remove high spots. The end of the tenon should protrude slightly all around. Mark and match legs and holes for a permanent match; they're *not* interchangeable. I use stick-on colored dots.

Insert all four legs in the seat with light mallet taps. You'll need to get the seat up on blocks, so the leg tenons will go to depth in

their mortises. Orient the legs properly, turn the assembly upright and mark the top of the leg tenons for the direction of the sawkerf (note the orientation of legs and stretchers in figure 4 on p. 92). Kerfs must be perpendicular to seat grain.

Now flip the assembly back over, so the seat is back on blocks on your bench. Measure for stretchers at the centerline of the bottom node of the bamboo. To do this, choose a front-back pair, and mark the center of the mortise in one with an awl as you sight "through" its mate. Flip the assembly around and repeat. Now measure the distance between the two marks, add 2⅛ in. (for the tenons and chamfered shoulders) and you have the length of your stretcher. Repeat for the other side. It doesn't matter if the two stretchers are different lengths.

To get the length of the medial stretcher, first measure the distance between the front legs and the distance between the back legs. Use the same awl marks you made to drill for the side-stretcher mortises. Add those two lengths, divide by two and add ⅝ in. That's the length of your medial stretcher.

Cut stretcher stock to exact lengths and turn, making tenons exactly 1 in., chamfers ⅛ in., but leave the tenons slightly thick. Center the nodes on the side stretchers; space two equidistant from each other and the chamfers for the medial stretcher. Sand them on the lathe, and make sure to turn a couple of extras for test-fitting. Now wrap legs and stretchers tightly in aluminum foil, leaving just the tenons exposed, and dry them in your kiln for 48 hours—no more. Then re-chuck all legs and stretchers, and sand lightly to take down the grain raised by heating them in the kiln.

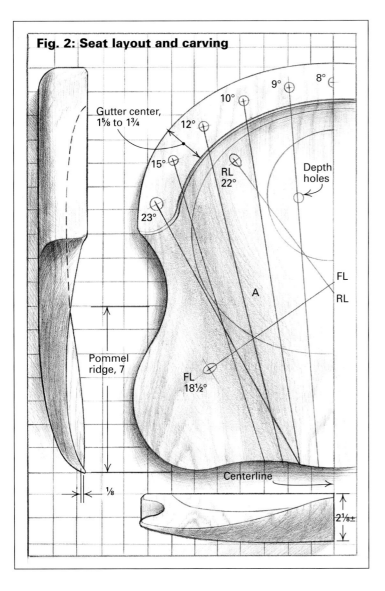

Fig. 2: Seat layout and carving

Gutter center, 1⅝ to 1¾

8°
9°
10°
12°
15°
RL 22°
23°
Depth holes
FL
RL
A
Pommel ridge, 7
FL 18½°
Centerline
⅛
2⅛±

Much of a Windsor's alluring grace is found in the seat, particularly in the S-curve on the side. The transition from a horizontal to nearly vertical surface over just a few inches requires a good eye and sharp tools to make it feel natural. Hodges uses a draw-knife for starters, followed by rasp, file and spokeshave.

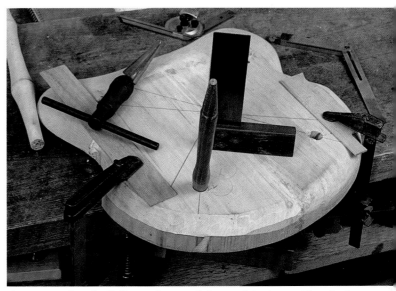

A reamer (to the left, on the seat) is used to taper the chair-leg mortises. Bore the mortises for the chair legs, using a mirror to get the angles right. Then use a bevel gauge, protractor, square and test taper to check the angles and mortise depth as you ream. A reamer in a tap wrench can be used to pare selectively within the mortise to get the angles just right.

Assembling the undercarriage

Boring and assembly require concentration and speed. Assemble the chair upside down on the bench on blocks, orienting each leg properly in the correct mortise. Scribe around each leg at the seat.

To check the leg-stretcher angles, set a rule along each side pair of legs. Then set a bevel gauge against the rule, and adjust it so the blade is in line with the center of a leg, rear first, then front (see the photo on p. 92). Record these angles for boring the side-stretcher mortises.

Lay another rule across the first, snugging it against either both back or both front legs. With the bevel gauge, record the acute angle where the two rules meet. This is the medial-stretcher angle.

Place side stretchers on the seat with their tangential planes up. Put the medial stretcher between them, radial plane up. Pick up side stretchers with your thumb and middle finger opposing, each in the middle of an "ellipse," right at the center of the tangential face of the stretcher. Now prick a mark with an awl on the node ring halfway between your fingers, or right in the middle of the radial face, to locate the mortise for the medial stretcher.

The next step is to size tenons. Accuracy is a must. Use test pieces until you get a perfect fit, and *then* go for the real thing. File a test tenon very slightly in the radial planes, exaggerating the oval. Chamfer ends slightly, so they won't bind just as your tenon enters a test board. Use a piece of scrap maple with a ⅝-in. hole in it to test the fit. If the tenon slips right in, try a smaller bit. If it won't penetrate with moderate blows, it's too wide. A drive plate is wonderful for sizing tenons because it removes such a small amount at

a time. Failing that, either file or re-chuck in your lathe. When you have a tenon that fits well, record its diameter with dial or vernier calipers. Then file flats on its radial planes, swab glue in the ⅝-in. hole in the maple test board and on the end of the tenon, and pound it home in the test mortise. Wait a minute. Try to pull it out or twist it. If you can't—and the mortise didn't split—that's your tenon dimension. Now size all tenons for real.

To avoid confusion in drilling, point the leg tenons toward you. For the two stretchers you'll mortise, draw arrows that will point toward you as you drill at an acute angle. You don't need jigs: Hands and eyes are capable of more than enough accuracy. Set the seat on blocks upside down on the bench for test fits. Do the stretcher assembly first. Pick up a side stretcher, note the angle you wrote down for the medial stretcher, set your bevel gauge and place the stretcher in a vise to hold it without rocking while you drill. I use a three-peg vise, which works well and takes only minutes to make (see the photo at left on p. 93). Place the bevel gauge alongside the stretcher, the acute angle pointing toward you. Set a mirror to the side, so you can see both bit and bevel gauge simultaneously while drilling. Don't worry about being a little off. This step is forgiving, too.

Bore the mortise so it's at least 1⅛ in. deep. Relieve the acute-angle side of the mortise, so the chamfer on the medial stretcher doesn't get hung up. Clean any chips or sawdust out of the mortise. Orient the medial stretcher correctly, and coat its tenon thinly with glue, particularly the end. White glue's a good idea until you're confident you can deal with the quicker set-up time of yel-

MAKING THE UNDERCARRIAGE

Double-check the leg angles before boring the stretcher mortises. Using a straight-edge to establish a plane between the front and back legs, the author checks the leg-to-seat angles to make sure that the stretchers will be parallel to the seat.

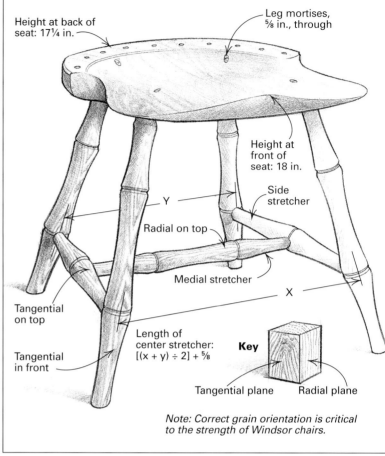

Fig. 4: Seat and undercarriage assembly

Height at back of seat: 17¼ in.

Leg mortises, ⅝ in., through

Height at front of seat: 18 in.

Side stretcher

Radial on top

Y

Medial stretcher

Tangential on top

X

Length of center stretcher: [(x + y) ÷ 2] + ⅝

Tangential in front

Key

Tangential plane   Radial plane

Note: Correct grain orientation is critical to the strength of Windsor chairs.

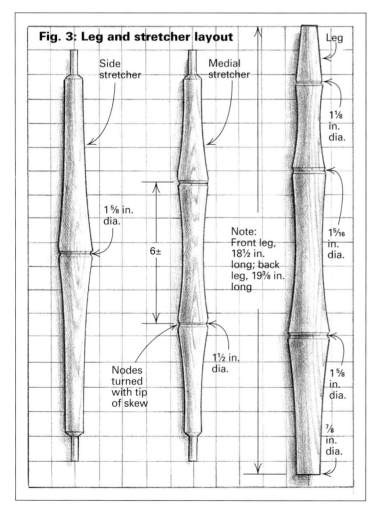

Fig. 3: Leg and stretcher layout

Side stretcher

Medial stretcher

Leg

1⅛ in. dia.

1⅝ in. dia.

6±

Note: Front leg, 18½ in. long; back leg, 19⅜ in. long

1⁵⁄₁₆ in. dia.

1½ in. dia.

Nodes turned with tip of skew

1⅝ in. dia.

⅞ in. dia.

low glue. Pound the tenon home with a mallet. Now bore the other stretcher, and pound in the other tenon in the same plane. If it needs correction, twist as you pound.

Take up a rear leg, bore the side-stretcher mortise, glue its tenon and pound it into the leg mortise a little. Seat the leg (dry) in its hole with the stretcher assembly attached. The medial stretcher should be parallel with the seat. It probably won't be, so correct it by pounding at the other end of the stretcher assembly while twisting it (see the photo at right on the facing page). Check again. Remove the leg from the seat, and pound the stretcher home. Be quick because the kiln-dried tenon is swelling from the moisture reintroduced by the glue. Bore the other rear leg, and keeping both legs in the same plane, pound the glued stretcher tenon home.

Reset the bevel gauge for a front leg, bore the mortise, glue its tenon and insert it in a little way. The top of the front leg should fall slightly to the outside of the line described by the back leg as you look across the pair. Treat the last leg in the same way—except now you can use its mate for alignment.

Kerf the leg tenons almost to the scribe line you marked showing their depth in the seat. Turn the seat upside down on blocks, swab the mortises with glue and work glue into the sawkerfs. Set the lower assembly in place, each leg tenon in its mortise. Pound legs down alternately, listening for the thunk that says it's done. Turn what is now half a chair over. Hammer in glue-smeared wedges.

Back assembly

The next step is to bend the back-bow. I steam the piece for about 45 minutes in a length of 4-in., schedule 40 PVC pipe with a cap glued on one end and a couple of rags in the other end. My steam generator is a tea kettle on a hot plate. The steamed back-bow goes into a plywood bending form the shape of the interior of the bow.

Holding parts securely is more than half the battle. Hodges uses three pegs and a wedge in her shaving horse, but a shoulder vise with wooden jaws also could be used. Either way, blocks should be used to keep the workpiece from rocking while you're drilling.

Work quickly once you've started attaching the legs to the stretcher assembly because glue in the leg joint will cause it to swell in no time, freezing the joint in place. Once you've adjusted the stretcher assembly so that it's parallel with the bottom of the chair, pound the tenon home.

After drying the back-bow in the bending form for about a week, stick its tenons into hot sand or under a light bulb in an aluminum reflector for at least four hours. Sand can be heated easily in a cake pan or skillet on an electric range top. After four (or five or six) hours, test-fit the back-bow tenons in the seat mortises. Pare the tenons until they protrude below the seat at least ³⁄₁₆ in. Mark tenons left and right, scribe around them at seat level and mark kerf lines, perpendicular to the seat grain. Chamfer the tenon ends.

While the tenons are drying, make a simple support fixture to steady the back while you drill for spindles (see figure 7 on p. 94), but wait to notch the top until after you've fitted the bow. Set the back-support fixture in place 90° to the seat in the center-spindle mortise. If the top of the back's arc doesn't coincide with the center of the seat, mark the true center. The center spindle must be perpendicular. Mark off spindle locations with dividers and pencil using the measurements in figure 2 on p. 91. Fix each line with your eye over its respective spindle mortise in the seat, and without moving your head or your gaze, use an awl to mark on the line at its center on the bow. This center is important because there's not much wood to spare.

Bore the spindle holes with a ³⁄₈-in. auger bit. In addition to the back-support fixture, I sometimes use a ½-in. dowel or a pair of all-thread rods connected with washers to steady the bow further and to drill true (see the photo on p. 94). I also use the mirror to stay true in the other plane. What you're trying to do is to sight "through" the bow to the spindle mortise in the seat, even though the bow's obscuring it. Begin perpendicularly to an imaginary tangent at the bow's surface, and then bring the bit gradually up to the correct angle within 10 turns. Bore until you can just feel the tip of the drill. Repeat for the rest of the spindle mortises in the bow, and then remove the back and finish the holes from the other side.

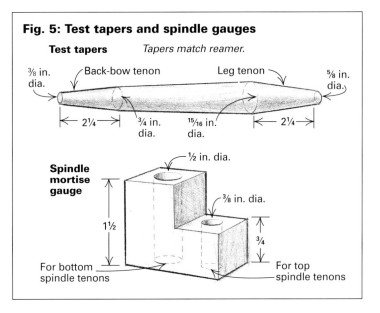

Fig. 5: Test tapers and spindle gauges

Test tapers   *Tapers match reamer.*

³⁄₈ in. dia. Back-bow tenon   Leg tenon   ⅝ in. dia.

2¼   ¾ in. dia.   ¹⁵⁄₁₆ in. dia.   2¼

½ in. dia.

Spindle mortise gauge

³⁄₈ in. dia.

1½   ¾

For bottom spindle tenons   For top spindle tenons

Make a spindle-tenon test gauge (see figure 5), and size all the bottom ends of spindles to fit snugly. Insert them in the spindle mortises in the seat, place the back just behind the spindles and arrange the spindles, so they're lined up with their corresponding back-bow mortises. Mark spindles with a pencil where they intersect the back-bow bottom and again ½ in. above the back-bow top. Cut them at this top mark. Now mark them, L1, R1 and so on, and scribe a line around each at its penetration into the seat.

Remove the back-bow. Remove the spindles and shave their tops, so they will slide easily into the spindle mortises in the back-bow down to the lower intersection. Chamfer the spindles heavi-

ASSEMBLING THE BACK

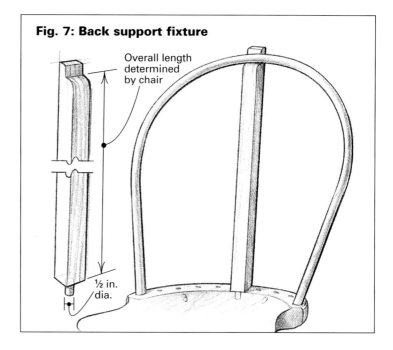

A wooden back-support fixture keeps the back-bow steady as Hodges drills spindle mortises in it. Two pieces of metal rod connected with nuts serve as a visual guide to keep her bit aligned with the spindle mortise in the seat.

Fig. 7: Back support fixture

Overall length determined by chair

½ in. dia.

Fig. 6: Back assembly

Thickness dimensions are green and will shrink.

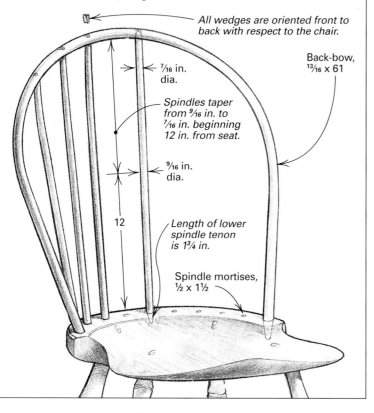

All wedges are oriented front to back with respect to the chair.

Back-bow, 13⁄16 x 61

7⁄16 in. dia.

Spindles taper from 9⁄16 in. to 7⁄16 in. beginning 12 in. from seat.

9⁄16 in. dia.

12

Length of lower spindle tenon is 1¾ in.

Spindle mortises, ½ x 1½

Further reading

Magazine articles

"Working Green Wood" by Harriet Hodges, *Fine Woodworking* #108, pp. 90-93 [this book, pp. 85-88]

"Steam-Bending Basics" by Andrew K. Weegar, *FWW* #107, pp. 62-66

"Milk Paint" by A. Richard Fitch, *FWW* #91, pp. 62-65

Books

Make a Chair from a Tree by John D. Alexander Jr., Astragal Press, Mendham, N.J., 1994

Make a Windsor Chair with Michael Dunbar, The Taunton Press, Newtown, Conn., 1984

ly on top, and replace them in the seat. Test-fit the back, reaming spindle holes very lightly or shaving from a spindle as necessary. Draw a line down the spindle fronts and onto the seat, so you can replace them in the same orientations. Now cut them off level ¼ in. (on the short side) above the chair, and mark for a kerf across their tops—perpendicular to the grain of the back-bow. Make sure the line at the intersection of the underside of the bow and the spindles is well-marked. Now disassemble the back; re-chamfer the spindle tops; kerf all spindles at the top, nearly to the line below the bow; and kerf the back-bow tenons nearly to the seat-depth scribed lines.

Lightly brush glue in seat holes, two at a time. Insert spindles. Brush glue in the back-bow holes, and with a mechanic's feeler gauge (or anything else that's thin, flexible and won't self-destruct with glue on it), work glue into all the wedge kerfs. Start spindles into their mortises in the back-bow, and then start the back-bow into its mortises in the seat. Pick up the mallet and a scrap of wood, and moving from side to center to alternate side, hammer the back down. Wiggle recalcitrant spindles. Sometimes the sharp points of the bow tenons hang up in their holes. If they do, pull forward on the bow while hitting it. When the bow tenons reach their depth mark, that's it.

Smear glue on the spindle wedges, and hammer them home. Turn the chair upside down, and insert wedges in the bow tenons. Look for gaps in the fit, inserting little wedges wherever you can get them. When the glue has set, saw the spindle, back-bow and leg tenons almost flush; then chisel, scrape and file to finish. Level the legs, and chamfer their bottom edges so they won't split when great-grandchildren skate the chair over a floor. Finally, sand, raise the grain, sand again (to 180-grit) and fill small gaps.

Finish

Paint makes the chair read as sculpture. I use milk paint, which is not like other paints. Practice with it. Penetrating-oil topcoats will make a chair water resistant. This finish gives off a soft glow and is extremely durable. Virtually unchippable, it is only burnished by the years.

In addition to building Windsor chairs and settees, Harriet Hodges raises sheep and harvests chair wood on a Craig County, Va., farm. She is also the indexer for Fine Woodworking.

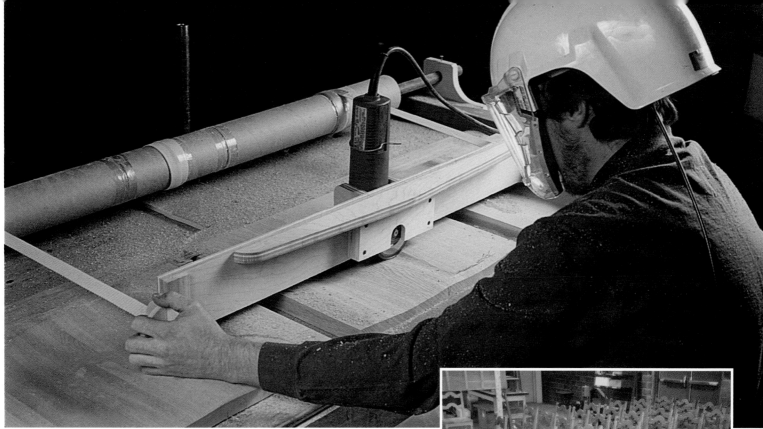

To simplify a production run of Yorkshire chairs with contoured hardwood seats (inset), Dan Trimble devised a seat duplicator. The jig's cutterhead, an angle grinder fitted with a wood-carving wheel, dishes out the central seat blank, reproducing the shape of the two seat patterns that are located left and right of the blank. When copy carving a seat (10 minutes from start to finish), Trimble wears long sleeves and an air helmet.

Sculpting Chair Seats with a Shop-Built Duplicator

Angle-grinder drives this high-production jig

by Dan Trimble

Shaping a flat slab of wood to fit the human behind is nothing less than sculpture. Doing it 30 times the same way is production sculpture. This was one of the tasks I faced when asked to reproduce more than two dozen Yorkshire-style chairs (see the inset photo above) for a new restaurant. Although I had built lots of chairs before, these were the first with contoured solid seats. Hand-chiseling the seats was out of the question, and I wasn't ready to invest in a designated machine for one run of chairs. So I set out to find a more practical way to carve the seats.

I knew that a chainsaw could do the job and remove wood rapidly, but control was questionable. I also knew about a power-carving wheel that had chainsaw-like teeth and fit a standard angle grinder (see *FWW* #87, p. 124). I reasoned that a less-aggressive version of this cutter would be just the ticket. I rushed an order off to King Arthur Tool, 3225 Earl Dr., Tallahassee, Fla. 32308;

(904) 893-8550. After receiving the 22-tooth Lancelot cutter, I mounted it on my angle grinder and experimented on a piece of wood. The wily little tool surprised me with its effortless cutting, removing stock both in line and side to side. But controlling the cut for 30 exact copies still presented a problem. Necessity being the mother of invention, I built a duplicating jig using this power carver and two pattern followers (see the photo above).

Making a linear carving duplicator

Based on three points on a line, I figured that when two outside points followed identical patterns, a center point would trace the matching contour on a blank. Allowing 3 in. between the patterns and a 17-in.-wide blank put the distance between the blank centerline and the center of each pattern at 20 in. To assemble the patterns and jig, I mounted a plywood base on a large worktable.

From *Fine Woodworking* (November 1992) 97:67-71

Tables and Chairs **95**

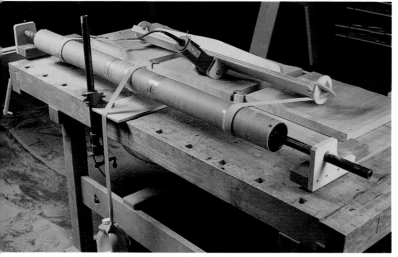

When duplicating a seat, Trimble moves his jig with the grain, taking ¼ in. at a pass. In actuality, the carving wheel cuts across the grain. To minimize grain tearout, Trimble makes an initial L-shaped swath with the cutter, which reveals the seat's pommele. Here, part way through a seat, he adjusts the guard.

At the back side of the jig, a pair of nylon straps wrapped around a tube keep the two followers parallel to the front edge of the patterns. This alignment ensures that the cutter copies the contour on the blank. The tube spins around an axle (¾-in. iron pipe) that is supported by two yokes. A counterweight (water jug) suspended at the end of a central strap puts tension in the system.

Frame and cutter—I made the jig's frame, which holds the followers and angle grinder, from a piece of ¾-in. cabinet-grade plywood. To straighten the frame, I added a plywood stiffener to go along its top edge. The neck on the head of my grinder fit nicely into a 1¾-in.-dia. hole drilled in the frame. To hold the grinder (with its screw-on handles removed) in place, I bolted a couple of ¾-in. plywood blocks to each side of the grinder reusing the tool's handle holes. Then I screwed on a piece of plywood to act as a guard for the cutter, as shown in the photo at left. I also notched the guard so that I could access the arbor nut of the grinder.

Pattern followers—To transfer the patterns correctly, I made round followers the same diameter as the cutter wheel. I cut two 4½-in.-dia. discs of ⅜-in. Baltic-birch plywood and added pairs of 4½-in.-dia. semicircles at right angles to the sides of the discs (see the drawing below). To keep the discs aligned and rigid, I glued on some corner blocks. Then I shimmed the discs in line with the cutter wheel. I screwed the sphere-like followers to the frame's ends, so the bottom of the discs were tangent with the edge of the cutter and 40 in. apart, center to center. The discs don't roll. Instead, they slide over the contour, much like the stylus of a lathe duplicator, pushing wood chips out of their way as they go.

Parallel guide system—The line between followers has to stay parallel to the front of the seat patterns and blank (see the drawing detail below); otherwise, the three-point follower/cutter principle fails. I originally thought I could hold the duplicating jig in line by hand but quickly found this very hard to do. So I came up with a system for guiding the jig using non-elastic straps attached to the ends of the frame. I used a pair of 4-ft.-long nylon straps rolled around a 5-ft.-long cardboard tube (see the photo at left). I ran a 5½-ft. length of ¾-in. iron pipe through the 4-in.-dia. plugs on each end of the tube to act as an axle. Supported on two plywood yokes that were screwed to blocks fixed onto the base, the tube spins on its axle and winds the straps in. When the straps are adjusted taughtly, the jig stays parallel to the front of the base. To tension the straps, I wrapped another strap in the opposite direction at the tube's center and weighted the other end of this strap with a plastic jug of water, letting it hang off the back of the table. To make the guide system operate more smoothly, I simply adjust counter balance by putting more or less water in the jug.

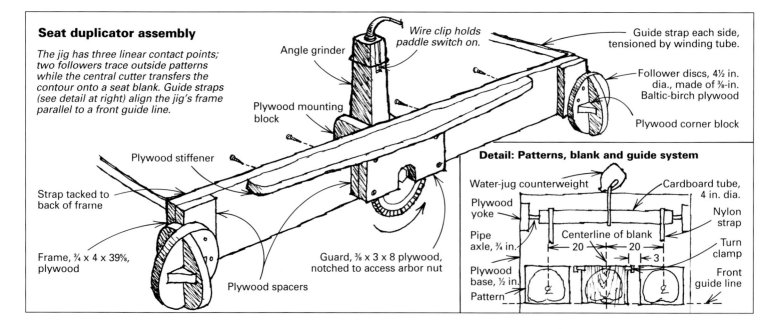

Seat duplicator assembly

The jig has three linear contact points; two followers trace outside patterns while the central cutter transfers the contour onto a seat blank. Guide straps (see detail at right) align the jig's frame parallel to a front guide line.

Wire clip holds paddle switch on.

Angle grinder

Guide strap each side, tensioned by winding tube.

Follower discs, 4½ in. dia., made of ⅜-in. Baltic-birch plywood

Plywood mounting block

Plywood corner block

Plywood stiffener

Strap tacked to back of frame

Frame, ¾ x 4 x 39⅝, plywood

Plywood spacers

Guard, ⅜ x 3 x 8 plywood, notched to access arbor nut

Detail: Patterns, blank and guide system

Water-jug counterweight

Plywood yoke

Pipe axle, ¾ in.

Plywood base, ½ in.

Pattern

Cardboard tube, 4 in. dia.

Nylon strap

Turn clamp

Front guide line

Centerline of blank

20   20   3

Photos except where noted: Alec Waters; drawing Maria Meleschnig

*Laminated patterns and topographic prototypes—*In my initial attempt to make seat patterns, I built two frames for plaster-of-paris molds. The pair came out fine, but after I applied a coat of varnish to harden their surfaces, the molds were still too soft, and the followers scored them easily. (I've since found that a thick piece of Baltic-birch plywood makes an ideal prototype material; the even layers produce rings that resemble topography lines, which let you know when the two halves of the seat are symmetrical.) Luckily, my plaster molds lasted long enough for me to copy carve (duplicate) two laminated maple patterns that work superbly. Because my blanks were thicker (1³⁄₁₆ in.) than the patterns, I used the contact points of my jig as a guide and shimmed the patterns at their corners until the cutter just grazed the blank. While I was at it, I measured my cutter wheel and found that it was slightly out-of-round. I marked where the high spot was so that in the future, I'll always use the same reference point when leveling the patterns. Once shimmed, I just screwed the two patterns to the base. Then, to hold the blank down, I made a pair of turn clamps from blocks of scrap and some metal clips.

Copy carving and finish-sanding the seats

Thinking that I should carve blanks in their grain direction, I first set up the patterns with the seats facing sideways. I plowed into a blank and got a fairly smooth cut using a to-and-fro motion while taking about ¼ in. at a pass. But after shaping a few oak blanks, I found that I couldn't keep the grain from tearing out excessively on the uphill cuts. So to make the cutterhead carve cross-grain, I removed the patterns, rotated them 90° and remounted them perpendicular to a front guideline (see the drawing on p. 96). I then cut an L-shaped swath (down the left side and across the bottom), which prevents the cutter from tearing out grain on subsequent passes.

To use the jig, I hold one hand on each follower (see the photo on p. 95). Because this position places me near all the dust, I wear a respirator/face shield (available from Airstream Dust Helmets, Highway 54 S., Elbow Lake, Minn, 56531; 218-685-4457). I also wear a long-sleeved shirt—the chips come off the cutter at a hellish speed, giving a good sting to bare flesh.

The jig is quite forgiving when cutting cross-grain, and in less than ten minutes, I can produce an accurate seat shape. I've found that I can smooth out any slight imperfections and give a flowing seat contour through sanding. I first rough sand with a pneumatic orbital sander using a 24-grit disc that's mounted to a soft pad. Then it's on to finish-sanding with a sequence of 40-, 80-, 120- and 220-grit discs. After the sanding is done, even a sharp eye (or a sensitive behind) cannot detect variation from seat to seat. □

Dan Trimble runs a woodworking business in Indiana, Penn.

Depth holes guide consistent seat carving

by Alec Waters

Confronted with six time-consuming Windsor chair seats, Bill Turner of Stonington, Maine, came up with a method that transfers a seat shape from prototype to blank using depth-governed pilot holes. He first lays out and drills a 1-in. grid of holes through a prototype pattern (see the drawing at right). With the prototype clamped atop a seat blank, he drills through a hollow spacer back through each hole. The resulting hole depths conform to the seat contour. To remove wood in a connect-the-dots fashion (see the photo at right), both Turner and Canadian furnituremaker Mac Campbell use grinders with chainsaw-tooth cutters. (Cutters are available from Woodcarver, c/o Ryobi America Corp., 1424 Pearman Dairy Road, Anderson, S.C. 29625; 800-323-4615.)

Freehand power carving: When carving with his grinder, Campbell shifts the tool's safety guard to a 45° angle to its axis. After he clamps the workpiece to his bench, he power carves up to about ¼ in. away from a pencil guide line that he marked at the back of the seat. To maintain control, Campbell orients the cutting wheel at a 90° angle to the work while holding the tool's auxiliary handle. To deflect chips, he wears a glove and face shield. Starting at the back of a seat, Campbell moves toward the front, scooping to a 1 in. depth about 3 in. from the rear of the carved area. Unlike traditional Windsor chairmakers, Campbell slightly rounds his seat's front edge to give more comfort to the back of a sitter's legs. After the seat is sanded, he also eases the bottom edge with a rasp or roundover router bit. □

Alec Waters is an assistant editor for FWW.

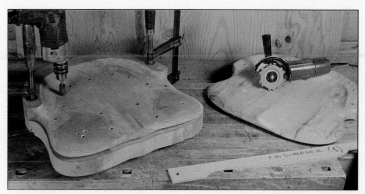

Both Bill Turner and Mac Campbell use depth holes to guide them when roughing out seats. Campbell modified the shape of this pattern (left) several times by adding fiberglass auto-body compound and grinding away wood. As he's carving, he periodically checks the seat's profile with a centerline template.

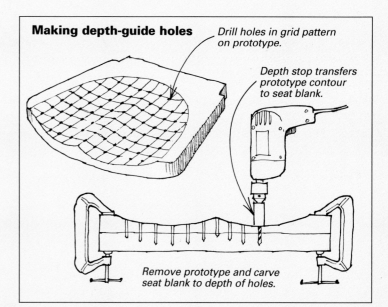

Making depth-guide holes

Drill holes in grid pattern on prototype.

Depth stop transfers prototype contour to seat blank.

Remove prototype and carve seat blank to depth of holes.

Step 1: Rough the seat hollow with an adze.

Step 3: Shape convex surfaces with a drawknife.

Hand tools shape a traditional seat

by Mario Rodriguez

For the sake of authenticity, when I'm reproducing an 18th-century chair, I use traditional hand tools and techniques. This is especially true when I'm scooping the chair's seat. I conduct workshops on making traditional-style seats, and people are often surprised that I can hand-shape a Windsor, or any other style chair seat, in 40 minutes or less. Here's how I do it.

Most antique chairs have seats carved from a single piece of wood. For my seats, most of which are to be painted (see the photo of the Connecticut comb-back Windsor chair on the facing page), I begin with a 2-in.-thick slab of pine that's sound and relatively clear, except for maybe a few small knots. First, I bandsaw the pine blank roughly to shape (use a bowsaw if you're a pure traditionalist). Then I mark out the pattern to be carved on the blank's top and an edge guide line at the circumference. I also drill holes for the legs and arm posts (stumps) at this time.

1) Adze: To begin roughing out a seat, I use a long-handled adze. I straddle the blank, so I can hold it down with my feet (clad in steel-toed boots) while I swing the adze (see the photo above left). Using shallow cuts and fairly short strokes to break up and shorten the grain, I hollow the center of the seat (well within my outline) to about ¾ in. deep.

2) Inshave: Next I clamp the seat to my bench and use an inshave to smooth out the seat cavity that's splintered and rough from the adze. Along the edges, I cut to within ¼ in. of my pencil line, easing the transition to the ¾ in. depth at the middle. To avoid tearing out grain, I shave from the rim down to the hollow (see the top photo above). For clean cuts, I keep my inshave sharp and my strokes light. I also keep tuned to the grain direction and restrict my shaving to the seat's concave area.

3) Drawknife: I use a drawknife to shape the seat's raised curved areas. The drawknife leaves an attractive faceted surface (see the bottom photo above) that needs little further work. I also use the knife to shape the seat's convex underside and back, working to the perimeter guide line.

4) Spokeshaves: I have two spokeshaves for seat-shaping work: One has a flat bottom and the other is round. I use the round-bottom shave to smooth out the curved surfaces, removing un-

Step 5: Carve definition and details with gouges.

wanted ridges and tool gouges (see the top left photo above); with the flat-bottom shave, I smooth the seat's front and back edges and its underside. Both spokeshaves leave a silky surface with slight tool marks such as those found on original Windsor chairs.

5) Carving gouges: A carving gouge is great for fine detail cutting, carving knotty areas and getting into tight places where other tools won't. I prefer shallow gouges (#2 and #3 sweep) for carving down from the rim outline into the seat. I use ½-in. and 1-in.-wide gouges, as shown in the bottom photo above. If a chair design calls for a rain gutter, I'll go to a ¼-in. veining gouge.

6) Hand-sanding: Finally, I use sandpaper to give the seat smooth flowing contours. I start with 60-grit to remove any grain tearout and finish up with 100-grit for a paint-ready surface. In keeping with the 18th-century chair look, I sand only the seat's top and front edge while keeping the edge crisp (see the top right photo above). On the seat's back edge and underside, I leave the tool marks showing. ☐

Mario Rodriguez is a cabinetmaker and 18th-century woodworking consultant. He teaches toolmaking, furnituremaking and antique restoration in New York City.

Making a Rocking Chair with Dowels

Alignment techniques for drilling at odd angles

by Ken Oldfield

This chair, based on a photograph of a Shaker rocker, was made with commercially available dowel stock for the rungs, legs and back uprights. The author steam-bent the back slats and uprights.

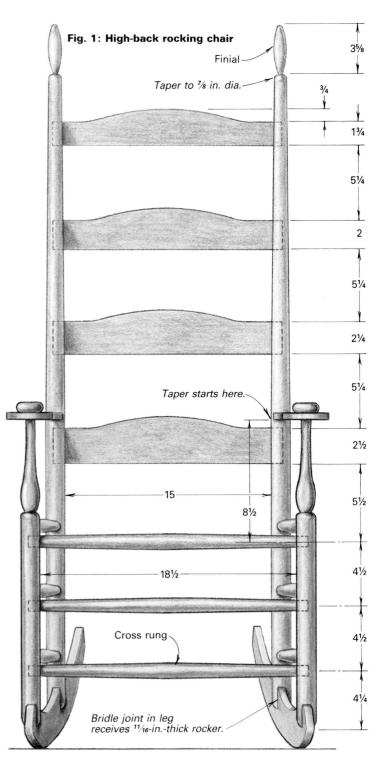

Fig. 1: High-back rocking chair

Finial

Taper to ⅞ in. dia.

3⅝

¾

1¾

5¼

2

5¼

2¼

Taper starts here.

5¼

2½

15

8½

5½

18½

4½

Cross rung

4½

Bridle joint in leg receives ¹¹⁄₁₆-in.-thick rocker.

4¼

Drawings: Heather Lambert

I'm an amateur woodworker, but I enjoy the challenge of chair building. After making two different styles of straight chairs, I was considering building a rocking chair for a spare room when I came across a photograph of a late-19th-century Shaker rocker. This design appealed to me because the basic construction looked straightforward and I thought I could build the chair relatively easily and quickly in my basement shop.

However, as I considered the construction, I discovered that the bed of my lathe was too short to handle the 46¼-in.-long back uprights. I realized I could avoid this problem by using hard-maple dowel rod (readily available at my local lumberyard) for these long pieces. I could have turned all the other parts from square stock in the conventional manner, but I opted to also make them from pre-turned doweling; I used 1⅜-in.-dia. dowels for the back uprights and front legs, and 1-in.-dia. dowels for all the rungs.

The biggest challenges I encountered when building the chair shown here were drilling the holes in the legs at the correct angles for the side rungs and cross rungs, and routing the mortises for the back slats. Because I only wanted to build one or two chairs, I didn't see the need for any elaborate jigs or fixtures. Instead, I made a V-block to hold the legs on the drill-press table and devised some low-tech alignment methods that served me well for drilling and routing at the proper angles.

The measurements given in figure 1 can be scaled up or down to suit your requirements. But keep in mind that the seat is wider at the front than at the back and that the seat angles given are based on the rung lengths shown. If you change any of the rung lengths, you should draw the seat full scale on graph paper and measure the resultant angles with a protractor (unless you change all rung lengths in equal proportion).

Stock selection and preparation—If you use preturned dowels as I did, take your time selecting the stock. These dowels are often bowed and you want the straightest pieces you can find, especially for the two 1⅜-in.-dia. back uprights. You may be tempted to look for two dowels with identical bows and skip the steam-bending process, but drilling the rung holes and routing the back-slat mortises on pre-bent stock will only add to your problems. I began by trimming the two straightest dowels to 46¼ in. long for the back uprights and cutting two 22½-in. lengths for the front legs. I mounted each of the front legs between centers on the lathe, turned tenons on their top ends and added the simple shaping, as shown on these two pages, to add a touch of style. If you don't have a lathe, you can use the dowels just as they are for the front legs and insert a ½-in.-dia. dowel in their top ends for joining the arms and the decorative knobs.

You need six side rungs, 16¼ in. long; three back cross rungs, 16¾ in. long; and three front cross rungs, 20¼ in. long. I turned these 1-in.-dia. dowels so they tapered to ¾ in. dia. at both ends. If you don't have a lathe, you can use ¾-in.-dia. dowel for the rungs. Because dowels are seldom precisely dimensioned or completely round, size their ends by forcing them through a hole drilled in a metal plate. And to ensure adequate strength, I advise using 1-in.-dia. stock for the top rungs, which support the woven seat. The ends of these rungs can be tapered with a spokeshave to fit into the ¾-in.-dia. mortises drilled in the legs.

Drilling—I made the 90° V-block shown in the top photo on the next page by ripping two maple 2x2s at a 45° angle and gluing them to a 10-in.-sq. plywood base. The plywood base is clamped to the drill-press table so that a leg laid in the V-block is centered beneath the spindle.

I began by drilling three cross-rung holes in each leg. First, I marked the centers of these holes on all four legs. The first hole is 4¼ in. up from the bottom of each leg and the other two holes are at 4½-in. intervals (see figure 1). For the first hole in each leg, I chucked a ¾-in.-dia. Forstner bit into the drill press and set the spindle stop to allow a ⅞-in.-deep hole. To ensure the next two holes were drilled in line with the first, I used a 4-in. length of ¾-in.-dia. dowel as an "alignment peg." I placed the peg in the first hole and aligned it with a try square standing vertically on the V-block base, as shown in the top photo on the next page. Then I clamped the leg to the V-block and drilled the cross-rung hole. I repeated this process for the cross-rung holes on all four legs.

Before marking the side-rung holes, clearly identify each leg as right or left

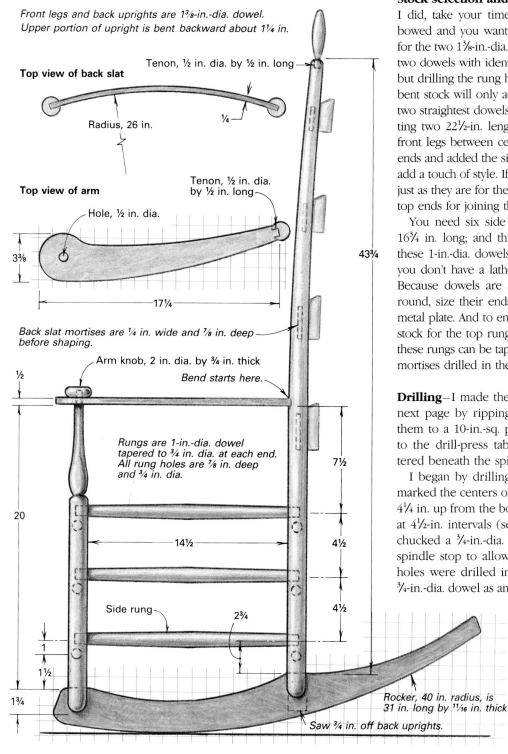

Front legs and back uprights are 1⅜-in.-dia. dowel. Upper portion of upright is bent backward about 1¼ in.

Top view of back slat

Tenon, ½ in. dia. by ½ in. long

Radius, 26 in.

¼

Top view of arm

Tenon, ½ in. dia. by ½ in. long

Hole, ½ in. dia.

3⅜

17¼

Back slat mortises are ¼ in. wide and ⅞ in. deep before shaping.

Arm knob, 2 in. dia. by ¾ in. thick

½

Bend starts here.

Rungs are 1-in.-dia. dowel tapered to ¾ in. dia. at each end. All rung holes are ⅞ in. deep and ¾ in. dia.

43¾

7½

20

14½

4½

Side rung

2¾

4½

1

1½

1¾

Rocker, 40 in. radius, is 31 in. long by ¹¹⁄₁₆ in. thick

Saw ¾ in. off back uprights.

to avoid confusion when drilling. With this right/left designation in mind, mark the centers of the side-rung holes approximately 90° from and 1 in. above the center of the cross-rung holes. When standing in front of the chair and looking down on the seat, the side rungs in the front legs will actually be centered 83° from the cross rungs: clockwise for the right front leg and counterclockwise for the left front leg. For the back legs, the side rungs will be 97° from the cross rungs: clockwise for the left back leg and counterclockwise for the right back leg. Another way to look at this is that the side-rung holes are placed -7° from 90° for the front legs and +7° from 90° for the back legs.

To align the legs for drilling the side-rung holes at the correct angle, I used a block of wood with lines running at a 7° angle, as shown in the center photo. With a leg in approximate position to drill the top side-rung hole, I put the alignment peg in the adjacent cross-rung hole and rotated the leg until it aligned with the 7° lines on the wood block (+7° for the front legs and -7° for the back legs). Then I clamped the leg to the V-block and drilled the hole. For the left front leg and the right back leg the block will be behind the V-block, and for the other two legs it will be in front. As you can see in the center photo, you need to cut away a portion of the V-block to accommodate the alignment peg. You'll only need to use the 7° block for the first side-rung hole in each leg, and then you can put the alignment peg in the side-rung hole you just drilled and use the try-square alignment method for the other two holes.

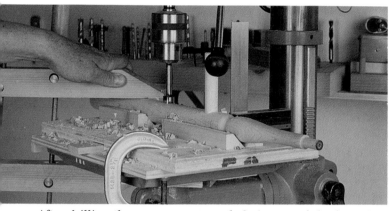

After drilling the upper-cross-rung hole in one of the front legs, the author inserts an alignment peg into this hole. To ensure that the next hole is drilled in the same plane as the first, he rotates the leg until the alignment peg is parallel with a square standing vertically on the base of the V-block fixture.

The correct angle for the first-drilled side-rung hole is established by referencing the alignment peg, inserted into a cross-rung hole, to a line drawn at a 7° angle on a block of wood.

To determine the angle for the slat mortises, the author assembles the back uprights with the cross rungs and then holds one of the steam-bent slats up to the ends of the uprights and marks the angles.

Steaming the slats and uprights—As is typical of Shaker ladderback chairs, the ¼-in.-thick back slats have a gentle curve on the top edge, and beginning with the bottom slat, each successive slat is slightly narrower than the one below it. The slats will be inserted into ⅞-in.-deep mortises in the back uprights, just like the 16¾-in.-long back cross rungs, but the slats should be crosscut about 2 in. longer to allow for their curvature. You will trim them to exact length after steaming and bending them. I used ash for the slats in the chair in the photo on p. 100, but oak would also be fine.

I built my steamer, shown in the bottom photo on p. 104, from 4½-in.-dia. plastic pipe with two electric kettles as sources of steam. I found that soaking the chair parts in hot water for 15 minutes prior to steaming greatly increased the efficiency of my steamer. After steaming each slat for about 30 minutes, I clamped it over a bandsawn 4x4, which was cut to the desired curvature, and then let it dry overnight. The slat will spring back somewhat after it is removed from the form, and so your form should have a tighter curve than what you want for your finished slats. A word to the wise: I learned the hard way that the harmless looking mist escaping from the kettles and the end of the steamer pipe is not so harmless; leather work gloves are now a permanent part of my steaming equipment.

I rout the mortises in the uprights to receive the slats with a ¼-in.-dia. up-spiral mortising bit. Because of the curve of the slats, the angle of entry of these mortises is not the same as the back cross-rung holes. To determine the angle, dry-assemble the back legs with the three cross rungs and lay this assembly on the bench. Draw a circle on the ends of the uprights to designate their size after they are tapered and hold a slat against the ends so you can mark the angle at which the slat should enter the upright (see the bottom photo). You may have to block up the slat to center it on the uprights. At this time you can also mark the slat for length based on ⅞-in.-deep mortises, and then use it to mark the length of the remaining slats.

Next, glue a ¼-in.-wide by 6-in.-long piece of wood (a Popsicle stick is ideal) to the end of each upright along the lines you just marked to act as a temporary guide while you rout the mortises. After laying out the mortises, put an upright in the bench vise flush with the benchtop and with the Popsicle stick pointing straight up. Then, stand a square against the stick so that its blade is vertical, and rotate the upright until the stick is aligned with the square's blade, as shown in the top photo on p. 104. Now you can rout the mortises.

I made an adjustable jig to guide the edge of the router base and provide stops at both ends (see the top photo on p. 104). I clamped the jig to the bench and routed the first mortise, and then moved the upright and reset the jig's stops to accommodate the different length of each mortise. Then I chiseled the ends of the mortises square and dry-assembled the chair back with the three cross rungs and four slats to check their fit.

Before steam bending the uprights, taper their upper ends and

(continued on p. 104)

Weaving a rush fiber seat

I used rush fiber for the woven seat on my rocking chair. This extremely strong and durable cord is actually tightly twisted paper that comes in a continuous 150-yd. roll. I ordered mine from Lewiscraft, 40 Commander Blvd., Scarborough, Ont., Canada M1S 3S2, but it's also available in the United States from most handicraft-supply houses and many mail-order woodworking supply firms. Although the instructions suggest lightly dampening the cord before weaving, I found this to be no improvement over using it dry.

The actual weaving process is quite simple, but the pattern is based on 90° corners and the seat is not; so first you must "square up" the opening by filling in about 1¾ in. from the sides at both front corners. To make the description easier to follow, I'll refer to the top rungs by number, as shown in figure 2 below, beginning with the top front rung as #1 and proceeding clockwise around the chair so that the top right rung is #4.

To begin filling in the corners, cut a 6-ft. length of cord, double it and tack it at the fold to the inside of rung #2 about 3 in. back from the front leg. Take one of the 3-ft. lengths and while maintaining moderate tension, bring it forward and over the top of rung #1 right next to the left leg. Go around the rung, so the cord is now pointing toward the rear of the chair, and then go left over the top of the cord strand and over rung #2. Bring the cord around the rung, and coming from underneath rung #2 go all the way to the right and over the top of rung #4. Go around the rung and come from underneath and cross over the cord and the top of rung #1, keeping the cord tight. Now, go around rung #1 and from underneath run the cord back about

3 in. and tack it to the inside of rung #4.

Repeat this pattern with the second half of the original 6-ft. length of cord, keeping it tight alongside the first cord. It will end up being tacked to rung #4 about 1 in. back from where the end of the first length was tacked. Now take a second length of cord (about 6 in. longer since it will have farther to go), and repeat the process. Concentrate on keeping the cords close together and making 90° bends in it as it goes to the right and left. With ¼-in.-dia. cord, about six turns over each end of the front rung will be required to create a rectangular opening with square corners.

Now that the opening is squared up, you can start the weaving process. From the hank of cord, coil up as much as you can handle conveniently and cut it off. Tack one free end to the inside of rung #2 and proceed as you did before. However, after you have gone over rung #1 on the right, you take the cord all the way back to and over rung #3. Come from under rung #3, go to your right over rung #4, come from under this rung, and across and over rung #2. Go around rung #2, and then up and over the cross cord and rung #3. Come from under rung #3 to the front, going over rung #1, and start the whole process again.

Keep the 90° angles sharp and accurate by pulling the cord tightly with your thumb and finger as you weave and form them. Viewed from the top, all lines formed by the cord must be parallel or square to each other (see figure 2). A block of wood and a hammer are useful for periodically knocking the cord strands together to keep them tight to each other on the rails. When you run out of cord, tie on another length underneath the seat using a

square knot somewhere that subsequent weaving will cover.

When only about 4 in. of space remains on rungs #2 and #4, fill the "pockets" that have been formed between the upper and lower levels of cord on the sides of the seat with pieces of cardboard (cut from corrugated boxes) to keep the seat firm and give it shape. Lay the cardboard along rung #2 and cut it to a triangular shape as shown. Insert this into the opening and do the same on the rung #4 side. You'll need several pieces of cardboard in each pocket, but don't overdo it or the seat will be very stiff and hard.

Continue with the weaving until about 4 in. of space is left on rungs #1 and #3. Now pack the front and the back of the seat with cardboard in a similar fashion to the sides. Here you will find that fewer pieces of cardboard can be inserted.

Resume weaving until the sides of the seat are completely covered. At this point there will still be about 1½ in. of rung in the front and back to be covered. To do this, bring the cord up through the center opening (you may have to cut the points off the packing pieces if they extend too far into the center) and forward and over rung #1. Go around this rung and, coming from underneath, go up through the center opening and then to the back and over rung #3. Go around rung #3 and then from underneath go back up through the center opening again. Continue in this way until the front and back rungs are filled in. Tack the end of the cord underneath the seat to rung #3.

When the seat is complete, give both the top and bottom two coats of white shellac to add to its durability. Now sit back and "rock around the clock." —K.O.

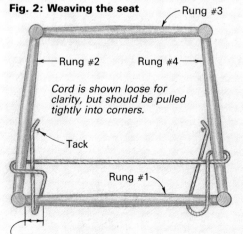

Fig. 2: Weaving the seat

Rung #3 · Rung #2 · Rung #4

Cord is shown loose for clarity, but should be pulled tightly into corners.

Tack

Rung #1

Fill in about 1¾ in. on each front corner to square up seat area.

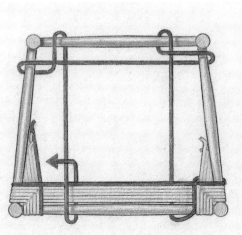

After squaring, the weaving cord continues on to rung #3 and on around seat.

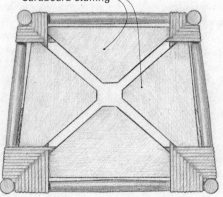

Cardboard stuffing

As you weave, keep the pattern on 90° lines.

then drill a ½-in.-dia. hole in the top of each one for the finials. I roughed out the taper with a handplane, beginning at the lowest slat mortise and tapering to ⅞ in. dia. at the top. Then I refined the shape with a spokeshave and smoothed away any facets left from the tools with 80-grit paper on an electric palm sander.

Since only the upper portion of each upright is bent, I didn't bother to steam the whole length. I made a pine plug with a 1⅜-in.-dia. hole in it for one end of the steamer pipe and inserted the tapered end of the upright only up to the point where the arm will join it, as shown in the bottom photo. As with the slats, I soaked the tapered portion of the upright in hot water for about 15 minutes and then steamed it for about 40 minutes. When I removed the upright from the steamer, I clamped it in the bench vise with wedges between the upright and the side of the bench to force the bend, and then I let the upright dry overnight. To ensure that I bent the upright in the proper direction, I inserted the alignment peg used for drilling into one of the cross-rung holes before steaming. Then I made a mental note of which way to orient the plug when I clamped the upright in the vise: either up or down, depending on whether I am bending the left or right upright. This way I didn't have to think about it too much as I hurried to bend the upright after removing

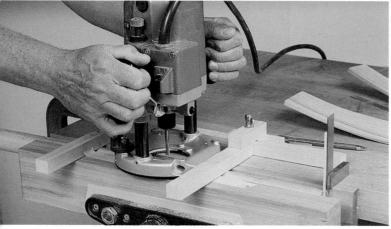

Oldfield glues a Popsicle stick onto the end of the upright along the line of the mortise angle and aligns the stick with a square standing on the bench. Then he routs the mortises with the aid of a jig that guides the router base and adjusts to set stops for the mortise length.

The author's steamer consists of two kettles with built-in electric hot plates that feed steam through dishwasher hose into a length of plastic pipe. Because only the upper end of the back uprights are bent, Oldfield made a wood plug through which he could insert the tapered upper portion of the upright. The short alignment peg in one of the rung holes reminds him of the direction of the bend.

it from the steamer. Springback is always a factor when steam bending. To give you an idea of how much springback you can expect, I bent my uprights about 2¼ in. immediately after steaming, and when I took them out of the vise the next day, the bend came back about 1 in., resulting in a total curve of about 1¼ in.

When both uprights were dry, I sawed ¾ in. off their bottom. This tilted back the seat and worked with the arc of the rockers to provide a pleasing center of balance for the chair, whether empty or occupied. Then I bandsawed the 1¾-in.-deep by ¹¹⁄₁₆-in.-wide bridle joint on the bottom of both legs so they would fit over the rockers.

Rockers and glue-up—After some experimentation with rockers, I found that a 35-in. to 40-in. radius provides a good range of rocking motion. I used a 40-in.-radius arc on the rocker in the photo on p. 48 and it provides an easy rocking motion; a smaller radius would let the chair tip further back. The rockers are bandsawn from ¹¹⁄₁₆-in.-thick hard maple for durability, and are 31 in. long measured from tip to tail end (see figure 1 on pp. 100-101). I used a spokeshave to break the top edges of each rocker, except for the short flat surfaces where the legs' bridle joints fit. To ensure that the legs seat squarely on these flat areas, dry-assemble the two chair sides (three side rungs and a front and back leg), fit them onto the rockers, and then mark and trim the rockers if necessary.

Next, I disassembled the chair sides and sanded all the parts, finishing up with 120-grit in preparation for glue-up. I glued up the front legs with their three cross rungs first and then the back uprights with cross rungs and slats. Check both of these assemblies by eye to make sure the legs are in the same plane with no twist, and then stand them on the bench with one of the legs against a framing square to make sure the assembly is not racked. When the front and back assemblies were dry, I glued them together with the side rungs, pulling all the joints tightly home with a web clamp. When gluing a chair together, you should make sure that the assembled chair stands on all four legs and then view it from the top and sides to ensure that the angles have not been distorted by clamping pressure.

The curved arms, which I bandsawed from ½-in.-thick stock, fit over the round tenons on the top of the front legs and are joined to the back uprights with a ½-in.-dia. hand-cut round tenon. I drilled the hole to accept the back of the arm at the appropriate angle based on the arm's curve as seen from above. After fitting the arm to the curvature of the upright, I marked around the front-leg tenons and drilled the holes through the arms so they would drop over these tenons. I glued the arms in place and then rounded the bottoms of the legs with a rasp, file and sandpaper and glued the rockers into the bridle joints. To top things off, I turned the finials with ½-in. by ½-in. tenons, rounded the tops of the uprights and glued the finials in place. Finally, I turned the decorative arm knobs, drilled a shallow ½-in.-dia. hole in the bottom of each and glued them onto the tenons that extend up through the arms.

I gave my chair two coats of blue milk paint that I ordered from The Old Fashioned Milk Paint Co., Box 222, Groton, Mass. 01450. This paint is made from lime, milk, clay and earth pigments and contains no lead, chemical preservatives, fungicides, hydrocarbons or other petroleum derivates. The paint has a slight milk odor after it's mixed with water, but this disappears as the paint dries. All other ingredients are basically inert organic materials except for the hydrated lime, which is strongly alkaline when wet, but becomes totally inert when dry. After the second coat was dry, I rubbed it down with 0000 steel wool and then coated the entire chair with Watco Danish oil to deepen the color and give the finish a slight sheen. □

Ken Oldfield is a marketing manager for IBM and an amateur woodworker in Toronto, Ont., Canada.

Windsor Settee
Stretching a traditional design to seat two

by Mac Campbell

The author redesigned the traditional Windsor settee so the bow would flow more smoothly in a continuous curve from the arm. He also fanned out the spindles evenly, eliminating the usual gap between the third and fourth spindles on each side, and extended the arms by 3 in.

The continuous-arm Windsor is my favorite chair. The graceful curve of the back bow, uninterrupted by attached arms, is a masterful use of wood. Thus, I was delighted when a client who had previously bought several chairs asked me to design a matching settee with an overall width of about 50 in. I was determined that the settee would possess the qualities I most admired in the chairs—exceptional visual lightness and delicacy, strength and durability, and flexibility and design integrity for longevity and comfort.

I had to modify my basic design slightly to make it more suitable as a settee. My Windsors have relatively short arms, so they can be pulled up to a dining table. Since settees are more likely to be used as narrow couches, however, I added one spindle to each side and extended the arms 3 in. This meant changing the end profile of the seat, so the stumps supporting the ends of the arms would tilt forward as they do on the chairs.

In addition, when I designed my chair, I softened the bend between the upper and lower portions of the back so the bow would flow more smoothly, even though this meant sacrificing some of the flat arm section to the beginning of the upward sweep. I also changed the spindle arrangement. Continuous-arm Windsors usually have two spindles plus the stump supporting each arm, and

these three components tilt forward. Then there is a noticeable gap, and the back spindles (usually nine) are fanned out and tilted back from the seat. But to emphasize the flow, I fanned out all 13 spindles evenly, eliminating the gap between the second and third spindles on each end. This means that the third spindle on the chair pierces the back bow diagonally from corner to corner. On the settee, the fourth spindle has this same problem, because of the extra spindle I added on each end. I ruined several back bows trying to drill this hole on chairs and discovered, I suspect, one reason why the gap was originally left between the spindles. Eventually, with the help of a friendly welder, I devised a drill guide, shown in the top, left photo on the next page, for boring this awkward hole. This spindle arrangement is, I think, unique to my chairs, and so I wanted it in the settee.

The back and seat angles of the chairs, arrived at over several years of tinkering, are quite comfortable, and I transferred these angles directly to the settee. I didn't have to measure the angles for the middle legs; I just set the outside legs in place without glue, tied a string tightly between them as a drill guide, as shown in the top, right photo on the next page, and bored the holes.

The contour of the settee seat is taken from the centerline of the chair, with the front somewhat rounded off, since there is no pommel. Many Windsors have a relatively slight hollow in the seat, but this reduces the comfort of the chair. I prefer to hollow the seat to a depth of about 1 in. (see the seat pattern detail in figure 1), with the deepest part about 3 in. from the rear edge of the carved area. Keeping the deepest portion this far to the rear prevents the sitter from sliding forward, and thus improves comfort. I also round the front of the seat to eliminate the more traditional sharp edge that can cut off circulation in the legs, particularly for short people.

I think back-brace spindles are unnecessary on chairs, because they limit the flexibility of the back, which adds to the comfort. With the settee, however, I feared that the long, straight back might bow backward when two people leaned against it. The settee back could

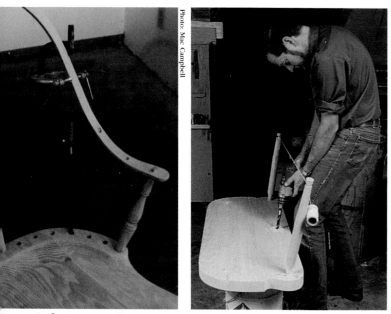

Left: *Fanning the spindles out evenly causes the third spindle on chairs, shown here, and the fourth spindle on the settee to pierce the back bow diagonally from corner to corner, making the hole difficult to bore. So Campbell fabricated this guide from metal tubing, rod and a C-clamp. Putting the bottom rod into the seat hole makes it easier to align the bow hole.* Right: *To align the middle legs with the outside legs, Campbell stretches a string between the two outer legs and uses it to sight the hole with a hand-held power drill.*

The settee bow bending form is a simple system of blocks and cleats mounted on a 3/4-in.-thick plywood base that can be secured with the dogs on a workbench. The ends of the bow are secured by U-shaped pieces of plywood, which can be slipped on faster than clamps. Cleats and rotating blocks also save time, so the steamed bow can be secured before it cools.

withstand this, but the bowing action could be uncomfortable on the human back. So I opted for a double set of bracing spindles, supported by blocks fit into mortises centered between spindles E and F.

Steam-bending—The most difficult piece in the settee is the back bow, and so I did this first. I prefer straight-grained ash, oak or hickory; ideally, a 94½-in.-long strip should be split from the log and worked down to ¹⁵/₁₆ in. thick by 1½ in. wide. Since the stock is bent in both planes, grain orientation is not important, as long as the grain is straight from end to end. I often bend stock green, and let it air dry on the bending form shown in the bottom photo.

The arm pattern detail in figure 1 shows how to lay out the flat portion of the arm and the beginning of the bow. Since the arms and the bow are cut from the same strip, the stock must be wider and flatter at each end and then taper toward the middle. I formed this double taper by fixing the stock on a special jig that runs through the thickness planer, but you could bandsaw it. To make the jig, taper a 1⅝x4x100½ strip of ⁸/₄ hardwood to the dimensions shown in figure 2. Then all you have to do is place the stock in the planing jig and make repeated passes until the planer is set at 1⅝ in. (the thickness of the jig). Feed roller pressure will bend the blank to conform to the jig and cut a smooth, even taper. Once the blank is tapered, round the edges on one side with a ¼-in.-radius roundover bit. On the side *not* rounded over, mark the center of the blank to help align the piece in the bending form.

Make the bending form out of any ¾-in. material; mine is fir plywood. The back of the form, which is 14 in. high by 45 in. long, with the corners rounded to an 8-in. radius, is screwed to a larger plywood base (see the bottom photo). The arm forms are rounded to a 7-in. radius so that the curve covers 80°. At the outer end of this curve is a straight, 4-in.-long portion. Attach the arm forms to the back form with corner blocks, screws and glue; the arm form should be located so its curve starts 12 in. below the top of the back form.

The bending blank is so thin that it will lose its heat quickly and must be locked into position within 25 to 30 seconds of being taken from the steamer. To reduce wasted motion, screw 2x2 turn-buttons on the form to guide the blank around the back corner and to minimize twisting. In addition, screw tapered cleats just above the corner bend of the back, so mating wedges can be driven between the cleats and the blank to lock the steamed stock in place. Turn-buttons on the side forms keep the lower part of the back bend snug to the form, and the ends of the arms are secured with small U-shaped pieces of plywood, shown in the bottom photo, which are slipped in place once the bend is complete.

After clamping the plywood base in the dogs of my workbench, I started cooking the blanks in the steamer. It will take between one and two hours until the blank is limber enough to bend. The exact time will depend on moisture content, steam temperature, etc. When the blank is limber, remove it from the steamer and place it on the form, aligning the center marks on the form and blank. The unrounded edges must be facing up, and the arm pads should be facing away from the form. Drive in the two tapered wedges, and draw one end of the blank around the form, tucking it under the rear turn-button on the way. Rotate the side turn-button as you go by it, and then continue the bend for the arm and slip a plywood U-clamp over it. Now do the other end.

Constructing the base—While the back is drying in the form, a process that can take several days or even weeks depending on the season and the original moisture content of the green wood, laminate the pine seat blank. I began with a 20-in.-wide by 48-in.-long rough ⁸/₄ block and machined it to 1¾x18½x46½. Next, draw the seat outline, as shown in the seat pattern in figure 1, and mark the

Photos except where noted: Dick Burrows; drawings: Kathleen Rushton

Fig. 1: Windsor settee

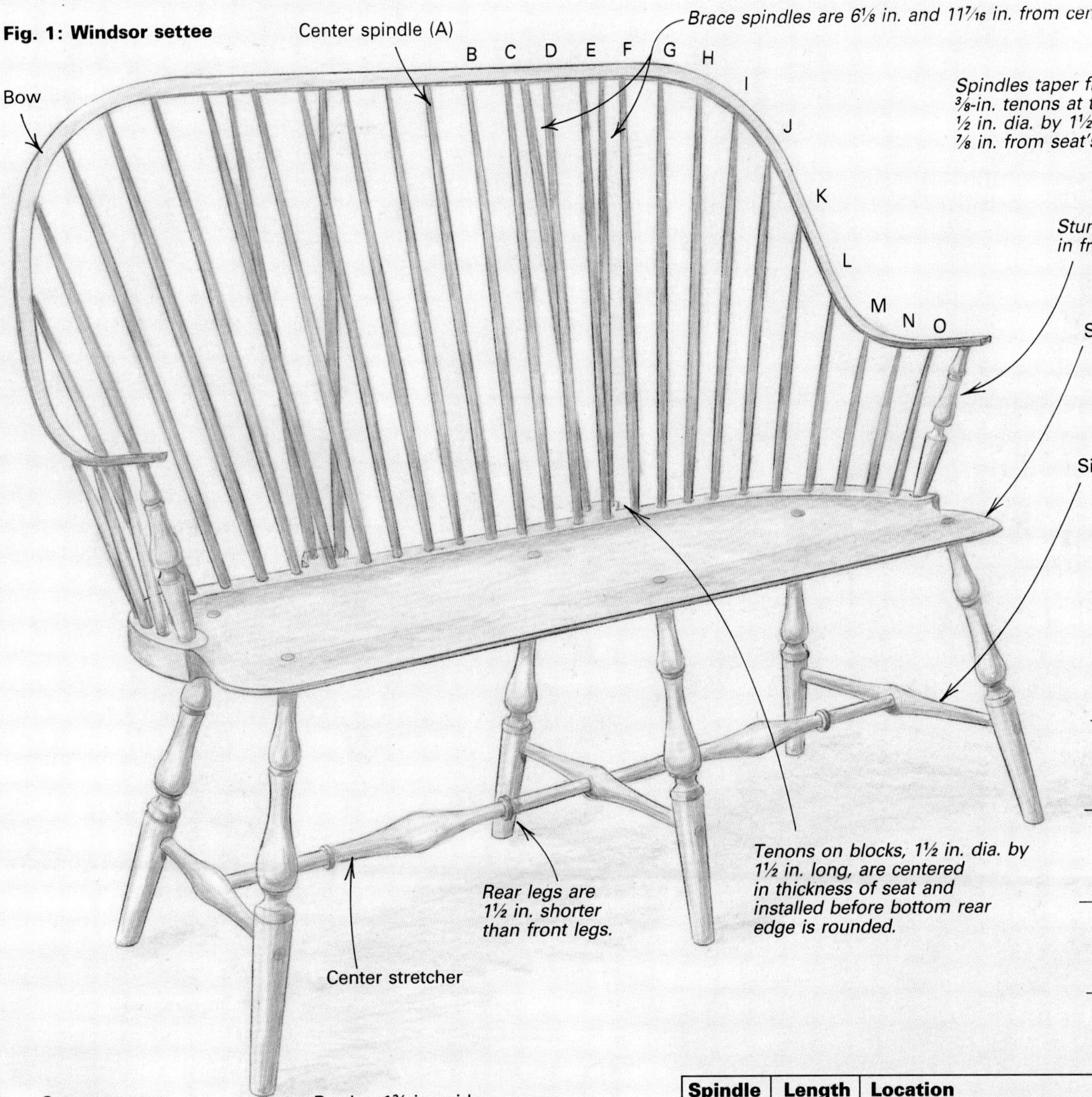

Center spindle (A)
Brace spindles are 6⅛ in. and 11 7/16 in. from center spindle on top of bow.
Bow
B C D E F G H
I
J
K
L
M N O
Spindles taper from ⅝ in. at bottom to ⅜-in. tenons at top. Tenons for seat are ½ in. dia. by 1½ in. long and are located ⅞ in. from seat's back edge.
Stumps are set 1½ in. in from end of bow.
Seat, 1¾x18½x46½
Side stretcher
Tenons on blocks, 1½ in. dia. by 1½ in. long, are centered in thickness of seat and installed before bottom rear edge is rounded.
Rear legs are 1½ in. shorter than front legs.
Center stretcher

Brace spindle blocks

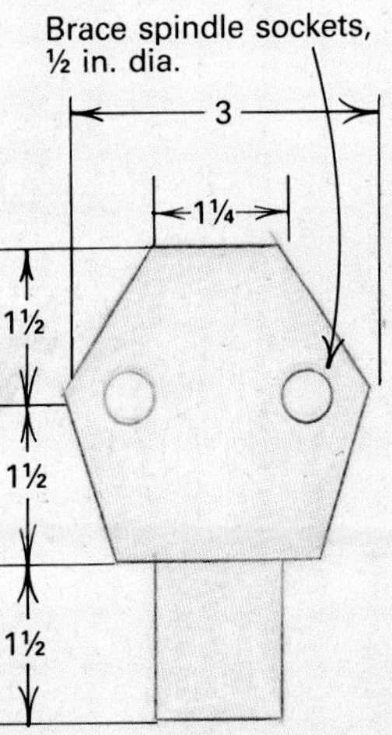

Brace spindle sockets, ½ in. dia.
3
1¼
1½
1½
1½

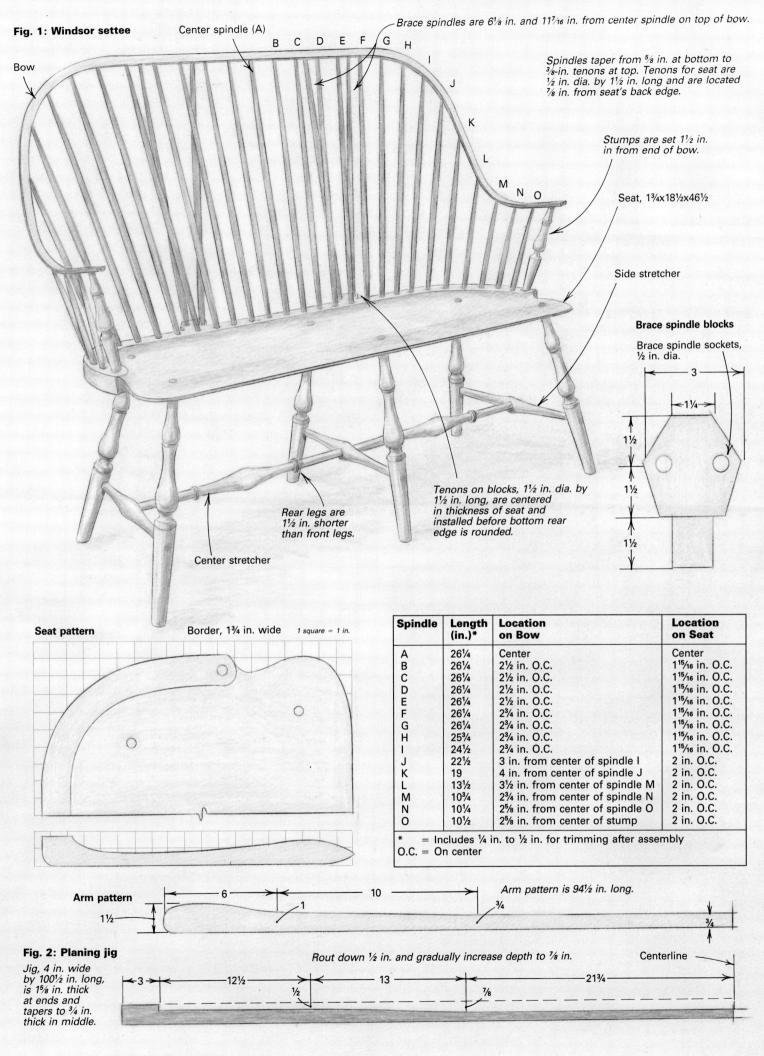

Seat pattern

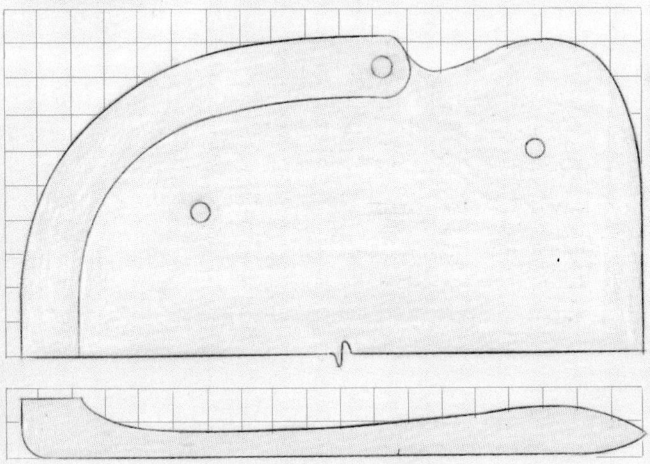

Border, 1¾ in. wide
1 square = 1 in.

Spindle	Length (in.)*	Location on Bow	Location on Seat
A	26¼	Center	Center
B	26¼	2½ in. O.C.	1 15/16 in. O.C.
C	26¼	2½ in. O.C.	1 15/16 in. O.C.
D	26¼	2½ in. O.C.	1 15/16 in. O.C.
E	26¼	2½ in. O.C.	1 15/16 in. O.C.
F	26¼	2¾ in. O.C.	1 15/16 in. O.C.
G	26¼	2¾ in. O.C.	1 15/16 in. O.C.
H	25¾	2¾ in. O.C.	1 15/16 in. O.C.
I	24½	2¾ in. O.C.	1 15/16 in. O.C.
J	22½	3 in. from center of spindle I	2 in. O.C.
K	19	4 in. from center of spindle J	2 in. O.C.
L	13½	3½ in. from center of spindle M	2 in. O.C.
M	10¾	2¾ in. from center of spindle N	2 in. O.C.
N	10¼	2⅝ in. from center of spindle O	2 in. O.C.
O	10½	2⅝ in. from center of stump	2 in. O.C.

* = Includes ¼ in. to ½ in. for trimming after assembly
O.C. = On center

Arm pattern

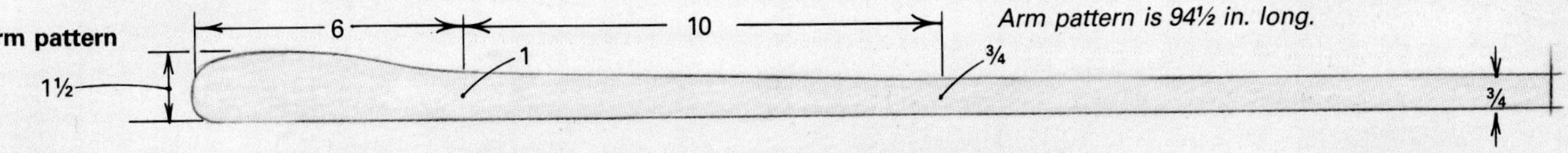

6
10
Arm pattern is 94½ in. long.
1½
1
¾
¾

Fig. 2: Planing jig

Jig, 4 in. wide by 100½ in. long, is 1⅝ in. thick at ends and tapers to ¾ in. thick in middle.

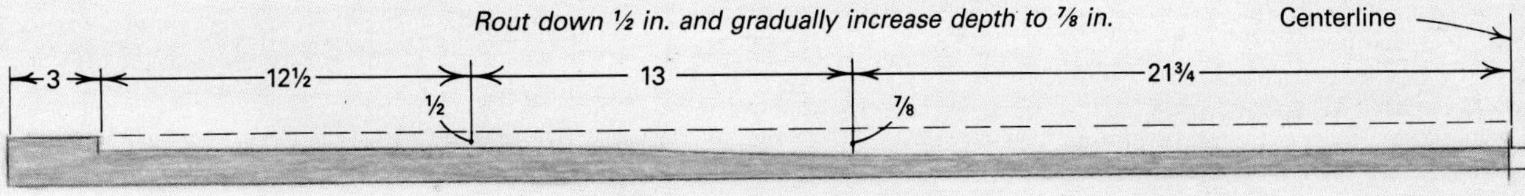

Rout down ½ in. and gradually increase depth to ⅞ in.
Centerline
3
12½
13
21¾
½
⅞

The leg and stump holes are bored from the top down, so any tearout is hidden on the bottom. The drill is guided by a notched scrap of 2x3x8 hardwood, crosscut on one end to the desired angle. Pencil lines drawn on the seat indicate the direction in which the angled legs lean.

locations for the legs, stumps and spindles on top of the blank. I laid out the holes in the seat using a compass to step off the center points of the holes about ⅞ in. in from the rear edge of the seat. The chart in figure 1 gives measurements for locating the spindle centers along the top of the seat, as well as the bow.

I drilled the leg and stump holes from the top down, so any tearout would be hidden on the bottom. The easiest way to get the holes at the right angle is to take a scrap of 2-in.-thick hardwood, about 3 in. wide and 8 in. long, and crosscut one end to the desired angle; I have one block with its end cut at 16° for the front legs and another cut at 22° for the back legs, and a separate 20° block for stumps. Cut a V-groove in the angled ends. After drawing the angle-guide lines on the top of the blank, place the guide block on the seat so that the drill bit rests in the V-groove and lines up with the center of the hole, as shown in the photo above. Make sure the other end of the block is centered on the angle-guide line, and drill away. Using the same system, drill the hole for the center spindle at 8° off vertical.

The seat can be carved with whatever tools you have: traditional gutter adze, chainsaw, body grinder or router-based carver. My favorite is the Woodcarver, a cutting head that fits on a small body grinder and removes wood at a ferocious pace (see the review in *FWW* #87, p. 124). I followed this with progressively finer sanding discs on the grinder and then hand-sanding. Regardless of method, start with a marking gauge fitted with a pencil to lay out the 1¾-in.-wide border supporting the spindles and stumps. When refining the seat shape, rely on your hands to find high and low spots, and sand them out. Finally, mortise the blank for the blocks that support the brace spindles, shown in figure 1.

The next phase of construction is lathe work—33 spindles, plus 6 legs, 5 stretchers and 2 stumps, as shown in figure 3. For strength and visual unity, the spindles should be from the same stock used for the bow. Turning spindles that taper from ⅝ in. dia. to ⅜ in. dia. can be a challenge; you'll need to use a steady rest or your hand to prevent the slender pieces from whipping. Sometimes I rough out the spindle with regular lathe tools, and then do the final smoothing on the lathe with a handplane, used like a skew chisel, and a body grinder (see *FWW* #69, p. 45).

Legs, stretchers and stumps are straightforward spindle turning, with dimensions as shown. Any hardwood can be used, although I prefer maple for its hardness and abrasion resistance. The legs are all identical, save those at the rear, which are cut 1½ in. shorter so

the seat will tilt backward comfortably. The center legs should be marginally shorter than the outer legs, to ensure that the bench doesn't rock from the center, but I simply trimmed them slightly after assembly. Once the turning is completed, bandsaw a slot in the end of each tenon to receive a wedge. I've found that cutting two slots ⅛ in. apart in the top tenon of the stumps is good insurance against any loosening from seasonal humidity fluctuations. Slots for the tops of the spindles are cut later; bottoms are not slotted.

Now is a convenient time to assemble the seat, legs and stretchers. Begin by dry-fitting the legs, aligning the wedge slots perpendicular to the seat grain. Now drill for the front to back stretchers. I did this freehand, using an extra-long auger bit in a slow-speed electric drill (see *FWW* #69, p. 46). Drill until the lead screw just begins to exit, and then remove the drill and complete the hole from the other side. Remove the legs, reassemble them with the front to back stretchers in place, and drill for the center stretchers. Now bandsaw some wedges: ½ in. wide for the stumps, ⅝ in. wide for the legs and ⅜ in. wide for the tops of the spindles; I prefer walnut for a visual accent, but you can use any hardwood. Swab all the mortises in the seat and undercarriage with glue, put a dab on the tenons and put it all together, driving a glue-coated wedge in each projecting tenon. Because of the long assembly time, I glued up everything with G2 epoxy, thickened with anti-sag powder and tinted with powdered stain, available from Lee Valley Tools Ltd., 1080 Morrison Drive, Ottawa, Ont., Canada K2H 8K7. Clean off squeeze-out with a rag dampened in glue solvent (alcohol works well with epoxy); after the glue has dried, trim the projecting tenons flush.

Assembling the back—You're now ready to drill the remaining spindle holes in the seat and bow. Before doing so, however, sand the bow to eliminate the fuzzy grain raised during steaming. If the grain has separated anywhere, line these splits with glue (stained with powdered pigments to match the final finish of the settee), and wrap them with waxed paper and several strips of inner tube.

Once the bow is completely smooth, dry-fit the stumps and the center spindle in their seat holes. As you recall, these holes were bored earlier before the seat was hollowed. Clamp the center of the bow to the top of the center spindle. To prevent splitting, clamp across the pad at the end of one arm. Now hold the arm in place on top of the spindle and drill the ½-in. hole for the stump, aligning the drill by eye. Once this is done, set the arm on the stump and repeat the process for the other arm. Now drill the ⅜-in. hole in the bow for the center spindle, and place the curved bow on the spindle.

The installed bow now becomes your guide for drilling the rest of the spindle holes in the seat, using the same extended auger bit as for the stretchers. Align the drill between the location marks on the seat and spindle and advance the bit until just the lead screw comes through the bottom of the seat; this guarantees that the hole is deep enough and provides an escape for hydraulic pressure when the spindle is inserted. Glue swept to the bottom of the hole during assembly fills the exit holes nicely.

After the seat holes are drilled, bore the matching holes in the bow with a brad-point bit mounted in a high-speed (2,500 RPM) drill. Traditionally, these holes were drilled by eye, but I built a jig (see figure 4) to make the process simpler and more reliable. This drilling jig is two blocks assembled with plywood squares and walnut strips. One block is fixed to a beam and one is movable. The outside strip on each is bored with a ⅜-in.-dia. hole. The hole in the movable block is a drill guide; the other houses a dowel or threaded rod protruding about 1 in. To use the jig, drop the dowel into a seat hole and clamp the sliding part just above the corresponding hole in the bow. Guide the bit through the hole and bore through the bow. Because of the angles of the holes, the bit may want to

Fig. 3: Lathe work

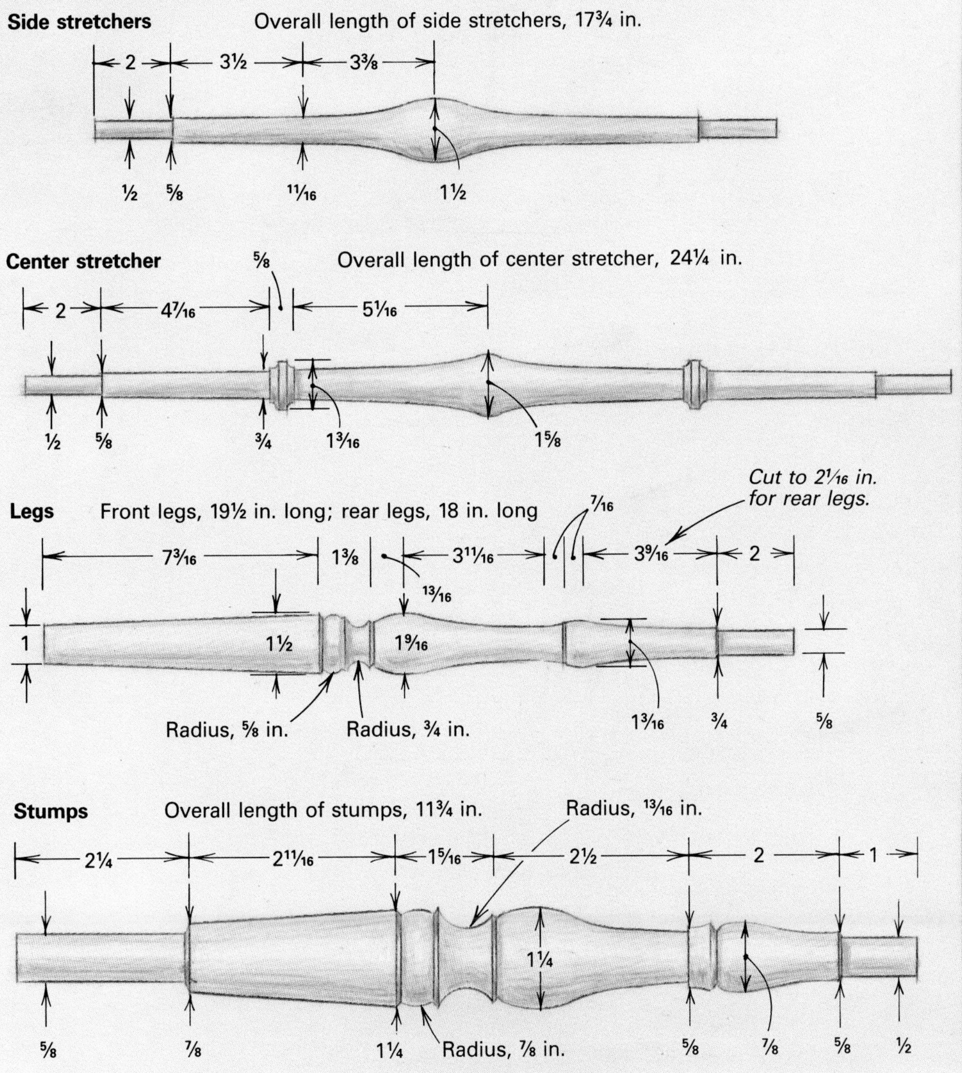
Side stretchers
Overall length of side stretchers, 17¾ in.
2
3½
3⅜
½
⅝
11⁄16
1½
Center stretcher
⅝
Overall length of center stretcher, 24¼ in.
2
4 7⁄16
5 1⁄16
½
⅝
¾
1 3⁄16
1⅝
Legs
Front legs, 19½ in. long; rear legs, 18 in. long
Cut to 2 1⁄16 in. for rear legs.
7⁄16
7 3⁄16
1⅜
3 11⁄16
3 9⁄16
2
13⁄16
1
1½
1 9⁄16
Radius, ⅝ in.
Radius, ¾ in.
1 3⁄16
¾
⅝
Stumps
Overall length of stumps, 11¾ in.
Radius, 13⁄16 in.
2¼
2 11⁄16
1 5⁄16
2½
2
1
1¼
⅝
⅞
1¼
Radius, ⅞ in.
⅝
⅞
⅝
½

Fig. 4: Drilling jig

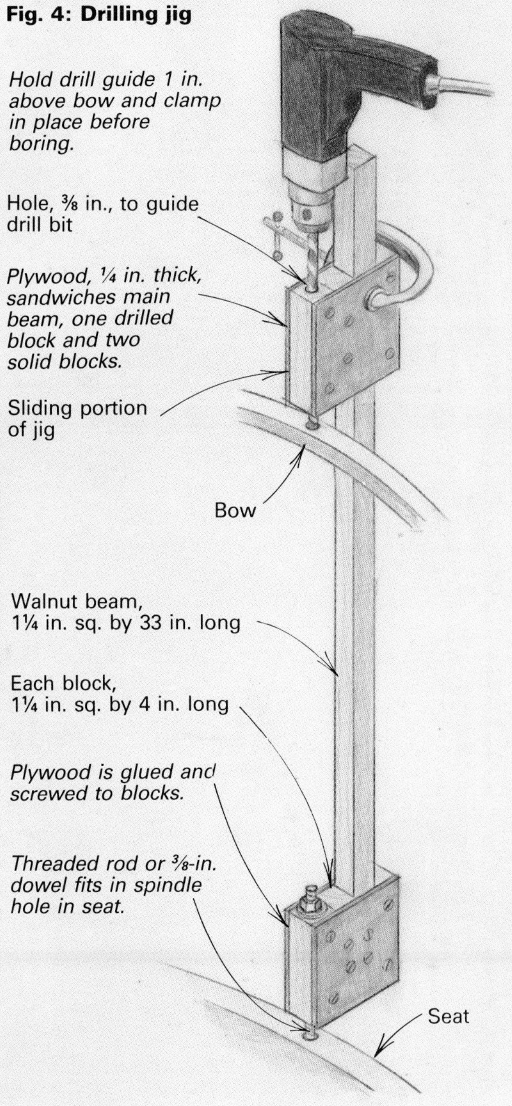
Hold drill guide 1 in. above bow and clamp in place before boring.
Hole, ⅜ in., to guide drill bit
Plywood, ¼ in. thick, sandwiches main beam, one drilled block and two solid blocks.
Sliding portion of jig
Bow
Walnut beam, 1¼ in. sq. by 33 in. long
Each block, 1¼ in. sq. by 4 in. long
Plywood is glued and screwed to blocks.
Threaded rod or ⅜-in. dowel fits in spindle hole in seat.
Seat

skitter off to one side. You can get around this by starting each hole by eye, holding the bit nearly perpendicular to the bow until the spurs begin to bite, and then slowly raising the drill into the proper line as the bit rotates. Use the drill guide to finish the hole.

When all the spindle holes are bored, you are ready for final assembly. First, dry-fit all the spindles in the bow (the extra-long tenons will slip well through). Then place the bow on the chair and insert the spindles one by one into the seat holes; this takes patience. When all the spindles are bottomed out in the seat, mark where each enters the bow. These marks are guides for trimming the spindles and cutting the wedge slots. When all the spindles are marked, use a rubber mallet to remove the bow, leaving the spindles in the seat. The spindles must remain in order, since each length is different. Remove one spindle at a time and slot it for a wedge, stopping each slot cut just above the mark where the spindle enters the bow. When you have done this, take a deep breath, disconnect the phone and get ready to glue up the back of the settee.

Start with the stumps. Swab glue into the holes in the seat and insert the stumps. Trim the projecting tenons close (not flush) to the bottom of the seat, drive a glue-coated wedge into the tenon and wipe off excess glue. Remove the spindles one by one from the seat and insert them in the corresponding holes in the bow, making sure that the slots in the spindles are perpendicular to the bow. Next, put glue in all the seat holes and on the upper tenons that project through the bow, and then set the spindle-and-bow assembly in place. Gradually work the spindles into the seat holes, drawing glue into the hole and fitting the arms to the stumps as you go. When everything is snug, wedge all the tenons in the bow and wipe off excess glue. Because the fourth spindle from each end enters and exits the bow at such an extreme angle, it is often reluctant to seat properly, even with a wedge. The solution here is to drive the wedge in delicately, and then wrap the protruding tenon with a couple of layers of waxed paper, followed by several wraps of tightly stretched strips of inner tube to clinch the bow on the tenon. This keeps everything where it belongs and eliminates any need to fill the joint later. Leave everything alone until the glue is thoroughly dry, and then trim the projecting tenons with a coping saw and smooth everything with a 120-grit disc on a body grinder and with hand-sanding. Your settee is now ready to finish.

Traditionally, Windsor chairs were painted, but most of my clients prefer clear finishes. This can be a problem since the woods used—ash, pine and maple—don't react to stain the same way; a wiping stain emphasizes differences, rather than blends them together. I use spray-on alcohol- or lacquer-base stains (non-grain-raising stains are available from many local and mail-order suppliers). Although they don't penetrate very deeply, I haven't experienced any chipping or wearing through, and they blend the wood colors without masking figure. After staining, apply a topcoat. I like tung oil-varnish mixtures, which develop a lovely soft patina over time. □

Mac Campbell designs and builds furniture in Harvey Station, N.B., Canada.

Design a Chair that Fits like a Glove

*An adjustable rig supplies
the critical dimensions
for comfort*

by Glenn Gordon

One size does not fit all, *whether you're talking shoes or chairs, and that's the premise behind John and Carolyn Grew-Sheridan's chair-fitting rig. The rig makes it possible to tailor a chair's contours and size to fit individuals, one at a time.*

"The problem of chair design is considered to be the most demanding in furniture—and for good reasons," says John Grew-Sheridan, who has thought about it a lot. Structural integrity is critical, even more so than for other furniture. At the same time, a chair must be comfortable and pleasing to the senses. The world has no shortage of ugly chairs that are comfortable or pretty chairs that aren't, so we have plenty of evidence that combining strength, comfort and comeliness in one design is not without its difficulties. San Francisco furnituremakers Carolyn and John Grew-Sheridan have worked out an approach to chair design that ensures a chair will be comfortable while demonstrating that "the dictates of comfort need not interfere with aesthetic considerations because," as John says, "there are an infinite number of ways to connect the critical structural and support points of a chair."

The Grew-Sheridans have been making chairs since 1975, and teaching others how to make them since 1980, when the University of California invited the couple to give a seminar on the subject. In preparing for the seminar, the Grew-Sheridans designed an adjustable rig for measuring individuals for custom-fitted chairs (see the photo above) and developed an inexpensive way of making full-scale mock-ups of their designs. Using the adjustable rig, they determine various chair dimensions, plot them as points on a graph and then transfer the coordinates onto a perspective drawing grid (available from art-supply stores). The result is a skeletal perspective

From *Fine Woodworking* (September 1992) 96:88-91

sketch, or stick figure of the chair, showing all the critical dimensional relationships but still devoid of any form or structure (see the drawing at right).

After working through the aesthetic and structural aspects of a chair's design on tracing paper over the grid, the Grew-Sheridans next make a full-scale model of the chair by laminating ordinary corrugated cardboard into "lumber" with thinned white glue, shaping the cardboard lumber into chair parts and hot gluing the "joints" (see the center photo). This technique allows them to make modifications with a minimum of effort, saving wood, money and grief.

From the general to the specific

The Grew-Sheridans gathered their information on essential body measurements for chair design from two publications. Most works on ergonomics, in trying to get to the bottom of seating comfort scientifically, proceed from an engineering mentality that tends to pay serious technical attention to everything except the seat of the pants. However, there are two classics in the field that Carolyn and John say they find tremendously useful. The first, a homely little pamphlet without the slightest aspiration to scientific importance, is called *Basic Design Measurements for Sitting* (by Clara Ridder, University of Arkansas, Agricultural Experiment Station, Fayetteville, Ark., 1959). The second is *Humanscale 1/2/3* (by Niels Diffrient et al., Cambridge, Mass., The MIT Press, 1978), a portfolio containing a booklet and three cleverly laid-out plastic reference cards with rotating dials. Turning these dials reveals all sorts of biometric data through numerous windows cut into the plastic cards. All the parts of the Grew-Sheridan's rig were sized, and the ranges for its various adjustments determined, from data in these two publications. The rig can accommodate just about any size human being, from the tiniest nymph to a nose tackle the size of a bison.

The beauty of the Grew-Sheridan's rig is its specificity because ideal chair dimensions—based on averages—exist only on paper. When a class of the Grew-Sheridan's chairmaking students averaged all their own measurements together and set up the rig accordingly, the result wasn't comfortable for a single person in the class. The chair industry (one size fits all) necessarily has to work to a happy medium, which will inevitably entail a certain amount of individual unhappiness. The Grew-Sheridans, meanwhile, have worked out a way for a custom chairmaker to make people happy, one at a time.

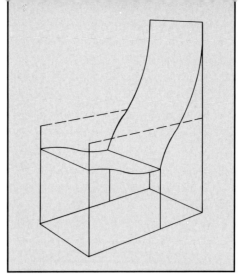

Photo below: Carolyn Grew-Sheridan

From plotted points to cardboard mock-up to finished chair, the Grew-Sheridan's process not only ensures that a chair will fit its owner perfectly but also that the chair's design will have been considered from every perspective, not just side and front views. By designing a chair in the round and building a prototype, a better-looking chair is almost guaranteed.

Finding and mapping a fit

The first step in the Grew-Sheridan's fitting procedure is to get a series of rough measurements of the person for whom the chair is being designed (see the sidebar on the following page for a detailed explanation of the fitting process). These initial measurements are taken with the person seated not in the rig but on a flat picnic bench or anything similar. The Grew-Sheridans then make preliminary adjustments to the rig based on those initial measurements and ask the person to have a seat. With the person seated in the rig, the Grew-Sheridans proceed to refine the rig's adjustments. Working by trial and error, and relying on their experience, they first establish an optimal seat depth, height and angle to the floor (in that order), and then they establish the height of the armrests (when appropriate) and the angle of the back to the seat. Then they adjust the series of back supports on the back rail, working from bottom (sacral support) to top (head support).

When all adjustments have been made so that the rig feels right to the sitter, the settings of the rig (in side view) are plotted on graph paper, along with distances measured from the floor to various points on the body (to determine a horizontal reference). Connect the dots, and you have a side view of a chair—or, more accurately, not of the chair itself, but of the "comfort-curve" for the person being fitted.

The next step is to render that view in a three-quarter front view using a perspective grid, as shown in the drawing above. This provides a three-dimensional skeletal view of the chair, a perspective armature over which can be drawn, on tracing paper, any number of structural and stylistic variations. Every chair sketched will be in scale, will show the correct curves and angle for the back, and will have the seat the right height and angle off the floor. Each variant drawn will be the same size and depicted from the same point of view as all the rest for clear, side-by-side comparisons.

From paper to prototype

The Grew-Sheridan's adjustable rig can help a designer resolve questions about a chair's size, proportions and comfort, but neither the rig nor the perspective sketches generated with it can give you a realistic representation of the chair in the round. A perspective sketch can take you part of the way, but it's easy to ruin lumber: If you have a change of heart about a detail halfway through building a chair, it can cost you.

It's helpful, therefore—before you cut

any stock—to see what a chair will look like in three dimensions. One way to do that is to make a scale model. A better way is to make a full-size mock-up. The Grew-Sheridan's technique for making full-size mock-ups is quick, cheap and surprisingly effective at evoking the look of the finished chair. The material they use—corrugated cardboard, found just about anywhere—usually for free—has good modeling properties: body, thickness and even a certain amount of strength. Using thinned white glue, they laminate the cardboard to whatever dimension of stock they need, then draw the pattern for, say, a chair arm on it, and bandsaw it out just as though they were working a piece of wood. They then use disc sanders, rasps and files to shape the arm, which goes quickly because the corrugated cardboard is really mostly air. Because the material is so easily worked and can usually be had for nothing, there's no reluctance to experiment.

Form follows function

Practicality, directness and an economy of means characterize the Grew-Sheridan's work as chairmakers. Their premise as designers is reflected in some passages John quotes from *Form and Function*, by Horace Greenough, first published in 1843: "The most beautiful chairs," wrote Greenough, "invite you by a promise of ease, and they keep that promise; they bear neither flowers nor dragons nor idle displays of the turner's caprice."

Fitting the chair to the customer

by Carolyn and John Grew-Sheridan

The first step in the fitting process is to measure the person sitting on a plain flat bench. This provides a set of starting measurements of the person's body that we can transfer to the rig. We're careful to make absolutely clear to the person we're fitting that this is *only* a preliminary setting or starting point. We've found if we don't emphasize this point, often people will refrain from telling us that the seat-to-back angle's too acute or the thoracic support is too low. We try to loosen them up and get them involved in the fitting process.

Taking measurements

The first measurement, known as the popliteal, is taken by measuring from the floor to the underside of the thigh at the knee. The customer should have on the same shoes that will typically be worn when sitting in the chair. Then we measure from that same point in the crook of the knee to the surface of the back. Next, holding a yardstick against the person's back with the end of the yardstick on the bench, we measure the height of the waist. We determine the location of the waist by having the customer bend to the side while seated. As it turns out, if you carry the waist measurement around to the back, that's just about where most people like to feel lumbar support.

We measure from seat to elbow to determine armrest height and note the relaxed spread of the arms as well for the width of the armrest at the elbows. The angle of the armrest is less predictable, we've found, so we just experiment until we hit upon a comfortable angle. Next, we measure from the seat to the underarm. This measurement is required for dining chairs in particular because it tells you approximately where to position upper back support.

Just as a dining chair requires upper back support, each type of chair has its own special traits and requirements. All chairs need to be wide enough in the seat—obviously—to get in and out of, so we take a seated hip width measurement; shoulder width isn't that significant a measurement unless you're building a chair that will partially envelop its owner, such as a large stuffed chair or recliner. Nevertheless, while we're measuring, we get all the information we can; there's no telling when a client we're fitting for a reading chair will want to order a set of dining chairs.

The final two vertical measurements that we take are from the seat to the nape of the neck and from the seat to the back of the head. These measurements are most critical for a chair designed primarily for relaxing in, where head support is absolutely essential.

Next, with the yardstick (or some other straight edge) still in place against the person's back and the person sitting up straight, we measure the horizontal distance from straight edge to lumbar (waist measurement transferred to the back), then from straight edge to the juncture of head and neck (the nape) and last, from straight edge to the back of the head.

Adjusting the rig

Setting the rig is straightforward once we've got all the above measurements (see the drawing on the facing page for information on where various parts of the rig are adjusted). The measurements and angles vary for different kinds of chairs, but for the sake of explanation, let's presuppose we're designing a reading chair. (Information on the requirements for various types of chairs can be found in the book, *Basic Design Measurements for Sitting*, mentioned on the previous page.) We set the seat depth first to about 2 in. less than the measured under-thigh length and then set the seat height at the knee to about 3 in. less than the popliteal measurement. We drop the rear of the seat 3 in. from the front setting (or 5 in. from the popliteal). We set the arm width at the elbow next (this generally falls in a fairly narrow range—between 21 in. and 23 in.) and then set the arm height at the elbow about 1 in. to 2 in. greater than the seat-to-elbow measurement.

For this preliminary setting, we position the back at 105° to the seat. Since we're adjusting the rig to fit the customer, this seat-to-back angle will often change. If we run out of range as we're adjusting the settings of the back supports, we can change the seat-to-back angle.

We adjust all the back supports using the measurements just taken, beginning with the sacral (1 in. forward of the back rail, 3 in. up from the seat). Proceeding up the back, we adjust the lumbar support—probably the most important— (usually 8 in. to 10 in. up, 1 in. to 2 in. forward of the back rail), thoracic support (set at the height of the underarm, at the same distance from the back rail as the sacral adjustment) and, finally, the neck and head supports. These last adjustments vary widely: a survey of 55 of our former and current chairbuilding students revealed a vertical range of 14 in.

From this point on, it's really just a question of using your common sense and making increasingly finer adjustments. The chair's intended use, how it will relate to other furnishings (such as a dining or end table) and whether the chair's owner wears heels, flats, sneakers (or is barefoot) all need to be considered when translating the information gathered on the rig into a chair design. When we schedule a fitting, we encourage the customer to bring whatever is necessary to make the fitting absolutely realistic. That might mean a pair of slippers and a book or a newspaper—or even a bowl, spoon, box of corn flakes and a quart of milk. Pretending to eat a bowl of cereal while reading the paper just isn't the same as actually doing it, and we want the chair to be comfortable in use. □

_____

Carolyn and John Grew-Sheridan design and build furniture and teach furniture-making in San Francisco.

"Greenough was searching for great principles of construction," explained Carolyn. "He argued that one should first look at the use and only then turn to the decorative elements. He believed the conflict in design is between the essential and the pretentious." In other words, everything in the design of an object, whether it's a canoe or a shoe or a chair, ought to be subordinate to function. If this idea is respected—if function is clearly understood and sympathetically addressed and the consciousness of it extended to such considerations as the chair's interaction with the sitter's body, the finish of the wood, the feel of the fabrics, the intention in the flare of the curves—form will flow from it. The most comfortable (and the most beautiful) chairs aren't conceived as cakes to be decorated with a pastry tube. The beauty of a chair—whether it's the ancient Greek Klismos chair or one of Hans Wegner's contemporary pieces—comes instead from the character of its response to structural necessity. They maintain a tradition in the design of functional objects in which practicality and beauty aren't at odds but are rather in equilibrium—are, in fact, one and the same, a tradition that John and Carolyn Grew-Sheridan are helping to sustain. □

Glenn Gordon, a writer and craftsman, lives in St. Paul, Minn. His past contributions to FWW include articles on James Krenov and Gerritt Rietveld.

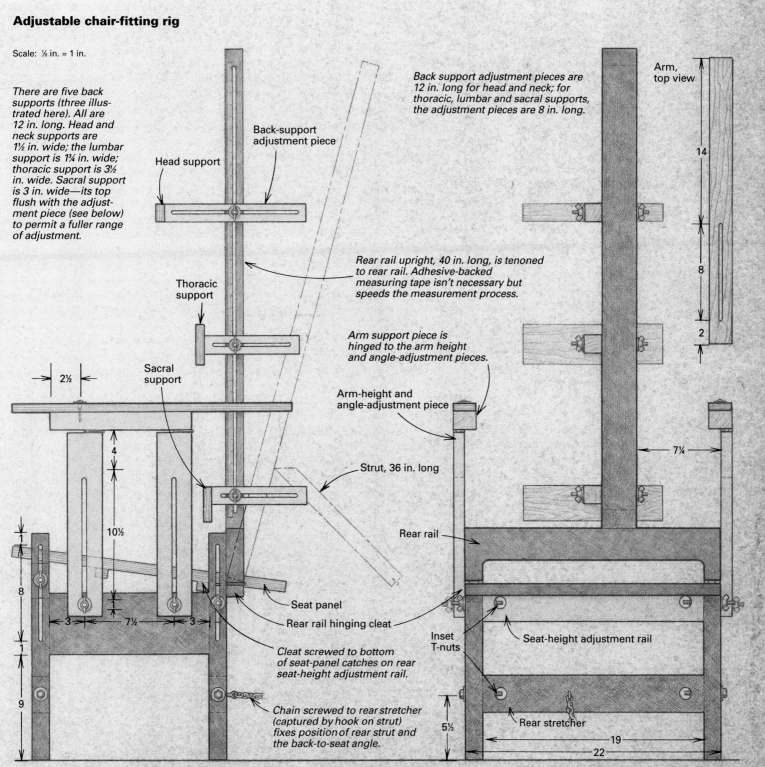

Adjustable chair-fitting rig

Scale: ⅛ in. = 1 in.

There are five back supports (three illustrated here). All are 12 in. long. Head and neck supports are 1½ in. wide; the lumbar support is 1¼ in. wide; thoracic support is 3½ in. wide. Sacral support is 3 in. wide—its top flush with the adjustment piece (see below) to permit a fuller range of adjustment.

Head support

Back-support adjustment piece

Thoracic support

Sacral support

2½

Back support adjustment pieces are 12 in. long for head and neck; for thoracic, lumbar and sacral supports, the adjustment pieces are 8 in. long.

Rear rail upright, 40 in. long, is tenoned to rear rail. Adhesive-backed measuring tape isn't necessary but speeds the measurement process.

Arm support piece is hinged to the arm height and angle-adjustment pieces.

Arm-height and angle-adjustment piece

Strut, 36 in. long

Rear rail

Arm, top view

14

8

2

7¼

4

10½

1
8
1

3   7½   3

1
9

Seat panel

Rear rail hinging cleat

Cleat screwed to bottom of seat-panel catches on rear seat-height adjustment rail.

Chain screwed to rear stretcher (captured by hook on strut) fixes position of rear strut and the back-to-seat angle.

Inset T-nuts

Seat-height adjustment rail

Rear stretcher

5½

19

22

Side elevation

Rear elevation (seat removed)

Built for Comfort: The Three-Slat Chair

Correct curves are key to comfort, durability

by Christian H. Becksvoort

Shaped seat and curved back slats provide comfort, while curved, laminated back legs ensure the chair will be able to withstand lots of racking and abuse.

Comfortable chairs, especially wooden chairs, are notoriously difficult to design. Consequently, I'm always on the lookout for good chairs. Whether in a restaurant, at a friend's house or in a waiting room, every time I sit down, I instinctively analyze what makes my seat comfortable, or not.

Several years ago, my wife bought a double folding chair at a flea market for the grand total of $2. The chair is of a style that was mass-produced around the turn of the century and used almost everywhere, in auditoriums, schools, Grange halls and libraries. Although not much to look at, it's a very comfortable chair. The two contact points, the seat and back, are well-formed and provide support right where it's needed. I decided to borrow the back curve and seat shape, the elements that make the chair so comfortable, and incorporate these features into a nonfolding, four-legged dining chair with mortise-and-tenon construction.

I also adjusted the back angle to 14° from vertical because the original was a little too "laid-back" for a dining chair. After a series of sketches, I came up with the chair shown above and in the drawing on pp. 116-117. Once I'd worked out the details, I made a full-sized drawing from which I later made patterns for each chair part.

Simple form makes bent-lamination easy. Plywood scraps form two mating halves with square outside edges to provide even clamping pressure over the length of the back-leg lamination.

Laminating and shaping the legs

One of the first decisions I made was to laminate the curved back legs rather than cut them from a big blank. Having repaired countless older chairs, I've learned that curved back legs cut from solid stock are extremely vulnerable to breaking: The short grain where leg meets floor invariably breaks, sometimes with the slightest tap.

I made a form for the leg-blank lamination from six pieces of scrap ¾-in. plywood. I bandsawed the plywood to rough shape and then disc-sanded the two halves of the glued-together form until I had a fair, smooth curve on each half with a nice match between the two.

I cut ⁵⁄₁₆-in.-thick strips for the lamination from a 4-in.-wide piece of 16/4 stock that was 38-in. long. That way, I was able to match the grain from front to back and get both back legs from the same lamination. I marked each bandsawn strip in order of cut, applied glue between each, wrapped them in plastic wrap so they wouldn't stick to the form and clamped them in the form for 24 hours (see the photo at left). The next day, I cut the lamination in half lengthwise along its face, ran the outside edge of both pieces over the jointer and then ripped them to 1½ in.

I cut the back legs so that the tops are

35 in. high and the bottoms are at 73° to the floor (see the drawing on p. 117). Then I marked and disc-sanded a flat section perpendicular to the floor on the front faces of the back legs, where the side rails will intersect the legs.

Next I bandsawed a taper on the inside edges of the bottom section of the back legs, from 1 in. sq. at the floor to 1½ in. sq. just below the flat at the side-rail intersection (about 12½ in. from the floor). I also tapered the tops of the back legs to 1 in. wide on their inner edges, as viewed from the back (see the drawing on p. 116), and to ¾ in. front to back, cut from the back and originating just above the flat for the side-rail intersection. If I'd tapered the tops of the back legs on their front edges, I would have changed the seat-back angle, making the chair slightly less comfortable.

I prepared the two front legs of the chair by jointing, planing, ripping and crosscutting rough 8/4 stock to end up with two 1½x1½x17½ blanks. Then I tapered them on their inside faces from 1 in. sq. at the floor to 1½ in. sq., 3 in. from their tops.

Leg-to-rail joinery

I used mortise-and-tenon construction on this chair because it has no stretchers, so the strongest possible leg-to-rail joinery was necessary. I laid out all the rails with a ³⁄₁₆-in. reveal at the leg intersections except the back rail, which I made flush to the inside of the chair.

I cut the four rails from rough 4/4 stock that I planed to thickness and cut to shape from my full-sized patterns. The front and back rails start out as 2¼-in.-wide blanks, but the side rails start out 3¼ in. wide to allow for the bandsawn curve that dictates the seat's contour. This takes the side rails down to 2¼ in. Also, I cut the side rails at 5° on both ends (85° in the front and 95° in the back), which makes them parallel, though slightly skewed uphill.

At this point, I cut the tenons to fit the mortises. All tenons are centered on the rails except for the back rail. I offset it to within ¹⁄₁₆ in. of the back face to keep it from being too close to the inside corner of the leg, thus compromising the integrity of the joint. Next I dry-fitted the legs and rails together. I held the chair together with band clamps while I checked the fit of the joints, dimensions of parts and angles. While the chair was dry-clamped, I also cut a wooden pattern of the seat profile (from the side) and of the back slats (from the top) from my full-sized drawing. I drew the pattern for the back slats by swinging a pair of 18-in.-long arcs, ½-in. apart, using a piece of string to create a 41¾ in. radius. Then I laid this pattern onto the top of the two back rails so that the back of the pattern intersects the front outside corners of both back legs. I scribed this line of intersection onto the top of the back legs, extended the line down the insides of the legs and then jointed down to the line, using the jointer fence to maintain the angle. Given the leg spacing and the radius of the back slats, the scribe marks formed about an 11° angle from the front edges of the legs, allowing the back slats to sit flush against the back legs. At this stage, I finish-sanded the four legs

and rails to 320-grit. Then I assembled the back legs and rail as a unit, pinned the joints and set the assembly aside to dry. I did the same for the front assembly. When it was dry, I connected the two assemblies by gluing and pinning the two curved side rails.

Making the seat

I cut the seat from a 6-in.-wide, 17-in.-long piece of 16/4 stock, choosing a piece with nice color and devoid of sapwood. I also laid out the pattern on the flatsawn face of the board so that the seat surface would be quartersawn (see the top photo on p. 116). This reduces the amount the seat will move side to side, and it's quite attractive. Also, the parallel grain makes it less obvious that the seat is glued up from a number of pieces. I jointed the edges and glued the seat blank together. When the blank was dry, I bandsawed the seat to match the pattern and then disc-sanded to fair in the four curved edges.

Shaping the seat top and bottom is probably the most time-consuming step in the whole chairmaking process. I clamped the seat upside down between two bench dogs and beltsanded across the grain with an 80-grit belt. I've found that by holding the sander perpendicular to the grain but moving it in a rocking motion with the grain, I can remove stock quickly without gouging the workpiece. As it turned out, the concave portion of the underside of the seat near the front legs was just about the tightest radius possible with this technique, but it worked. I flipped the seat over and sanded the top using the same technique. The top went much faster because its concave section was so much shallower.

Next I use a 1-in. by 5-in. soft sanding pad (available from Econ-Abrasives, P.O. Box 865021, Plano, Texas 75086; 800-367-4101) chucked into an electric drill. This soft pad, with a 100-grit disc on it, took out the 80-grit cross-grain scratches and conformed well to the contour of the seat. I repeated on the front and the back of the seat through 180-grit paper. Then I switched to a round, 5-in. orbital finish sander at 220-grit because it leaves fewer and smaller swirl marks. I continued with the finish sander through 320-grit.

When the seat was smooth and scratch-free, I beveled its sides and back edge. I shaped the front edge to a rounded point (see the drawing on p. 117). This went quickly using a combination of block plane, rasp, file and sandpaper. The seat was now ready to be fitted to the chair. I did this with a couple of sheets of carbon paper, using a technique similar to one used by machinists with their bluing (see the box above).

Because the back of the seat is beveled and has such a pronounced curve, the ends of the back rail are exposed (see the drawing on p. 117). This doesn't provide as much support for the seat as I'd like, so I added a second rail on the inside of the back of the chair. I glued and screwed it to the inside of the back rail and made sure it's tight and flush to that original rail. For additional strength and because the chair has no stretchers, I added corner

---

Fitting a shaped seat

To fit a seat that isn't flat onto a base that is takes a bit of trial and error. I place the seat in position on the chair base, its back edge touching the back legs and its sides centered. By looking beneath the seat on the sides, I can see where the high points are and where I need to remove stock from the rails and legs. Most of the fitting involves fairing into the front legs and hollowing out the side rails where the back of the seat is lowest. With the chair base clamped into the bench vise for stability, I use my belt sander with an 80-grit belt to do most of the work. After one or two test-fittings, the seat begins to look like it belongs on the chair.

By now, points of contact have become difficult to see. To circumvent this, I take two sheets of carbon paper (yes, its still available at office-supply stores) and place them, carbon side down, on the front edge of the chair. I press the seat down and move it slightly back and forth, which leaves dark patches at the points of contact. I work down these points with a rasp and file. After just a few more fittings, I've got a custom fit between seat and chair base. —C.B.

Photos except where noted: Charley Robinson

Quartersawn blank from flatsawn stock. Quartersawn lumber is more stable than flatsawn and is easier to grain-match, but it's hard to come by and more expensive. By starting with thicker stock and laying out adjacent seat parts on top of each other across a board's width, the author created quartersawn parts.

Achieving a nearly perfect grain and color match is possible by sawing the pieces from the same board. A steady hand and slow feed rate will keep the cuts on line, and sanding will take out the slight bandsaw ripple seen on the outside face of this board.

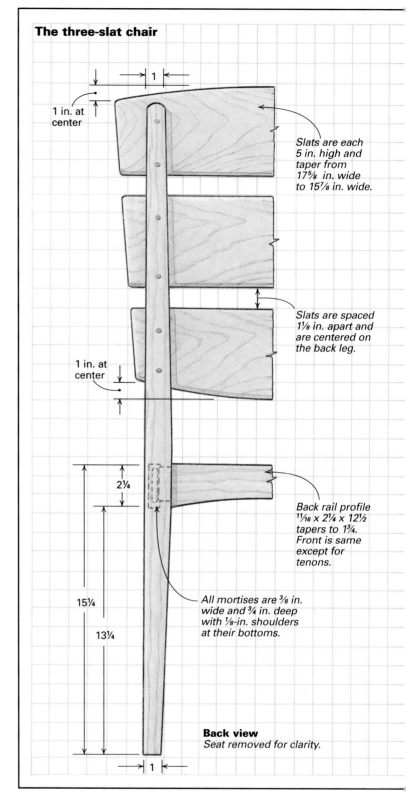

The three-slat chair

1 in. at center

Slats are each 5 in. high and taper from 17⅝ in. wide to 15⅞ in. wide.

Slats are spaced 1⅛ in. apart and are centered on the back leg.

1 in. at center

2¼

Back rail profile ¹¹⁄₁₆ x 2¼ x 12½ tapers to 1¾. Front is same except for tenons.

15¼

All mortises are ⅜ in. wide and ¾ in. deep with ⅛-in. shoulders at their bottoms.

13¼

1

Back view
Seat removed for clarity.

blocks to the inside of each corner, notching the front blocks on the bandsaw to accommodate the leg corners. When screwing these blocks into place, I'm careful not to mount the blocks too high, which would interfere with the fit of the seat.

At this point, I finish-sanded the seat by hand to 600-grit. Then I screwed the seat to the chair base with two screws up through the front rail and two through the auxiliary back rail, both of them about 6 in. apart.

Preparing the back slats

I took my pattern for the back slats from the full-sized drawing, transferred the shape three times onto a piece of 18-in.-long, 5-in.-

wide 12/4 stock and bandsawed the slats out (see the bottom photo). This keeps the grain and color nearly the same on all three slats, from top to bottom. I shaped the top and bottom slats by giving them the same radius at the corners (viewed from the front) that I gave them front to back by cutting them on the bandsaw (see the drawing above). I also tapered the slats' width from top to bottom. I set the slats on my bench and used spacers to keep the slats 1⅛ in. apart as they will be on the chair. I marked a 1¾-in. taper from the top corner of the top slat down to the bottom corner of the bottom slat, bandsawed to the line and then smoothed the taper with rasp and file.

I repeated the sanding process I used on legs, rails and seat, ex-

Drawing: Heather Lambert

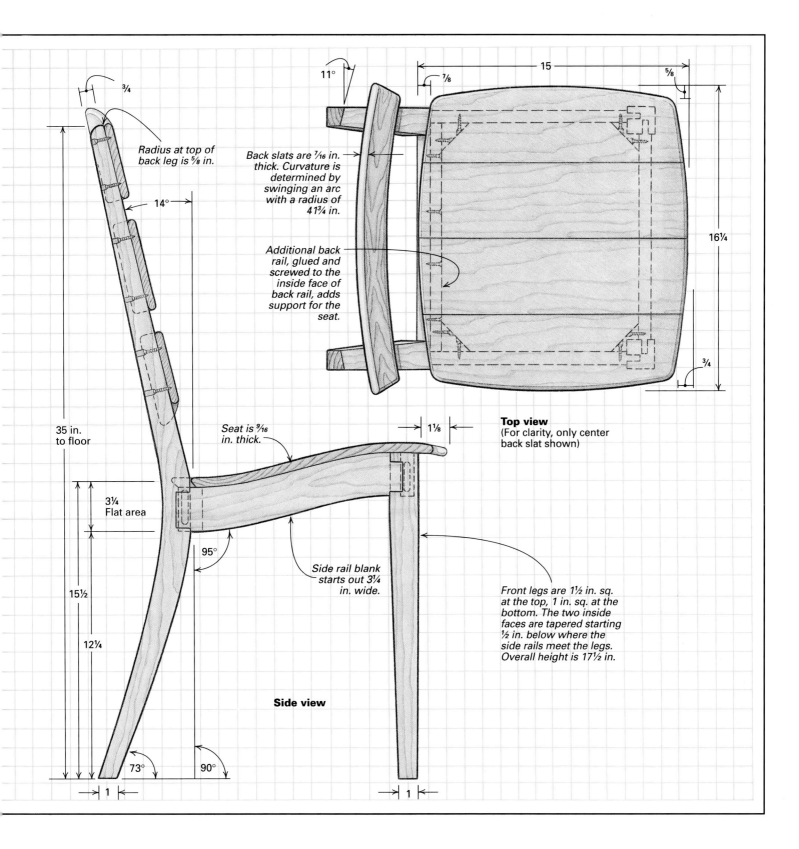

3/4

11°

15

5/8

Radius at top of back leg is 5/8 in.

Back slats are 7/16 in. thick. Curvature is determined by swinging an arc with a radius of 41 3/4 in.

14°

Additional back rail, glued and screwed to the inside face of back rail, adds support for the seat.

16 1/4

3/4

35 in. to floor

Seat is 9/16 in. thick.

1 1/8

Top view
(For clarity, only center back slat shown)

3 1/4 Flat area

95°

Side rail blank starts out 3 1/4 in. wide.

15 1/2

12 1/4

Front legs are 1 1/2 in. sq. at the top, 1 in. sq. at the bottom. The two inside faces are tapered starting 1/2 in. below where the side rails meet the legs. Overall height is 17 1/2 in.

73°

90°

Side view

1

1

cept that I used a pneumatic spindle sander for grits 80 through 150. A random-orbit sander will also do the job, just not as quickly. I also rounded all the edges on the front faces of the back slats at this time to make the seat more comfortable and to give the chair a softer appearance overall.

I clamped the slats to the chair temporarily with spring clamps, the top one at 36 in. from the floor, the other two with 1 1/8-in. spaces separating them. Then I marked the centers of the back legs, top to bottom, and I located the screw holes, two per slat on each leg.

I removed the slats and drilled countersunk pilot holes for the screws from the back side of the legs. Because the back slats were

only 7/16 in. thick after sanding, I drilled through the leg just until 5/16 in. of the bit was showing. Then I reclamped the slats to the back legs and drilled into the slats until I felt the countersunk portion of the bit just bottom out. Finally, I glued and screwed the slats to the legs, plugged the screw holes carefully and resanded the backs of the legs.

I used three coats of tung oil as a finish. For a final touch, I added leather pads to the bottoms of the legs to protect fine hardwood floors from being scratched by the end grain of the chair legs. □

Christian H. Becksvoort builds custom furniture in New Gloucester, Maine and is a contributing editor to Fine Woodworking.

Craftsman-Style Comfort in a Morris Chair

Mortise-and-tenon joinery looks good and makes it last

by Gene Lehnert

Forerunner of today's recliners, this Morris chair built in the Craftsman tradition features an adjustable reclining back. The back, which pivots on pegs, rests on removable pins that slide into holes on the inside of the arms. To recline the back, simply move the adjustment pins to different holes in the arms. To make his chair even more comfortable, the author also built a matching footstool.

Photos: William Sampson

The Morris-style spindle chair is my favorite Gustav Stickley piece. In his popular *Craftsman* magazine, Stickley wrote, "No better or more comfortable and useful chair was ever designed." The chair, which features pinned through-tenon joinery, makes a comfortable, adjustable-back chair in the Craftsman tradition. I worked up this version (see the photo at left) after looking at a lot of museum pieces and studying examples in Stickley's *Craftsman* magazine, books and other magazine articles.

Although Stickley sometimes used other woods, his primary choice was quartersawn white oak, which he darkened by fuming with ammonia. Even in his day, Stickley commented that quartersawing was a wasteful method of woodcutting. Today, the wood is rather difficult to find. However, larger retail suppliers have it for about $5 a board foot. It should be selected for color match and figure. Be extra careful when choosing the stock because variations in wood tone mar color uniformity during the fuming process, a finishing technique I'll discuss later in this article. Sapwood should be eliminated as it tends not to darken when fumed.

Building the chair

The legs are composed of a solid core with ⅛-in.-thick veneers glued around them. Veneering this way provides uniform quartersawn figure on all four sides of the legs. The through-tenons at the leg tops are 1½ in. sq. with bevels on the ends, as shown in the drawing on p. 120. I use my motorized miter box set at an angle of 12° to cut the bevels. On the back legs, the tops are both beveled and slanted, using a disc sander, to match the angle of the arms. Note that the shoulders on these tenons are angled to support the arms. Because pinned through mortise-and-tenon joints are Stickley hallmarks, it is important they be properly executed. Also, note the corbels that support the rear arms are angled at the tops.

The bottom side rails are supported also using pinned through mortise-and-tenon joints. I use a hollow-chisel mortiser in my drill press to cut the mortises in the legs and the ½-in. spindle mortises in the rails. The work is held on an angle block clamped to the drill-press table. The slant of the angle block is 1 in. rise to 24¾ in. run. I clamp the same angle block to my tablesaw's sliding table to cut the angled tenon shoulders of the top and bottom side rails and the spindles.

Because of their angles, the upper and lower shoulders on the rails and the front and back shoulders on the spindles must be pared by hand. The tenons for the upper side rails are cut before their top slants are cut. I sometimes cut the tenons using an angled sliding table on my router table. These techniques ensure precisely fitting mortise-and-tenon joints for the legs, rails and spindles.

Making the arms—When you first look at one of Stickley's Morris chairs from the side, you get the impression the arms are sawn from thick pieces of wood. What else could explain the bend at the front of the arm? But upon close inspection, Stickley's ingenuity is apparent. To form the bend on the front of each arm, I follow Stickley's lead and glue a filler block to the underside of the arm board. Then I bevel off the top

What is a Morris chair?

Barbara Streisand melodically asked, "What kind of a chair is a Morris chair?" in her early 1960s recording of "My Honey's Loving Arms." Perhaps some listeners then pondered the answer to this question, but renewed interest in Morris chairs and in other Craftsman-style furniture did not really spark until the '80s.

Gustav Stickley and other furniture builders in the early part of this century produced several styles of chairs that were patterned after the designs of Englishman William Morris. *Morris chair* became a generic term for easy chairs with movable, slanting backs. These chairs were the forerunners of today's reclining chairs. Stickley's spindle chair, introduced in 1905, proved to be the most popular of all. Although the term *spindle* usually refers to turned posts, Stickley and Morris used square spindles.

A picture of the original Morris chair appeared in Gustav Stickley's *Craftsman* magazine. He said of it, "This chair has always seemed to be the best of its kind, and one especial advantage is that it harmonizes in structural effect with any good furniture."

Stickley was a successful furnituremaker for a quarter of a century until 1916 when he went out of business. His Craftsman furniture, sometimes called Mission style, is once again gaining great popularity. *—G.L.*

with repeated cross-grain passes on the radial-arm saw, as shown in the bottom left photo on p. 121. (You could also bandsaw away the waste.) Taking care to match color and grain will make the joint barely discernible. I cut the filler block from the same board to ensure the match.

To hold the arm at the correct angle on my radial-arm saw table when cutting the slope, I use an angle block. The angle is 3⅞ in. rise to 22¾ in. run. I also use this block with the drill-press mortiser to cut the through-mortises in the arms (see the right photo on p. 121).

To accommodate the upper rail, I cut a ⅞-in.-wide, ½-in.-deep groove from one mortise to the other and centered on those mortises. Though it's a tedious process, I use my hollow-chisel mortiser to cut the groove because the bend in the arm prevents me from plowing it all the way through with a router. A router and chisel could be combined to do the job.

Building the back

This part of the chair is perhaps the trickiest. It involves three things—bending the ⅜-in.-thick back slats, cutting long tenons that fit perpendicular to the back posts and assembling the unit so it lies flat.

You can steam the slats in preparation for bending, but I prefer to submerge the slats in boiling water for softening because it's faster and easier. If you do boil the slats, it is a good idea to add a small amount of baking soda to avoid prematurely blackening the wood. This reaction is characteristic of oak. If blackening should occur, the original color can be restored using oxalic acid, which is readily available at hardware stores (see *Fine Woodworking* #86, pp. 65-67).

The slats have a radius of 23 in. To bend them, I sandwich them in a shop-built form made from two bandsawn blocks that mate to create a 22-in. radius, which overbends the wood a little to allow for inevitable springback. Allow the wood to dry completely in the form to prevent excessive springback.

Before cutting the tenons perpendicular to the back posts, small oak wedges (1 in. by ¼ in.) have to be glued to the back of each slat where the tenons will be cut, as shown in drawing detail C on p. 120. The wedge provides enough stock for cutting the long tenons while keeping them perpendicular to the back posts.

I have to admit that I really enjoy devising machine setups. While creating fixtures and jigs to solve joinery problems initially takes more time, it gives me pleasure and ensures accuracy when working

Making a Morris chair

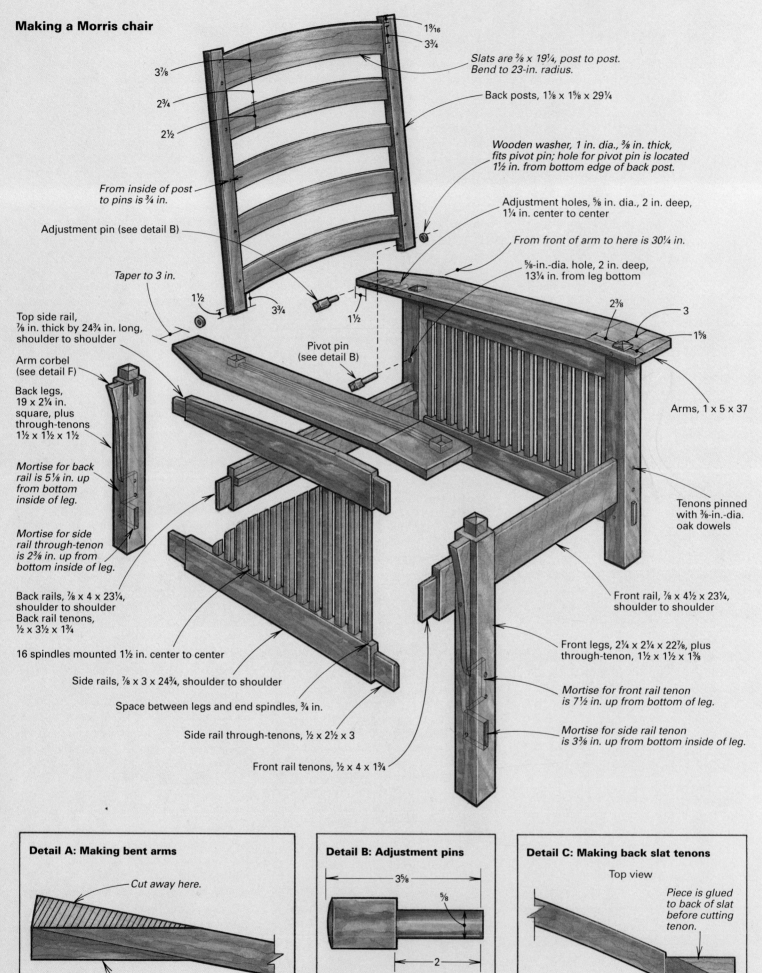

Slats are ⅜ x 19¼, post to post.
Bend to 23-in. radius.

1⁹⁄₁₆

3¾

3⅞

2¾

2½

Back posts, 1⅛ x 1⅝ x 29¼

Wooden washer, 1 in. dia., ⅜ in. thick,
fits pivot pin; hole for pivot pin is located
1½ in. from bottom edge of back post.

From inside of post
to pins is ¾ in.

Adjustment pin (see detail B)

Adjustment holes, ⅝ in. dia., 2 in. deep,
1¼ in. center to center

From front of arm to here is 30¼ in.

⅝-in.-dia. hole, 2 in. deep,
13¼ in. from leg bottom

Taper to 3 in.

1½

3¾

1½

2⅜

3

1⅝

Top side rail,
⅞ in. thick by 24¾ in. long,
shoulder to shoulder

Pivot pin
(see detail B)

Arm corbel
(see detail F)

Back legs,
19 x 2¼ in.
square, plus
through-tenons
1½ x 1½ x 1½

Arms, 1 x 5 x 37

Mortise for back
rail is 5⅛ in. up
from bottom
inside of leg.

Mortise for side
rail through-tenon
is 2⅜ in. up from
bottom inside of leg.

Tenons pinned
with ⅜-in.-dia.
oak dowels

Back rails, ⅞ x 4 x 23¼,
shoulder to shoulder
Back rail tenons,
½ x 3½ x 1¾

16 spindles mounted 1½ in. center to center

Front rail, ⅞ x 4½ x 23¼,
shoulder to shoulder

Front legs, 2¼ x 2¼ x 22⅞, plus
through-tenon, 1½ x 1½ x 1⅜

Side rails, ⅞ x 3 x 24¾, shoulder to shoulder

Space between legs and end spindles, ¾ in.

Mortise for front rail tenon
is 7½ in. up from bottom of leg.

Side rail through-tenons, ½ x 2½ x 3

Mortise for side rail tenon
is 3⅜ in. up from bottom inside of leg.

Front rail tenons, ½ x 4 x 1¾

Detail A: Making bent arms

Cut away here.

Add wood here.

Detail B: Adjustment pins

3⅝

⅝

2

Pivot pins for the back have the
same dimensions as the adjustment pins, except the shaft is
3½ in. long instead of 2 in.

Detail C: Making back slat tenons

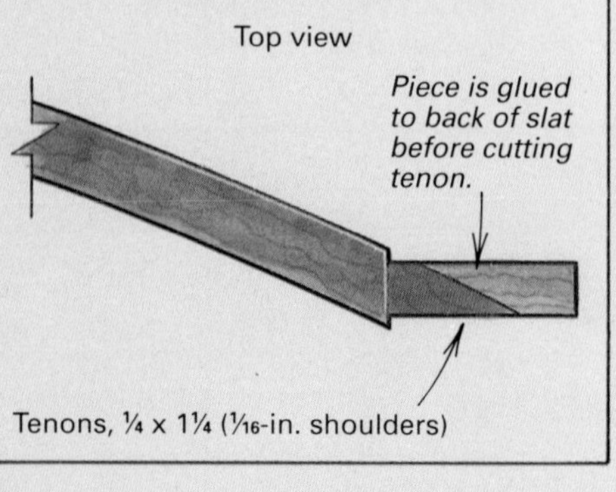

Top view

Piece is glued
to back of slat
before cutting
tenon.

Tenons, ¼ x 1¼ (1⁄16-in. shoulders)

Drawings: Mark Sant'Angelo

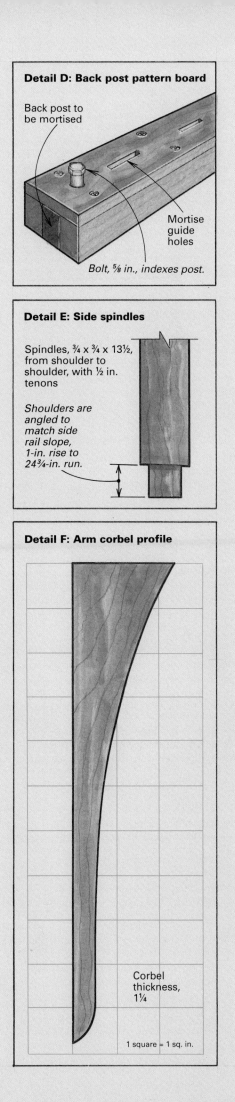

Detail D: Back post pattern board

Back post to be mortised

Mortise guide holes

Bolt, ⅝ in., indexes post.

Detail E: Side spindles

Spindles, ¾ x ¾ x 13½, from shoulder to shoulder, with ½ in. tenons

Shoulders are angled to match side rail slope, 1-in. rise to 24¾-in. run.

Detail F: Arm corbel profile

Corbel thickness, 1¼

1 square = 1 sq. in.

on multiple pieces. And, once I make the fixture, cutting a complex shape is elegantly simple and fast. That's why I cut the back slat tenons with a shopmade fixture that holds the router horizontally and lets me shear-cut tenons with a spiral fluted bit.

If you don't have an overarm router as an alternative or aren't inclined to devise a fixture, you can cut perfectly good tenons with a handsaw; then plane or chisel them for a good fit. The important thing is not how you cut the tenon; it's getting the tenon perpendicular to the side of the back post it goes into.

I cut the ¼-in.-wide mortises in the back posts (hollow chisel in the drill press again) using a mortising pattern board to hold the posts in position (see drawing detail D). The channel-shaped board has a ⅝-in. hole 1½ in. from one end that corresponds to the hole that will be used to mount the back to the chair. The posts slide into the channel and are indexed to the ⅝-in. holes to ensure uniformity between parts. The same holes also come into play later during glue-up.

Assembling the parts

To glue up the back, I use the fixture shown in the top photo on p. 122 to hold the entire back unit square, flat and in po-

sition until the glue dries. The posts are again indexed to the ⅝-in. holes for correct alignment of the back assembly to the back legs. The sides are glued using plywood fixtures to hold them flat and square. I cut holes in the plywood, so I can clean up the glue before it dries.

The rest of the assembly is conventional. The back is attached to the rear legs using turned pins and washer-spacers, as shown in the drawing on the facing page and in the top left photo below. To recline the back, simply move the adjustment pins to a rearward hole. Flat surfaces on the pins allow the back posts to rest firmly. As an alternative system, on earlier Morris chairs, Stickley sometimes used a back support rod that went from one arm to the other and rested in notched supports screwed to the tops of the arms.

Last, drill and pin the tenons using ⅜-in.-dia. oak dowels. The drawing shows the correct dowel placement.

Finishing touches

Stickley used ammonia fuming to add color to his furniture. He discovered the method by noticing that oak stable stalls changed in color over time. He figured that the ammonia in horse manure reacted with the tannic acid in white oak to shade the wood pleasingly.

Back adjustment pegs *(above) fit into holes in the arms. Moving the peg back allows the chair back to recline.*

A radial-arm saw cuts away waste *(below) to form the bend in a chair arm after a block of wood was glued underneath. An angle block holds everything in position.*

Using a hollow-chisel mortiser attachment on the drill press *makes quick work of cutting the through-mortises in the chair's arms to take the leg tenons. The same device also works to cut the groove under the arm to fit on the side rails, as shown on the already-cut arm in the foreground.*

Fuming the wood—I use the fuming tent shown in the bottom left photo. It is made of wood and heavy builder's plastic. Large and small garbage cans turned upside down over the furniture also work well. The chamber should be as small as the furniture put into it allows so as to concentrate the 26% ammonia fumes as much as possible. Ammonia is put in small cups around the items to be fumed. I usually leave the wood exposed to the fumes overnight to achieve the tone I like. But, by monitoring the process every hour or so, the chemical reaction can be shortened for lighter shades.

With some reservations, I am impressed with the pleasing color and grain appearance made possible with fuming. Fuming does not raise the grain. Because the chemical reaction penetrates about ⅛ in., the wood can be lightly sanded after fuming. The method is also quite economical.

A gallon of ammonia that costs about $10 could fume a houseful of furniture.

However, even Stickley had some problems with the method. Variations in tannic acid, sometimes present in even the same piece of wood, can cause variations in color shade. There are some things that can be done to ensure success. Select wood for maximum uniformity. If there are light spots after fuming, brush tannic acid and ammonia directly on the wood to touch it up.

I sometimes fume sanded furniture parts before assembling them. If extra parts are made and fumed, they can be mixed and matched for best color before final glue assembly. The chemical reaction from fuming does not affect gluing, and parts marred during gluing can be touched up. Fuming smaller parts before assembly also allows more parts to be fumed in a concentrated space. As a last resort, regular wood stains may be used to touch up lighter spots. Stickley did that quite often.

Industrial-strength ammonium hydroxide (NH$_4$OH 26%) can be obtained from Dietzgen, 250 Wille Road, Des Plaines, Ill. 60018, or from local blueprint companies. Be very careful handling this product, which is much stronger than 5% solution household ammonia. The Material Safety Data Sheet describes ammonium hydroxide as a poison that enters the body through ingestion, inhalation, skin contact or eye contact. Use it outside or in a well-ventilated area. Wear protective clothing, eyewear and a respirator. Follow all safety precautions recommended for it.

As a final finish coat, Stickley in some cases simply waxed the fumed wood. However, he usually coated it with shellac or lacquer. I use varnish and get good results, too.

Upholstery adds comfort—An upholstered seat and back cushion complete the chair. Stickley used a variety of materials, including leather, to upholster his furniture. I used cloth fabric for mine. Check the Yellow Pages directory in your community for upholstery supplies. The chair seat requires twelve 5-in.-dia. by 6-in.-tall coil springs sewn to 3-in. webbing stretched over a hardwood frame. Make the frame of ⅞-in.-thick, 2-in.-wide hardwood. The springs are securely tied, then covered with burlap, tow and curled hair. One-inch thick foam rubber and cotton can be substituted for the tow and curled hair.

Pack and shape the materials smoothly to a depth of approximately 2 in. Burlap or muslin is stitched in place over this. After sewing the seat cover and stapling it over the frame, I stapled a section of muslin to the seat frame to cover the bottom (see the bottom right photo). The completed seat slips into the chair frame and rests on cleats screwed to the front and back rails of the chair, so the seat slopes about 2 in. from front to back. The back is a loose cushion filled with cotton floss. Foam rubber 23 in. wide, 28 in. tall and 3 in. thick can be substituted for cotton.

See *FWW* #68 or books available at your local public library for more detailed information about upholstery techniques. If you—or your sewing machine—are not up to doing the upholstery work, you could have a local upholstery shop do the seat and back cushion for you. □

Back parts fit into a clamping fixture to keep everything straight during glue-up. Bolts through the back post peg holes not only help align the parts in this fixture, but they are used to index the back posts in another fixture for cutting the slat mortises.

Using 26% ammonia to fume the wood gives distinctive color, but rubber gloves, protective eyewear and breathing apparatus are a must. Cups of ammonia are placed inside the plastic-sheet fuming tent with items to be fumed and left overnight.

Stapling the bottom of a seat cushion, the author finishes the upholstery work for his Morris chair. Upholstery materials such as the cotton batting (right) or webbing and springs (foreground) are available from local upholstery supply stores.

Gene Lehnert teaches vocational cabinetmaking/millwork and builds furniture in La Marque, Texas.

Making a Child's Rocker

A tandem Windsor for two toddlers

by Mario Rodriguez

Rodriguez's 13-month-old daughter, Isabel, tries a tandem Windsor rocker. It's finished with latex paint and has oiled padauk armrests.

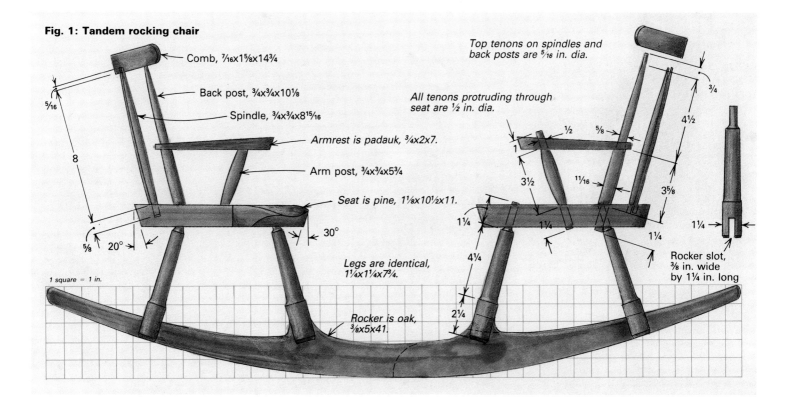

Fig. 1: Tandem rocking chair

Comb, $7/16 \times 1^5/8 \times 14^3/4$

Back post, $3/4 \times 3/4 \times 10^1/8$

Spindle, $3/4 \times 3/4 \times 8^{15}/16$

Armrest is padauk, $3/4 \times 2 \times 7$.

Arm post, $3/4 \times 3/4 \times 5^3/4$

Seat is pine, $1^1/8 \times 10^1/2 \times 11$.

Legs are identical, $1^1/4 \times 1^1/4 \times 7^3/4$.

Rocker is oak, $3/8 \times 5 \times 41$.

1 square = 1 in.

$5/16$

8

$5/8$ 20°

30°

Top tenons on spindles and back posts are $5/16$ in. dia.

All tenons protruding through seat are $1/2$ in. dia.

$3/4$

$4^1/2$

$1/2$ $5/8$

1

$3^1/2$ $11/16$

$3^5/8$

$1^1/4$ $1^1/4$

$1^1/4$

$4^1/4$

$2^1/4$

$1^1/4$

Rocker slot, $3/8$ in. wide by $1^1/4$ in. long

Photos: Gary Weisenburger; drawings: Aaron Azevedo

When I heard that friends were expecting twins, I set to work on a special gift for their joyous occasion: a toddler-size tandem rocker with two tiny comb-back Windsor chairs that face each other. Of all the Windsors I make, children's chairs are the most satisfying, but they pose a few unique design problems. For instance, the chairs look good with compressed, chubby legs and posts—like a baby's legs and arms—but they need proportionally stronger joints, since children's furniture takes more abuse than adult furniture. Furniture for little people should be easy to clean, because kids are sure to grab it with oatmeal-covered hands. So, even though I reduced the height of an adult chair by 50%, I reduced the diameter of the turned parts only 25%, and I simplified the shape of turned parts by not decorating them with coves and beads. The tandem rocker's turnings are pleasantly plump, so they have heavier tenons and thus stronger joints, and oatmeal doesn't have anywhere to hide. As you can guess, these design solutions work for single rockers, as well as for tandems.

I'll tell you how I built the tandem rocker shown on the previous page, and, where appropriate, I'll tell you how to adapt the design for a single rocker. In most cases I'll describe how to make parts for a single chair, but remember to double everything for the tandem version. You'll see that the posts and legs are simple to turn, and since there aren't any stretchers between them, you don't have to drill angled stretcher sockets in the legs. Drilling the seat's compound-angle post and leg sockets can be intimidating, but the process can be simplified if you break it down into two factors: the angle at which the member meets the seat and the direction in which the part leans, which I call the direction line. I simply use a hand-held drill with guide blocks to set the angles and then aim the drill along the direction line. And don't let steam-bending the seat back combs throw cold water on your desire to build this tiny Windsor, because that part of the project is fun. The same is true of scooping out the seat: it only has to look good, because little padded rumps don't stay in one place long enough to get comfortable anyway. In fact, this design is as forgiving as the toddler it's intended for and every part can be made to fit together during assembly, even if you've drilled a few holes a little off.

Drilling the seat—When drilling angled holes, imagine you're shooting them with a hand gun. I used shopmade guide blocks (described later), like the one in the photo below, to angle the drill bit accurately, and I aimed the bit and the guide block's plywood base along the direction line. I marked the seat top with direction lines, the centers of the post and leg sockets, and traced the seat's outline from a thin plywood pattern, as shown in figure 2. It's easier to mark the seat with direction lines and clamp the guide block on it before you scoop it out. Holes in the blank won't affect saddling (carving the seat) if you use wide carving tools, like an inshave.

If you drill 1/8-in.-dia. holes in the pattern to indicate the socket centers, a pencil point will fit in them so you can transfer the centers to the seat accurately. Likewise, saw 1/8-in.-wide kerfs on each angle direction line in the pattern edge, to transfer the lines. Select a pair of 1 1/8x11x14 clear pine seat blanks with the grain running front to back. This size will provide 3 1/2 in. of waste on the back of the seat for clamping when you drill it and scoop it out. Align the front edges of the pattern and blank, mark the hole centers and their direction lines, trace the seat's outline and bandsaw the waste from its front edge. Although I marked the pattern with an outline of the scooped out saddle, I drew it freehand on the seat blank. As I said, the saddle doesn't have to be carved accurately.

I made the drill guides by gluing and nailing 5/8x5/8x2 1/2 angled blocks on the end of 1/4x5/8x8 plywood strips, marking each block with the socket type and appropriate angle. To drill a 1/2-in.-dia. socket, align and clamp the block's plywood base to the seat on the direction line, with the block's angled front edge 1/4 in. (half the socket diameter) from the hole's center. Center the bit's point, align its angle with the block's angle and aim the bit in the direction of the line. Use the guides to bore the post and leg sockets through the seat into a backing block, and then drill the 3/4-in.-deep spindle sockets by eye, without guide blocks. Do this by putting the back posts in their sockets and align the bit angle parallel with the posts while you aim the bit along the direction line through the socket.

Carving the saddle—After drilling the seat, I clamped it to the workbench and scooped out the saddle, a simple dish about

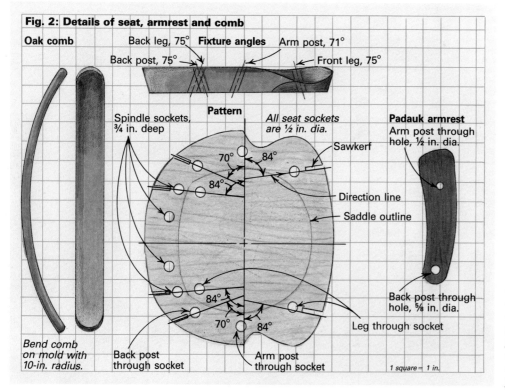

Fig. 2: Details of seat, armrest and comb

Oak comb

Back leg, 75°   **Fixture angles**   Arm post, 71°

Back post, 75°   Front leg, 75°

Pattern

Spindle sockets, 3/4 in. deep

All seat sockets are 1/2 in. dia.

Sawkerf

Padauk armrest
Arm post through hole, 1/2 in. dia.

70°   84°

84°

84°

Direction line

Saddle outline

84°

70°   84°

Back post through hole, 5/8 in. dia.

Leg through socket

Bend comb on mold with 10-in. radius.

Back post through socket

Arm post through socket

1 square = 1 in.

To drill through-sockets in the seat, for the legs and posts, the author uses a guide block to set the drill angle and points the drill bit in the direction of lines marked on the seat. He marked the direction lines and socket centers from a plywood seat pattern.

⅝ in. deep, with an inshave (see the top photo). The angle and length of the handles on my inshave prevented me from using it to make a steep cut into the seat, and so I finished carving the abrupt radius at the back of the saddle with a 1-in.-wide #3 carving gouge. Since the seat is small, you could use a wide gouge exclusively to scoop out the saddle.

I used a drawknife and a spokeshave to shape the front of the seat. The front of its top rolls over to the beveled (undercut) bottom edge to accommodate a seated toddler's legs. As shown in the center photo, the sharp corner on the front edge, where the top surface meets the bevel, is a curved line: it begins on the top adjacent to the arm post, curves down below the seat's mid-thickness at its round front corners, and then sweeps up to the pommel (the center of the saddle's front). To visualize this curve, use your finger as a guide to draw a straight line at the mid-thickness of the seat's bandsawn front edge. I then used that line as a guide to draw the curved sharp corner on the front edge. To make the tandem seats identical, I carved their rolled over fronts until they were symmetrical and looked alike, and then I carved their bevels. The bevel angle changes from 90° in the hollow curve near the arm post, to 45° around the seat's left and right corners, to 30° across the front. I clamped the seat on the benchtop to spokeshave the rolled over edge and then on edge in a vise to carve the bevel with a drawknife.

When you're finished carving, bandsaw the seat's back edge on the pattern line, setting the saw table at 20° to bevel the edge as shown in figure 1, and then smooth it with a spokeshave. While you're at the bandsaw, cut out the rockers and a pair of combs according to the dimensions in figures 1 and 2 on pp. 123-124. If you're building a single chair, refer to figure 1 to alter the rockers; the rest of the chair is the same. I laid out, bandsawed and smoothed the edges of the tandem rockers and the combs from single pieces of 1-in.-thick green oak. I then resawed them into matched pairs. By cutting out the combs now, you can steam bend and dry them while you turn the spindles, posts and legs.

Steam-bending the combs—It doesn't take much effort to bend these small combs and they are less likely to break than larger ones. As you can see in the bottom photo, I generated steam with an electric wallpaper steamer, which you can rent at most paint stores, and used a section of 6-in.-dia. plastic sewage pipe as a steambox. I supported this long pipe in the middle, to prevent it from sagging, and elevated the lidded end so condensation would drain through a hole at the opposite end. While waiting for steam to fill the box, wrap your combs in damp towels to keep them green—they will bend easier than dried wood.

When steam is billowing from the box, indicating that it's hot, put the combs in for about 45 minutes (or longer if they're dry). A good rule of thumb is 45 minutes to an hour per inch of thickness. Use caution and wear gloves when you open the steambox lid and insert or remove hot wood—scalding steam can be invisible. (I recommend that beginners wear a long-sleeve shirt to prevent burns on their wrists.) By the way, you can quickly heat your lunch in the steambox and this is a good time to break and eat it.

I bent both combs on a fixture that has two 10-in.-radius solid wood bending forms screwed to its 1-in.-thick plywood base, which you can see in the bottom photo. The fixture's plywood base has ¾-in.-dia. dowel holes that are ¾ in. from the bending forms. After I wedged an end of a hot comb against a dowel at one end of the form, I bent the comb and inserted a dowel at the other end to hold the comb loosely in place. I then hammered a wedge between the second dowel and the comb, driving it against the form. The solid bending form retards drying on the face of the comb against it, so wrap the hot comb with a wet towel for more

Above: Rodriguez scoops out the saddle with an inshave. Since the tool's long, angled handles prevent him from cutting steeply into the seat, he'll finish around the back edges with a wide gouge. Right: The author carves the front of the seat with a drawknife. He shaves to a line that is marked on the middle of the edge and that curves around the sharp corner where the top rolls over. Below: Rodriguez steam bends the combs for about 45 minutes in a closed plastic pipe connected to a wallpaper steamer. Then the combs can be wedged against forms on his plywood bending fixture.

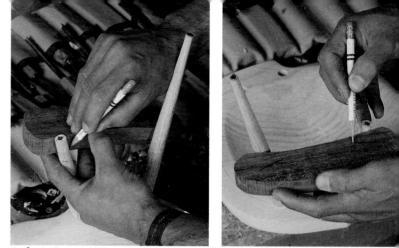

Left: Before drilling the armrest for the back posts and arm posts, the author holds it in position and marks the edge where each post will meet it. Then he sights the direction to point the drill, where each post appears plumb, and marks direction lines on the top of the armrest (right).

even drying. Although even drying retards springback when you remove the piece from the form, you'll still get a small amount, which is all right. Leave the comb wedged in place to dry for a couple of days and go to work on the turnings.

Turning the spindles, posts and legs—As you can see in figure 1 on p. 123, the turnings don't have any decorative coves or beads, as on most Windsors. And none of the parts are longer than 10⅜ in. or thicker than 1¼ in., so you can use hardwood cutoffs from your scrap box; any hardwood will do, because this chair, like a traditional Windsor, is painted. Eighteenth-century chairmakers used green wood, because it turns easily, but it is supple, and the limber spindles might whip as you turn them to their finished diameter. You can overcome this by using a steady rest or by following the tool's cutting edge with your free hand. If turning the spindles proves too difficult, you can whittle and scrape them smooth by hand.

Taper the tops of the spindles and back posts to fit holes in the bent comb, and taper the spindle bottoms to fit the seat sockets. To fit the posts to the armrest holes, turn a ½-in.-dia. by 1-in.-long straight section in the top of the arm post and a ⅝-in.-dia. by ½-in.-long straight section with a ¹⁄₃₂-in.-wide shoulder in the middle of the back post. Each post has a tenon in the bottom to fit its seat socket. Before taking any of the parts off the lathe, sand them to 100-grit, being careful to leave the shoulder in the back post crisp, for a good fit in the armrest.

All of the chair legs are identical: they flare to 1¼ in. dia. at the bottom, where they're slotted to fit the rockers, and they have a tenon at the top, which fits a socket in the seat. I sized each turning by holding an open-end wrench over it with one hand and slowly cutting to the diameter with a gouge I held in my other hand. Turn the legs from billets that are 3 in. to 4 in. too long and leave a square section on each end, to facilitate cutting the rocker slots. I cut these slots by guiding the legs' square ends on the bandsaw table. You can either bandsaw or chisel out the waste and then cut the square ends off the legs. If the slots aren't wide enough, plane the rocker slightly thinner, which is easier than opening the slot.

Assembling all the parts—Assembly is similar for a single or tandem rocker, since you only assemble one chair on the pair of rockers at a time. First, sand the seat with 100-grit paper. Leave the corners crisp and sharp, but use sandpaper to round them where the flat top curves down into the scooped out saddle.

Before assembling the posts and armrests, cut a shoulder on each post so it fits flush on its seat top. Set the post in its socket and mark around it at the seat top. Remove the post and refine the shoulder by sawing it to ¹⁄₁₆ in. wide at the line, and then put each post back in its socket to fit the armrests.

I bandsawed the armrests to the pattern lines shown in figure 2 from ¾-in.-thick padauk, and fit them to the back posts and arm posts before shaping them. I also drilled two holes in the armrests after marking their centers, an angle line and a direction line, again before shaping them. By doing it this way, you won't have invested time and effort shaping the armrests and you shouldn't feel badly throwing a piece away and starting again if the angled holes are drilled a little off. To set up for drilling, lay the seat on a flat benchtop with the back post and arm post in their sockets and hold the armrest parallel to the seat, against the posts and with the armrest at the height of the shoulder in the middle of the back post. Then, as shown in the photos above, draw a drill-angle line parallel to each post on the edge of the armrest and draw direction lines on the armrest top. When you sight along a direction line, its post should appear plumb. Drill the ½-in.-dia. arm-post hole and ⅝-in.-dia. back-post hole, and bend the posts so you can

slide the armrest down in place. Once it fits the posts, mark the excess length beyond the armrest, cut it off, apply glue on the post tenons and in the armrest sockets, and assemble the seat, posts and armrests. I wedged the top of the arm post and pinned through the armrest into the back post with a dowel.

Now, align the seats, legs and rockers by first assembling them without glue. Push the legs into the seats and rockers by twisting them into the correct holes. Fit the front leg slots over the humps in the rockers; then bend the rockers and fit the back-leg slots on them wherever the legs land. When both seats are in place, the rocker should look balanced, with the seats at symmetrical angles. If they aren't, change the seat angle by shaving the rocker's top edge. I checked the seat height symmetry with a measuring stick and then by eye; when everything looks right, it is. Next, mark a line from the seat bottom to the leg and around each leg where it protrudes through the seat. Disassemble everything, saw off the excess leg tenons (leaving the line), apply glue to the tenons and slots, reassemble everything, and align the marks on the seats and legs. Then drive wedges in the leg tenons to bear against the seat end-grain, and pin each leg to the rocker with dowels.

After you remove the steam-bent comb from the bending fixture, sand it smooth. Then, before putting the spindles in the seat sockets, hold the comb symmetrically against its two back posts and mark the comb's edge for the post socket centers on the surface of the comb for the drill angle. Then, drill the comb and put it on the posts, insert the spindles in their seat sockets (aligning them so they are symmetrical and spaced about equally), and mark the centers and angles of the comb's spindle sockets. Drill the spindle sockets freehand in the comb by aiming the drill at the marked angle and straight between the comb's surfaces. Now glue the comb to the posts and spindles.

Finishing the chair—I painted my tandem rocker with flat latex paint after I sanded it with 100-grit paper. Since the armrests aren't painted, I sanded them to 220-grit and rubbed Watco oil on them (you could coat armrests with clear lacquer) before applying any paint. Finish the armrests first, though; otherwise it would be difficult to remove any paint that might drip on the wood. Flat or satin latex paint comes in a variety of colors, it goes on easily by brushing or spraying, and it sands easily between coats. To make the painted surfaces more durable, you can spray it with a light coat of satin lacquer, but I prefer a flat finish rubbed with wax. ☐

Mario Rodriguez is a cabinetmaker and 18th-century woodworking consultant, and he teaches antique restoration in New York City.

Index

If you enjoyed this book, you're going to love our magazine.

A year's subscription to *Fine Woodworking* brings you the kind of practical, hands-on information you found in this book and much more. In issue after issue, you'll find projects that teach new skills, demonstrations of tools and techniques, new design ideas, old-world traditions, shop tests, coverage of current woodworking events, and breathtaking examples of the woodworker's art for inspiration.

To try an issue, just fill out one of the attached subscription cards, or call us toll free at 1-800-888-8286. As always, we guarantee your satisfaction.

Subscribe Today!
6 issues for just $29

Taunton
M A G A Z I N E S
for fellow enthusiasts

Taunton Direct, Inc.
63 South Main Street
P.O. Box 5507
Newtown, CT 06470-5507

Fine WoodWorking

1 year (6 issues) for just $29.00
— over 18% off the newsstand price

Outside the U.S. $38/year
(U.S. funds, please.)
Canadian res: GST included.

☐ Payment enclosed
☐ Please bill me

☐ Please send me a *Fine Woodworking* books and videos catalog. (BBBP)

Use this card to subscribe or to request a *Fine Woodworking* books and videos catalog.

NAME _____

ADDRESS _____

CITY _____

STATE _____

ZIP _____

PHONE _____

I am a 1. ☐ novice
2. ☐ intermediate
3. ☐ advanced
4. ☐ professional woodworker

Fine WoodWorking

1 year (6 issues) for just $29.00
— over 18% off the newsstand price

Outside the U.S. $38/year
Canadian res: GST included.

☐ Payment enclosed
☐ Please bill me

☐ Please send me a *Fine Woodworking* books and videos catalog. (BBBP)

Use this card to subscribe or to request a *Fine Woodworking* books and videos catalog.

NAME _____

ADDRESS _____

CITY _____

STATE _____

ZIP _____

PHONE _____

I am a 1. ☐ novice
2. ☐ intermediate
3. ☐ advanced
4. ☐ professional woodworker

Fine WoodWorking

1 year (6 issues) for just $29.00
— over 18% off the newsstand price

Outside the U.S. $38/year
Canadian res: GST included.

☐ Payment enclosed
☐ Please bill me

☐ Please send me a *Fine Woodworking* books and videos catalog. (BBBP)

Use this card to subscribe or to request a *Fine Woodworking* books and videos catalog.

NAME _____

ADDRESS _____

CITY _____

STATE _____

ZIP _____

PHONE _____

I am a 1. ☐ novice
2. ☐ intermediate
3. ☐ advanced
4. ☐ professional woodworker